SEP 1 8 2008

MORE
HAUNTED
HOUSES

Books by Joan Bingham and Dolores Riccio

Haunted Houses USA
More Haunted Houses

Published by POCKET BOOKS

MORE HAUNTED HOUSES

Joan Bingham

and

Dolores Riccio

POCKET BOOKS

New York London Toronto Sydney Tokyo Singapore

An *Original* Publication of POCKET BOOKS

POCKET BOOKS, a division of Simon & Schuster Inc.
1230 Avenue of the Americas, New York, NY 10020

Copyright © 1991 by Joan Bingham and Dolores Riccio

Bingham, Joan.
    More haunted houses / Joan Bingham and Dolores Riccio.
        p.   cm.
    Includes bibliographical references (p. 279).
    ISBN 0-671-69585-1 : $9.00
    1. Ghosts—United States. I. Riccio, Dolores, 1931–
II. Title.
BF1472.U6B56   1991
133.1'0973—dc20   91-23875
                                                      CIP

First Pocket Books trade paperback printing October 1991

10   9   8   7   6   5   4   3   2   1

POCKET and colophon are registered trademarks of
Simon & Schuster Inc.

Printed in the U.S.A.

*To all those people we love
and hope to haunt someday*

ACKNOWLEDGMENTS

Our warmest thanks to our editors, Claire Zion and Sally Peters, for their continued encouragement and their enthusiasm for good ghost stories! Our deep appreciation also to literary agent and friend Sue Herner, who helped bring our books about haunted places from vision to reality.

We're also very grateful to those wonderful librarians, archivists, psychics, investigators of the paranormal, and friends who generously helped us to research these stories. Besides those listed under specific locations, we also want to express our appreciation to the research staffs at the Warwick Public Library (Rhode Island) and at the Allentown Public Library (Pennsylvania).

Special thanks to Irene Somishka of Havasu City, Arizona, for all of her invaluable help.

Our appreciation goes to Raymond Nelke, founder of Collectors of Unusual Data International (COUD-I), for gathering and sharing so many wonderful news items about haunted places and other anomalies.

ALABAMA, Bladon Springs Cemetery, the Boyington Oak, Musgrove
    Cemetery
Bob Bahr, journalist, and Alice Bahr, librarian

ARIZONA, Haunts of the Hopi and Navajo nations
Carol Downey, Reference Librarian, Arizona Department of Library,
    Archives, and Public Records

CALIFORNIA, Lebec, Fort Tejon
Don Schmidt, State Park Ranger, Fort Tejon Historic Park
Richard L. Senate, author and psychic researcher

CALIFORNIA, Interstate 15, Barstow
Kelly Roberts, psychometrist

CALIFORNIA, Los Angeles, Hollywood Memorial Park
Richard L. Senate, author and psychic researcher

COLORADO, Denver, Cheesman Park
Dave Deame, researcher, writer, Mensan

COLORADO, Mesa Verde
Kelly Roberts, psychometrist

CONNECTICUT, Easton, Easton Cemetery
Ed and Lorraine Warren, psychic investigators

HAWAII, Oahu
Jean Hunt, President, Louisiana Mounds Society

ILLINOIS, Chicago, Bachelor's Grove Cemetery, Graceland Cemetery, Resurrection Cemetery
Norman Basile, paranormal investigator

KANSAS, Fort Leavenworth
Maurice Schwalm, psychic investigator, writer, lecturer

MARYLAND, Chessie, Moll Dyer's Rock, St. Andrew's Church Road Bridge
Lynda Andrus, psychic investigator

MISSOURI, Joplin, Neosho Spook Light
Elizabeth Baily, Reference Specialist, The State Historical Society of Missouri
Dale Kaczmarek, President, Ghost Researchers Society

NEBRASKA, Lincoln, Robber's Cave
Mary Ethel Emanual, Development Consultant, Department of Economic Development
Chris Nabower, Nebraska State Historical Society

NEW HAMPSHIRE, Derry, America's Stonehenge
Robert E. Stone, President, America's Stonehenge
Jean Hunt, President, Louisiana Mounds Society

NEW JERSEY, Ringwood Manor
Dan and Pauline Campanelli, owners of a haunted house

NEW YORK, Fort Ticonderoga
Mildred and Joseph Wilson

OHIO, Doylestown, Rogues' Hollow
Cal Holden, Chippewa-Rogues' Hollow Historical Society

PENNSYLVANIA, Chestnut Ridge
Stan Gordon, Director, Pennsylvania Association for the Study of the
    Unexplained (PASU)

RHODE ISLAND, Exeter, Chestnut Hill Cemetery
Debbie Nunnes, Research Librarian, East Greenwich Library

SOUTH CAROLINA, Bishopville
Ron Schaffner, member of COUD-I

SOUTH CAROLINA, Huntington State Park
Bill Oberst, Georgetown Chamber of Commerce

TENNESSEE, Adams, The Bell Witch
Don Wick, Director of Information, Tennessee Department of Tourist
    Development

TENNESSEE, Chickamauga and Stones River battlefields
Dale Kaczmarek, President, Ghost Researchers Society

TENNESSEE, Morgan County, Historic Rugby
Barbara Stagg, Executive Director, Rugby
Don Wick, Director of Information, Tennessee Department of Tourist
    Development

WASHINGTON STATE, The *Equator*
Jim Ardeth and Evan Bolin

CONTENTS

THE SOUTH CENTRAL STATES
◆

THE NORTH CENTRAL STATES
◆

THE SOUTHEAST
◆

THE NORTHEAST

◆

INTRODUCTION:
Mysterious America

Europe has its Stonehenge and Avebury, its Loch Ness Monster and puzzling concentric circles, its phantom carriages, haunted cemeteries, and specters wandering the moors. But on our vast and varied landscape, too, are scenes of the supernatural, the legendary, and the downright scary to rival the eeriest the Old World has to offer. "From the mountains to the prairies," there are enough mysterious places in our own country to fill an atlas of the weird and the wonderful.

While we were researching our book *Haunted Houses, USA,* we unearthed a number of intriguing scenes of American lore and legend that just weren't houses and so were outside the scope of that volume, but we promised ourselves we'd return to explore these phenomena at some future time. Now, for this volume, we've revisited these haunted or legendary sites to tell their fascinating stories.

What is it that makes certain locations vibrate with unseen forces, while other places remain neutral? Why do ghostly manifestations appear at one scene and not another? We may not be sure why some areas generate supernatural phenomena, but we do know that over the years such things have been reported by many reliable witnesses. We theorize that some places are more easily imprinted by events and people than others are, and that the emotional character of an event is a factor in impressing its image on that locale.

Cemeteries and Native American burial grounds, for instance, frequently are haunted by troubled spirits, and this is especially true if the graves have been disturbed. Shipwrecks are particularly potent in evoking the supernatural; phantom ships are often seen after such tragedies occur. The country-side around historic forts is liable to spawn tales of ghostly riders. Curious geological formations give rise to legends, manifestations, or mysterious lights. Certain roads and bridges are continually haunted by auditory or visual manifestations.

Perhaps haunted places contain portals to the past—cracks in time where previous events seep through to replay in the present. This is not so inconceivable; physicists tell us that the space-time continuum may contain minute holes where chronological time does not exist. They call these wormholes. Who knows what may be slipping through them?

Einstein's general theory of relativity abolished earlier, fixed concepts of time and space. His famous theory proposed, and subsequent experiments proved, that time depends on the distribution of matter in space. There are places in the universe called black holes, where the pull of gravity is so great that time, quite literally, stands still. The universe itself is timeless, but we humans, with our internal biological clocks, observe events in the universe in chronological sequence, making it difficult for us to comprehend timelessness. It's as if we were travelers on a train; the country we are moving through is present in its entirety, but we see only the part through which we are passing at the moment.

Taking this overview, past events have not vanished from the universe; we have simply traveled beyond them. In the haunted places we've written about in this book, it may be that witnesses are hearing and seeing things that happened long ago because some peculiar and unknown characteristic of the place itself admits these visions from another time.

Or it may be, as tradition explains hauntings, that the dead sometimes return in spirit to this life. In our research we have found that a strong personality, a dramatic event, or some important business left undone are the usual prerequisites of a haunting. If the spirit or life energy of a person is not dissipated at death, it may be attracted to important scenes of its past existence. Sometimes such a spirit is summoned by the living, which is what happens in a séance.

But hauntings are only one kind of phenomenon that occurs on these legendary landscapes. In this book we've also told the stories of other kinds of mysterious scenes. Here you'll also find locations where monsters (like Chessie or Bigfoot) have been seen repeatedly; places where you can view lights and fires of unknown origin; sites where UFOs are most likely to hover; and archaeological discoveries that offer some mysterious, unexplainable features.

There is much about these matters that we don't understand and that scientists, always leery of being thought fools, are reluctant to study. More sympathetic to strange or supernatural happenings are folklorists, reporters, and even some historians. We've drawn on their stories and newspaper accounts to piece together the facts behind some puzzling legends, and we're grateful to all those who presented such events in an open-minded fashion.

Many of the organizations and the psychics whom we wrote, called, or met also were helpful in introducing us to the mysterious phenomena in their region. We've included a listing of some (see pages 275–77) who could assist you if you wish to delve deeper into this subject or to take a tour of haunted places.

Since we each researched and wrote about different stories, we've signed each story with the individual author's initials.

If you're intrigued by mysteries, hauntings, and legends and want to experience these sites yourself, you can use the motorist's directions in this book as a tour guide to supernatural America. Or if you just like a good spine-tingling tale, curl up in a comfortable chair and read on! We hope you enjoy visiting (in flesh or in spirit) these legendary landscapes as much as we enjoyed discovering and telling their stories!

THE
PACIFIC
COAST

THE UNLIKELY GHOSTS
Everett, Washington

For me, all sailing ships are beautiful, poetic, and mystical. Their sensuous movement through the water captivates and delights me. In my opinion, no engine-driven vessel can match their grace or form. Old sailing ships, in addition to these qualities, usually have an aura of accumulated wisdom and experience. Each ship has a personality fashioned by her builders, the individuals who sailed her, the seas she has traversed, the storms she's encountered, and the ports in which she has moored. Only a landlubber would deny the anthropomorphous quality of a ship.

There are many types of sailing ships or boats. For example, there are catboats, sloops, cutters, yawls, ketches, schooners, brigantines, bark, and so on. Of all these and other ships, the vessel that would capture the title of Miss Universe of the Seven Seas would be the two-masted schooner. There are other types of sailing craft that may outperform her in some particular area of endeavor, but none comes close to her exquisite beauty. There is no compromise in her form—she is divine. To see her under full sail is enthralling, to say the least.

I am, as you may have guessed by now, unabashedly infatuated with two-masted schooners. So when I learned that such a ship was haunted by two well-known historical personages, I had no recourse but to investigate.

The lead came from an unexpected source: *The Antique and Auction News.* In an article in this trade paper, Leon Thompson described attending a séance on the schooner *Equator,* moored at the waterfront in Everett, Washington. The eighty-one-foot trading schooner was built in the Matthew Turner shipyard, up the bay from San Francisco, in the late 1880s. Her San Francisco owners had sent her off to the South Pacific to transport copra—dried coconut meat from which the oil is extracted—

3

under the command of Captain Denis Reid (Danny Reid, by some reports), a twenty-three-year-old Scot.

I was unable to discover how long the *Equator* remained active. However, the less aesthetic but more efficient diesel-driven ships had replaced all but a few of the commercial sailing craft by the outbreak of World War II. After millennia, the age of wooden ships and iron men had succumbed to the machine. Sails were replaced by pistons, lines by copper tubes, somnolent creaking of timber by the metallic clang of combustion, the stately masts by tubes of bellowing soot, and the fresh sea air by petroleum fumes. As they say, "That's progress." I wonder! Anyway, somewhere along the way the *Equator* was retired and tied to a wharf at Everett.

In the vein of "You don't miss the water 'til the well runs dry," the lovely old ships of sail are once again appreciated—after their almost total extinction. Now cities and communities up and down the coasts are salvaging neglected old vessels and restoring them for their appeal to tourists. This is *Equator*'s destiny, to be a dockside museum for the generations who missed the old schooners' quiet splendor—the better for her and the better for us, I say.

Even with the cosmetic surgery of restoration, the old girl shows her considerable age. The wrinkles and scars of more than a century of vicissitudes protrude through her skin of enamel, and her seams aren't as straight as they once were. But it just adds to her allure. The most ignorant novice can see she's no Hollywood replica. She wasn't built for show, she was built to work, and work she did, and it shows. She's been around, seen things in the raw, participated in a few questionable ventures, given aid and comfort to many damnable characters—as well as the good and true—in her day. You can tell by just looking at her that she has something to say, that the secrets of a hundred years are somehow encapsulated within her ancient frame. What a casual glance won't tell you is that she provides refuge for at least two incorporeal personas.

Over the years strange occurrences have been reported aboard the *Equator*. Guests have recounted seeing figures who could not be accounted for in various parts of the ship. Workmen have complained of missing tools and feeling that an eerie presence was beside them as they performed their tasks. Occasionally, nocturnal passersby reported seeing a floating light moving about the topside.

As each incident surfaced it was shrugged off with a rational explanation. However, as the reports continued to accumulate, interest in the *Equator* by the psychic community grew and finally culminated in a séance.

Leon Thompson reported that "three psychics were seated beneath her stern, holding hands and asking for the spirits that guarded the schooner to make known their presence."

According to Thompson, nothing happened for half an hour, then "two glowing spheres appeared just above the stern and floated gently down toward the psychics." From his vantage point Thompson could not clearly hear what was said, but he saw that "the glowing spheres did form into a strange shape (much like a human body) before they returned to the schooner."

After the séance had ended, the psychics told Thompson that the two forms were the ghosts of Robert Louis Stevenson and the Hawaiian King Kalakaua. Sounds pretty farfetched, doesn't it? But according to the three psychics, the ghosts related that Stevenson had leased the *Equator* and, while in Hawaii, had entertained the king aboard ship. Because Stevenson had enjoyed the time spent on the *Equator* as well as his friendship with King Kalakaua, and the king reciprocated, "The two return each year in spirit form to relive those happy, carefree days aboard the old schooner," Thompson said.

Now, all I knew about King Kalakaua was that he was the last king of Hawaii and father of Queen Liliuokalani. As for the author of such classics as *The Strange Case of Dr. Jekyll and Mr. Hyde, Kidnapped, Treasure Island,* and *A Child's Garden of Verses,* I knew he was born in Edinburgh, Scotland, was sickly and quite thin, and had died in Samoa. In other words, I didn't know enough even to guess at the plausibility of accepting the two ghosts as Stevenson and Kalakaua. After a few visits to the public library, I was at least able to venture some thoughts— however arbitrary.

A frail infant, Robert Louis Balfour Stevenson was born on November 13, 1850, and remained sickly the rest of his life. He nearly died of gastric fever at the age of eight. He studied to be a civil engineer, like his father, but gave it up because of its physical demands and switched to law instead, passing the bar in 1875. But there is no record of his ever practicing law. From Stevenson's earliest youth he had been drawn to literature. He later wrote: "It was not so much that I wished to be an author (though I wished that too) as that I had vowed that I would learn to write."

At sixteen he published his first public writing in the form of an anonymous pamphlet entitled *The Pentland Rising* and, two years later, *The Charity Bazaar.* Following his admittance to the bar, Stevenson spent two years journeying about France, Germany, and Scotland; the accounts of these travels were published as *An Inland Voyage* (1878), and *Travels with a Donkey in the Cévennes* (1879).

Physical restoration was the initial motive for Stevenson's travels, for his health always improved when he was away from Edinburgh and outdoors, and declined when he returned home to Scotland for any time. He became a pilgrim, moving from place to place, searching for his personal Utopia.

In 1876 Stevenson met Mrs. Fanny Osbourne at Fontainebleau, France. He spent most of his time with Mrs. Osbourne in France until she returned to her home in San Francisco in 1878. In August of the following year, Stevenson received word that she had become ill. He hurried across the Atlantic and the Continent to be at her side. They were married in May 1880 and briefly lived in a desolate mining camp that inspired the story *The Silverado Squatters.* The terrain was savage, their relationship serene. Before winter set in, Stevenson, Fanny, and her son returned to Scotland.

Stevenson's health was again in a state of decline, and after a brief stay with his family, the three continued on to Switzerland, where he was treated for his tuberculosis. In the summer of 1881, much improved, he again returned to Scotland, where he wrote *Treasure Island.* His summer stay in Scotland countered the better health he had gained in Switzerland, forcing him back to that country for another winter of treatment and rest.

In January 1884 Stevenson had a severe setback and nearly died. In August of the same year he moved to Bournemouth, England, where he lived for three years. During this time Stevenson published *The Strange Case of Dr. Jekyll and Mr. Hyde* and *Kidnapped.*

On August 17, 1887, Stevenson sailed from England for New York with his wife, stepson, and widowed mother. It was his final departure from Europe. Until June of the following year he rested in upstate New York and on the New Jersey coast. Having written so much about sailing, he decided to charter a boat in San Francisco and make an excursion to the South

Pacific. On June 28, 1888, the family left San Francisco on the schooner *Casco*, sailing first to the Marquesas Islands, then Tahiti, and north to Honolulu on Christmas Day.

Stevenson wrote to his editor and close friend, Sidney Colvin, that the six months on the *Casco* had been "incredible . . . I did not dream there were such places or such races." Stevenson thought life at sea on the *Casco* was horrible, but he wrote Colvin that "you are amply repaid when you sight an island, and drop anchor in a new world."

In a letter to the author Henry James, Fanny wrote that she hadn't believed the travelers' tales of the South Seas. Once there she found the stories were not exaggerated; to the contrary, only "the half" had been told her. Even her mother-in-law, a proper Victorian lady, had succumbed to the islands' enchantment. "I wish you could but just get a glimpse of that lady taking a moonlight promenade on the beach in the company of a gentleman dressed in a single handkerchief," she wrote James.

The Stevensons rented a large old Hawaiian house on the beach at Waikiki, just out of town. He wrote his friend and fellow writer, Charles Baxter, that he was "so well that I do not know myself—sea bathing, if you please, and what is far more dangerous, entertaining and being entertained by his Majesty here, who is a very fine, intelligent fellow. But Oh, Charles! What a crop for the drink!"

Kalakaua had succeeded a number of Hawaiian kings who had been democratic-minded and had worked to modernize the monarchy as well as the country. He, however, wished to restore the lost power and prestige of the throne. His court was ostentatious and his person flamboyant, but he was also highly civilized and had a keen, inquisitive mind. The king spent hours pumping Stevenson about the Marquesas and other islands below the equator, as well as Europe and America. However, fellowship with Kalakaua entailed much food and drink (particularly drink), and even Stevenson's mother was known to teeter away from the royal table. The king's position and personality made it impossible to say no to the next refill.

Stevenson wrote to Baxter that he planned to return to Europe. He said he felt duty bound to return home for the sake of his editor, Colvin, who required more frequent contact than every six months or so. Also Lloyd Osbourne, his twenty-one-year-old stepson, should not have to spend his formative years drifting in the South Seas. "And those two considerations will no doubt bring me back—to go to bed again—in England."

Stevenson and his wife knew that once they were back in Europe they would never be able to return to the Pacific, and there was so much they had not seen in the South Seas. The pull to sail south was further strengthened by the fact that even the mild climate of Hawaii was too temperate for Stevenson's health. So in the spring they decided to follow their hearts to the South. They would sail to Butaritari (now known as Makin, in the Gilbert Islands) or Ponape (Caroline Islands) and from there take a boat on to the Philippines or China.

Stevenson began negotiating with the Boston Missionary Society for passage on their vessel, the *Morning Star,* which was preparing to sail to Butaritari within the month. However, there were so many restrictions that Stevenson was having second thoughts when he learned that a trading schooner, the *Equator,* was due to stop over in Honolulu on its passage south. He contacted the owner and was able to arrange a "most obliging and liberal" agreement. Stevenson could stop the *Equator* at any port he desired, as long as it did not interfere with the ship's normal itinerary for trading at specific islands. Captain Reid proved most obliging, and the schooner was run like a private yacht for the Stevensons—alcohol, cards, smoking, and oaths were permitted.

The *Equator* sailed from Honolulu one night in late June, after a farewell visit from King Kalakaua with his entourage of cabinet ministers, his Royal Hawaiian Band, and a basket of champagne. The group now was composed of Stevenson, Fanny, her son, Lloyd, daughter, Belle, and son-in-law, Joe Strong (an unproductive artist with spendthrift habits). Stevenson's mother was homesick for Edinburgh and had left by steamer in May.

Stevenson wrote his friend Baxter that "this new cruise of ours is somewhat venturesome, and I think it needful not to be in a hurry to suppose us dead. In these ill-charted seas, it is quite in the cards we might be cast on some unvisited, or rarely visited, island" and remain there for months or years, only to "turn up smiling at the hinder end."

Life on the *Equator* was so superior to what it had been on the *Casco* that Stevenson made up his mind to remain in the South Seas for the rest of his life. Fanny later said that within the first ten days aboard the *Equator* he decided to buy his own trading schooner on which the family could live and travel to various islands. The vessel's name was to be *Northern Light,* and as a working boat it would pay all their living expenses from the trading of copra. However, the *Northern Light* bubble deflated when Stevenson observed at close hand the questionable methods of the copra traders. Fanny wrote, "South Sea trading could not bear close examination. Without being actually dishonest, it came a little too close to the line to please us. Our fine scheme began to fade away."

For six months the Stevensons sailed the South Pacific aboard the *Equator,* often spending weeks on an island while the schooner charged off to an unappealing port to pick up copra. Stevenson was in his glory. His health was better than it had ever been, and he loved the South Seas and its people.

On a calm day in the first week of December 1889, the *Equator* reached Samoa. Stevenson's intention was to stop over in Samoa for about two months and then continue on to other islands. This they did, leaving on April 10, 1890, on the trading ship *Janet Nicholl.* However, both Stevenson and his wife were so taken by the island that they purchased land on which to build their permanent home.

The voyage on the *Janet Nicholl* lasted until August and took them to thirty-five islands they had never visited, as well as several islands they had called upon earlier. In August they stayed on in Sydney and by October were "home" in Apia, Samoa.

Stevenson's property was, in his words, "314½ acres of beautiful land in the bush behind Apia." It had three streams, two waterfalls, a great cliff, a number of views of the sea and the lowlands, and an ancient native fort. A large house was built and the estate christened Valilima (a Samoan word meaning "five streams"). The site of Valilima had also been a bloody battlefield, and the area was believed haunted by *aitu*—ghosts of the slain.

In a footnote in his 1974 biography, *Robert Louis Stevenson,* James Pope Hennessy wrote, "It is today believed by some Samoans that Louis Stevenson is now himself an *aitu.*" He was recently seen by "a creditable English youth," peering through two bedroom windows at Valilima—now used as the official residence for entertaining guests of the Samoan head of state.

At the time, three native chiefs (Tamasese, Laupepa, and Mataafa) were claiming kingship. Mataafa was the oldest and most popular, and seemed to have stronger rights than the other two. Stevenson staunchly supported and gave aid to Mataafa, who in 1893 was banished to the German-controlled Marshall Islands. In 1899, five years after Stevenson's death, the Germans brought Mataafa back and established him as king. Stevenson had written in 1892 that there would be no peace in Samoa until Mataafa was in his true place—a prediction that proved to be correct.

On December 3, 1894, while helping his wife make dinner in the kitchen of Vailima, Stevenson suffered a stroke and never regained consciousness. He passed away that evening. The next day, sixty husky Samoans, who considered him a chief, carried his body up to the summit of the sheer peak of Vaea in relays. A concrete monument with bronze plaques now marks the site. It was the place he had chosen as his final resting place. But it's doubtful he remained there.

In *Voyage to Windward: The Life of Robert Louis Stevenson,* I. C. Furnas writes that Stevenson's mother contracted fatal pneumonia in 1897, at the age of sixty-eight, and quotes Belle, Stevenson's stepdaughter: ". . . thinking she saw her son at the foot of the bed, she exclaimed, 'there is Louis! I must go,' and fell back at once, unconscious, though she did not actually breathe her last until the next day."

What of the two ghosts on board the *Equator* tied up at a pier in Everett, Washington? Are they Stevenson and King Kalakaua? Some of the famous author's most pleasurable days were spent on the *Equator,* and I'm sure he equated the vessel with happiness. As for Kalakaua, he and Stevenson had developed a relationship as drinking buddies that may well continue to this day, and their last hours together on earth were spent on the *Equator.* However, a skinny Scottish intellectual and a corpulent Hawaiian monarch do make an incredible pair of ghosts.

DIRECTIONS: *From Seattle go north on I-5. At Everett take the Broadway exit. Go north on Broadway to Hewitt Avenue. Turn left on Hewitt and follow it all the way to Marine View Drive. Go north on Marine View Drive to 10th Street. The boat is at the 10th Street Boat Dock.*

—JB

THE MYSTERIOUS PHANTOM OF FORT TEJON

Kern County, California

Being mauled to death by a bear was not a pleasant way to go, even in the Old West, where grievous misadventure was an everyday occurrence. Although little is known about the restless phantom seen by many persons around Fort Tejon, local folklore maintains it's the ghost of Peter Le Beck, a legendary mountain man whose last encounter on earth was with a ferocious grizzly. An ancient oak tree in the northwest corner of the parade ground once carried a deeply carved inscription which read:

> PETER LE BECK
> KILLED BY A X BEAR
> OCTOBER 17, 1837

The "X" is believed to be an abbreviation for the grizzly, because of the X shape of raised fur on the California bear's chest. The epitaph is no longer visible on the old oak, because that section of bark has been cut out and is on display in the fort's small museum.

The old oak was Le Beck's tombstone; he was buried beneath its roots. But, as is often the way with ghosts, the Frenchman's bones weren't left to rest in peace. Perhaps that's why his spirit is seen wandering about this state historic park, particularly in the late afternoon. Information about this persistent apparition was brought to my attention by Richard L. Senate, a psychic investigator who lives in Camarillo, California. A student had reported to him that one of the park rangers always included the ghost of Le Beck as part of the fort's lore.

Le Beck's oak-tree epitaph was first discovered and noted in 1853, in R. S. Williamson's railroad route exploration report. The tragedy it commemorates happened long before there ever was a Fort Tejon. For those who established the fort, the Le Beck oak simply came with the territory and provided some pleasant shade and speculation.

11

Another opinion about the phantom seen lurking around the parade is that it's the ghost of a soldier who died at the hospital during Fort Tejon's occupation, which was actually rather short. The fort was constructed in the summer of 1854 and abandoned only ten years later—but then, military history is chock full of these expensive changes of mind.

The plan for the fort was conceived in 1852. Lieutenant Edward Beale, the Commissioner of Indian Affairs in California and Nevada, had been put in charge of erecting and maintaining San Sebastian Reservation in Tulare Valley, about twenty miles away from the present location of Fort Tejon. He recommended that a military post be located nearby to protect the Indians in the southern San Joaquin Valley and government property at the reservation from marauding raiders of other tribes. The proposed site would strategically control an important pass in the Tehachapi mountain range.

The post Beale envisioned was authorized and outfitted. Later, Fort Tejon was constructed on the post's grounds.

The story is told that just before the U.S. Army began construction a posse of irate mountain settlers drove a whole village of local Indians into the heavily mineralized waters of Lake Castac, where they drowned one by one. For months afterward, passersby on the stage road reported the eerie spectacle of partially preserved bodies floating in the waters of the lake.

In 1850 a visitor to the military post that predated the fort described a bucolic scene. "The post of Tejon is on a little plain, entirely surrounded by high mountains, beautifully situated in a grove of old oak; at this season the fort is most romantic and beautiful. The noble oaks are in full leaf. On the plains and mountain side, Mother Nature has almost excelled herself, carpeting them with flowers of every hue, giving to the eye one of the most beautiful prospects imaginable; and the air is bracing and exhilarating and inspiring. An oasis in the desert where all is freshness and life."

Of course, this poetic visitor probably went home to a well-appointed house in town. Wives of men stationed at this post were more likely to call the place "desolate" and "primitive."

Fort Tejon became the regimental headquarters for the 1st U.S. Dragoons, and they were kept quite busy. Patrols from this isolated mountain camp traveled as far as the Colorado River, penetrated unexplored regions of Owens Valley, escorted parties to Salt Lake City, and rode the supply route to and from Los Angeles. The troopers guarded miners, chased bandits, and offered their protection to southern California in general.

In 1854 Kit Carson visited the new fort. By the following year Tejon had a brass band good enough to be invited to play in Los Angeles. In its peak period over twenty buildings made up the fort, one of the largest settlements in Southern California. In 1858 the fort was a station of the Butterfield Overland stagecoach line that ran from San Francisco to St. Louis, a trip that took twenty-three days. The phantom of Tejon hardly disturbed the bustling activity at the fort.

One of the unique episodes in the fort's history was its unusual cavalry. Under the direction of U.S. Secretary of War Jefferson Davis (later president of the Confederate States of America), camels were imported in 1857 for transporting supplies to isolated posts in the arid Southwest. At first Beale (who was now a general) may have thought this was another weird idea out of Washington. But soon, after using twenty-eight of the awkward-looking beasts in a wagon-road survey party to Fort Defiance, New Mexico, Beale became a camel enthusiast. Favorably impressed by their splendid performance, he recommended that the camel corps be expanded. One camel was better than four of his best mules, he declared. The camels traversed stretches of country covered with the sharpest volcanic rock without injury to their feet and climbed with heavy packs over mountains where the unloaded mules found it difficult to go—even with assistance from dismounted riders. Surprisingly, the desert-bred animals plunged into rivers without hesitation and swam with ease. They even carried water for the flagging mules.

The camel corps experiment was put on hold when the Civil War broke out; it was never resumed. The transcontinental railroad was under construction, making the notion of loping about on camels appear rather out of date.

After the army abandoned the fort, those acres and buildings somehow became part of Rancho Tejon, a Mexican grant, which was purchased by General Beale. (He'd always appreciated that location's possibilities.) In 1939 the deteriorating buildings of the old fort were donated to the state. Restoration of the fort began in 1949, accompanied by occasional appearances of the phantom, whether a soldier or Le Beck.

There are two stories about the removal of Le Beck's remains. The first is related in Richard L. Senate's excellent book *Ghosts of the Haunted Coast.*

"After the military base was established, the good Christian women of the fort caused the soldiers to dig up the bones of the Frenchman from the base of the oak and move them to a proper cemetery, where he was given a Christian service. Peter is said to have begun his wanderings then in protest of the desecration of his grave. . . . Perhaps he wanders the fort longing for his old grave."

The second story was recently sent to me in a letter from Senate, who found it in a 1941 book by Clarence Cullimore, *Forgotten Fort Tejon.* In July of 1890 a group of campers, calling themselves the Foxtail Rangers, exhumed the bones buried four feet beneath the Le Beck oak. He'd been a tall man, perhaps six feet. Two of his ribs were broken. The right forearm, the left hand, and both feet were missing. This does sound as if Le Beck ran into a really vicious attack.

In 1915 a man named Sam Allen found a coin in one of the adobe bricks of the fort's hospital. It proved to be a five-franc coin dated 1837, engraved with the bust of Louis Philippe, then the ruling king of France. Since the year was the same as that inscribed on the Le Beck oak, it was thought the coin might have fallen out of the Frenchman's pocket while he struggled with the bear. This led some folks to believe that Le Beck was a French spy sent to help secure California for France. Another theory was that Le Beck was an officer in the French army, making maps for the planned seizure of the state.

Today the five-franc coin found at Fort Tejon is exhibited at the Southwest Museum in Los Angeles.

Psychic investigator Senate writes: "The isolation in the mountains makes this park ideal as a place to detect psychometry." Psychometry is the "reading" of inanimate objects, which are said to retain an imprint from former owners. Gifted psychics receive impressions of the personalities and emotions imprinted on an object, a building, or a place. (I have seen this ability demonstrated with surprising accuracy, not by professional psychics but within a group of interested amateurs. In our experiment, each person brought an object unknown to the others, and we all attempted to gather impressions from each of these objects in turn. Some of the group were able to "tune

in" to very specific and detailed histories just by holding a
pendant or a thimble.)

Senate organized a psychic exploration of the fort with a
group of his students. After meeting at the museum they split
up to gather individual impressions of the environs for almost
an hour before regrouping to compare notes and enjoy a picnic
by a rushing stream.

One of the psychic "hotspots" pinpointed by the group was
the small adobe building designated as the orderlies' quarters.
Nausea, anger, and frustration were just some of the strong
feelings experienced near this building. Another place that
Senate's group found abuzz with psychic activity was the former
officer's quarters. There, emotions of unhappiness and loneliness were pervasive, which the investigators attributed to the
officers' wives.

"The site of the hospital across the parade grounds seemed
to be charged with energy," Senate wrote. "Most hospitals are
haunted, so it did not seem inconsistent that strong traces of
emotion should remain on that site. . . . The hospital was built
near the haunted oak tree, leading us to speculate that the
ghost seen at the old fort is not the French trapper but the
spirit of one of the Dragoons who died in the hospital."

To me, the most interesting impression gleaned on Senate's
trip was that one of the group sensed the spirit of a Native
American named Chief Black Bear, who had been put to death
by hanging from an oak tree near the mess hall, about three
hundred yards from the haunted oak. Perhaps it was the chief
and not a grizzly who killed and mutilated Le Beck.

We are left with many questions about the phantom of Fort
Tejon. Is it the apparition of a dragoon who died at the hospital?
Le Beck the French trapper or Le Beck the French spy, who
was dispatched from this life either by a bear or a Native
American named Black Bear? Or could it be some unknown
spirit, a person the history books forgot but who strongly
resists that oblivion? Perhaps one of the Native Americans
driven into Lake Castac to drown.

The Fort Tejon Park and historic buildings are open all year
from 10:00 A.M. to 4:30 P.M. for a small fee. On the first Sunday
of each month, members of the fort's historical association and
docents in period clothing and uniforms illustrate the lifestyle of
the pioneers and servicemen who worked and lived at Fort
Tejon. Demonstrations of cooking, army drills, woodworking,

sewing, blacksmithing, and other crafts take place. On the third weekend of each month, from April through October, volunteers reenact Civil War battles on the parade grounds (although no battles actually took place at Tejon). For further information, write Fort Tejon State Historic Park, P.O. Box 895, Lebec, CA 93243 or call (805) 248-6692.

Perhaps on your visit you, too, will see the phantom of Fort Tejon near the haunted oak!

DIRECTIONS: *Fort Tejon is located in Grapevine Canyon, Kern County, on I-5. It is 36 miles south of Bakersfield and 77 miles north of Los Angeles, near the small community of Lebec.*

—DR

HOLLYWOOD'S IMMORTALS HAUNT THIS CEMETERY
Hollywood Memorial Park Cemetery
Los Angeles, California

Richard L. Senate, my ghost-hunting friend from California, dug up some fascinating evidence that Hollywood Memorial Park is haunted by a few special ghosts from the film community's colorful past.

Considered by cemetery aficionados to be one of the greatest in the world, Hollywood Memorial Park appears to be a serene island where tall palm trees and high walls shut out the frenetic city of Los Angeles. Yet one never forgets that this cemetery is part of hectic Hollywood. Within these walls one wanders past Greek temples, Roman temples, and Egyptian temples as from one movie set to another. No longer on theater marquees, the familiar names of yesteryear's stars are now featured on impressive stone monuments. Paramount Studios stands just outside the cemetery's southern wall. To the north the famous Hollywood sign looms over the Hollywood Hills.

As with Hollywood of the living, there's a hierarchy in this Tinsel Town of the Dead, too. The grandest graves surround a peaceful little lake on the eastern side of the park. Cecil B. DeMille and his wife, Constance, are buried beneath an imposing double marker. Right across from their memorial is an identical double marker for Columbia's Harry Cohn, which he shares with no one. Cohn, who died in 1958, had selected his own plot; he felt this particular location would allow him to keep a watchful eye, even after death, on his studios, then just a few blocks away on Gower Street. Perhaps if Columbia hadn't moved away from Cohn's ghostly surveillance in 1972, it wouldn't have been plagued with the scandals that rocked the studios in the later seventies. Poor Cohn must have turned over in his grave when the Coca-Cola Corporation bought Columbia in 1982.

Nelson Eddy, Tyrone Power, Adolphe Menjou, and Marion Davies (under her family name of Douras) are also resting beside the scenic lake in this memorial park.

Inside the Cathedral Mausoleum, in crypt number 1205, lie the remains of the cemetery's biggest drawing card—Rudolph Valentino. Dead at the height of his fame in 1926, from appendicitis and peritonitis, his memory was revered by thousands who had idolized the charismatic star of *The Sheik*.

One of the memorial park's enduring mysteries was the identity of the heavily veiled "lady in black" who made her pilgrimage to lay roses at Valentino's crypt every year on the anniversary of his death. Although she no longer appears in the flesh (apparently she has finally gone to join her hero), the flowers on Valentino's crypt are always fresh. And strangely, an insubstantial dark form is sometimes seen kneeling there. I believe that the veiled woman's intense feelings for Valentino have imprinted the crypt with her energy, like an emotional charge, resulting in this apparition.

Also in this mausoleum are the crypts of Peter Finch, Peter Lorre, and Eleanor Powell. Just outside is the tomb of Douglas Fairbanks, overlooking a beautiful reflecting pool paid for (they say) by his ex-wife Mary Pickford.

At the western end of the cemetery is the Abbey of Palms Mausoleum. Sisters Norma and Constance Talmadge are buried together here in the Sanctuary of Eternal Love.

Even here among the graves of the rich and famous, no one can say why one spirit and not another comes back to haunt the living. I might have expected Peter Lorre's hoarse, frightened whisper to be heard, but no. . . . Senate writes in his book *Ghosts of Southern California* that the ghostly voice heard in this cemetery is a sobbing sound above the simple grave of silent-film starlet Virginia Rappe.

The film comic Roscoe "Fatty" Arbuckle was implicated in Virginia's death. It was alleged that the young woman died after having been forced by Arbuckle to perform some rather unusual sexual acts in a San Francisco hotel room. The world's most popular comedian, who numbered among his ardent fans many schoolchildren, was tried for Virginia's rape and murder three times. In the first two trials the jury was unable to agree on a verdict. The third jury acquitted Arbuckle, but his career never recovered from the disgrace he suffered when his private life was made public in court. The press had enjoyed a field day with each sensational revelation of Arbuckle's—and the whole film community's—excesses.

There are a few questions still unanswered about the case. The Hearst newspapers had been instrumental in turning these trials into a nationwide scandal. As it happens, shortly before Arbuckle came to trial, the Hearst-Marion Davies affair was receiving universal criticism, and Miss Davies's films had lost money as a result. Rumor has it that Hearst gave the go-ahead to his newspapers to exploit every Hollywood scandal of the time—especially Arbuckle's—in order to take the heat off himself and Miss Davies. Buster Keaton reported hearing Hearst declare that he'd sold more newspapers during the Arbuckle trials than when the *Lusitania* went down.

Minta Durfee, Arbuckle's ex-wife, was his staunch supporter during his ordeal. She was quoted on the subject of Virginia in Kevin Brownlow's *The Parade's Gone By.* "Rappe . . . worked at Sennett [studios]; I knew her well. She was very sweet, but she was suffering from several diseases, one of which so shocked Sennett that he closed down the studio and had it fumigated."

Whatever really was the cause of Virginia's death, her promising life was cut short by this tragedy, and it's not surprising that anguished sobbing is heard at her grave site.

Of all the famous ghosts whose apparitions we might expect to find in Hollywood Memorial Park, it's the wry, sophisticated Clifton Webb who's been seen among the ornate gravestones on these manicured grounds, for reasons we may never know.

Most people remember Webb for his portrayal of the redoubtable baby-sitter Mr. Belvedere in *Sitting Pretty,* although his role in *Laura* always has been my favorite. That hysterical edge in his portrayal of the urbane newspaper columnist Waldo Lydecker wasn't all acting. Right after the production closed down, Webb suffered a nervous breakdown and had himself committed to a sanitarium in New England. His costar in *Laura*, Gene Tierney (who shared the same birthday as Webb, November 19), wrote about Webb's recovery in her autobiography. "He came out of it rested and restored, but the main effect of his analysis was to encourage him to treat his mother rudely."

Well, no one could be rude with as much panache as Clifton Webb. He was the only denizen of Hollywood ever to call Darryl Zanuck by a nickname; he called the Warner Bros. mogul "Bud."

When Webb was being considered for the Lydecker role, Zanuck's casting director sneered at the actor's test, saying "He doesn't walk, he flies." But Zanuck saw a film clip made of Webb onstage in *Blithe Spirit* and hired him anyway. Webb was later to become a close friend of Zanuck's.

Whether walking or flying around Hollywood Memorial Park, what a wonderful ghost Clifton Webb must be!

DIRECTIONS: *Hollywood Memorial Park is located at 6000 Santa Monica Boulevard in Los Angeles. The hours are 9:00 A.M. to 5:00 P.M. daily. Admission is free, and so is a map showing who's buried where, available at the main entrance.*

—DR

THE CASE OF THE MISSING HOUR
Interstate 15
Barstow, California

There is a stretch of Interstate 15 right outside Barstow, California, which many people who are interested in UFOs and other manifestations of life from other planets claim conceals an underground factory of sorts run by aliens. Psychic Kelly Roberts was driving along this highway when she had a highly unusual experience—even for her. This is how she related it to me.

"This experience really freaked me out, even though I should have been prepared for it.

"One afternoon four or five years ago I was traveling on Interstate 15 going from San Diego to Las Vegas. I stopped for gas in Barstow, and I was just coming back onto the freeway when I looked at the clock. It was a few minutes after three. After checking the time I looked down to get my Pepsi out of the holder in the door; I took a sip, lit a cigarette, looked back at the clock, and an hour had gone by. This took place in what I had thought was about ten seconds.

"I wasn't upset. Figuring it was the clock, I reached over and hit it with the palm of my hand. It wasn't a digital clock but the kind where the numbers flip over, so I thought maybe it had gotten stuck. I hit it again and it still didn't move. Then I looked at the watch on my wrist, and it showed the same time as the car clock. I really sort of came unglued. An hour was missing!

"Just then traffic got really horrendous and it started to rain. A strong wind was coming up, and the cars were hydroplaning all over the road on the wet pavement. I had to give all my attention to driving and to the other cars on the road. So I didn't think much more about the incident until an hour or an hour and a half later, when I got to Las Vegas. When I arrived at my hotel, I experienced a sense of complete disorientation. It was terrifying! I got lost in a hallway that was a straight shot from the parking lot to the front desk. For about forty-five minutes I just couldn't find the front desk. Here I was with my luggage, roaming back and forth like a rat in a maze. I finally got to the desk, registered, and settled into my room.

"After trying to calm myself I called my friends, who lived just across the street. I was supposed to go there for dinner, and I was anxious to see them. They told me to come right over. All I had to do was cross the street, go to the front door, and take the elevator to the third floor. When I got to their parking lot I could see the side door, but I couldn't reach it. Impossible as it sounds, I got lost in the parking lot for half an hour. By the time I made it to their apartment I was in tears. I didn't understand why I couldn't seem to get from point A to point B without getting lost. I explained to my friends about the lost hour and, because I still was disoriented, went into a room by myself to meditate. During meditation I could see myself coming back into the car and back into my body. I saw myself laughing because I knew that I wouldn't consciously remember what had happened and that it would cause great confusion."

"Was this an out-of-body experience?" I asked.

"Not exactly," Kelly answered. "I have out-of-body experiences all the time in my work. It's one of the methods I use when I'm helping the police [something Kelly often does]. This experience happened right around Calico Ghost Town, an old mining town that's now open to the public. I was told by my guides in meditation that from that point on, for almost the next thirty miles, there is an underground UFO habitation. I went there astrally and saw them actually taking minerals out of the ground. They were converting some of them, melting some of them. There was an assembly-line thing. But I couldn't see as much as I'd have liked to. Something was blocking me; perhaps those running the workshop were protecting their secret."

Kelly decided to try a second time to penetrate the underground UFO workshop psychically. This time she was met with resistance at every turn and she saw less than the first time. She told me laughingly, "I guess it's by invitation only."

Kelly says that over the last few years at least twenty of her clients have reported becoming disoriented on this same stretch of road, where, she says, "there's nothing to become disoriented about. It's a straight road going through the desert. But my clients had chills, goosebumps on the arms, and other signs of fright. They felt like they were being watched." And the clincher—the strangest and most convincing argument—is that none of Kelly's clients knew of the other clients' experiences on that thirty-mile stretch of Interstate 15.

DIRECTIONS: *Take I-15 North from Barstow toward Las Vegas. (Kelly adds, "I advise motorists to remain on the highway and not try to take any side roads. Usually in an area with a high concentration of UFO energy, the mechanics of a car or truck are apt to break down. This is not a stretch of desert you want to be stranded in.")*

—JB

GHOSTS ON THE GOLF COURSE
Aetna Springs, California

Aetna Springs is a plush resort town in the hills of California about fifty miles north of San Francisco. The resort was built near a mineral spring that boasts properties of a curative nature, and people go there from all over in the hope of finding relief from some malady or just to enjoy the atmosphere.

Noted psychic Hans Holzer tells of his visit there in his book *Ghosts of the Golden West*. Holzer's interest in the place wasn't to partake of the waters or to enjoy a vacation but because of a friend of his, Dr. Andrew van Salsa (who was well known and recognized not only as a medical doctor but for his amazing ability to take pictures in which the likenesses of people who had departed this sphere kept popping up). In 1963 the good doctor took a vacation at Aetna Springs resort and, since he was a loquacious fellow, soon became friendly with Mr. Heibel, who managed the place.

Andrew van Salsa took only two pictures; the remainder of the roll of film was used by Heibel. Most of the shots were of the beautiful golf course, and they'd all been taken within half an hour of each other. The pictures were soon developed and, to the amazement of all, even van Salsa, who'd had this type of thing happen many times before, two of the pictures (presumably those taken by van Salsa) showed two rows of monks. It was unclear whether there were four or five monks in each row. The monks had shaven heads and were adorned in white robes. Each was carrying a candle and had around his head a bright light that appeared to be flames. The expressions on the monks' faces indicated that they had died in terrible pain.

When Hans Holzer saw these pictures the agonized faces upset him, and so at the first opportunity he and his friend and fellow psychic Sybil Leek journeyed to Aetna Springs to try to unravel the mystery of the monks and find out just what they meant to the area. Accompanying them was Holzer's wife, Catherine, and Bill Wynn, a friend. Because Holzer didn't want Sybil Leek to have any preconceived feelings, he hadn't told her the purpose of their mission. She thought they were on vacation. As they were nearing the Aetna Springs area, Sybil closed her eyes for a moment, then reached out toward Holzer and told him that the place to which they were going had been some sort of religious sanctuary, a place where people had gone for survival.

On further questioning from Holzer, Sybil acknowledged sadly that the people had all been killed. She felt those people had crossed water to get there—a Huguenot influence was her conclusion.

Soon the little party had registered at the resort and set out to explore it. They drove to the golf course, left their car, and walked out onto the green. Once there, Sybil went into a trancelike state and started mumbling about fire, torture, and crucifixion. She felt, she said, that a bench under the trees by the side of one of the greens was a hotspot—where the evil activity had taken place. Gently prodding her for the facts, Hans Holzer asked what nationality the offending people were. Sybil's answer was quick: "They were conquistadores." After agonizing for a few more minutes, she said she saw the victims and that they were in women's clothes. Holzer translated this to mean the robes of the monks.

At this point, Sybil Leek became very upset and began crying—sobbing that she could feel the hatred that accompanied the killings there. She told Holzer that the spirits were there because there had been no justice—their deaths had not been avenged. A few minutes later she said they had been murdered by Hieronymus (Saint Jerome) because they had taken some silver. Holzer intoned some words of sympathy and beseeched the monks to leave and be at peace with their brothers. Sybil was muttering prayers and breathing heavily just before she came out of the trance. She remembered nothing of the hour in which she had labored to understand and free the spirits of the monks. Holzer took pictures of the area, figuring he'd get some shots of the monks, since he'd been quite successful at photographing ghosts in the past. But his camera wasn't working right. Or perhaps his words and Sybil's prayers had released the ghosts at last.

No one in the Aetna Springs area seemed to know about, or care about, the ghosts or their history, so Holzer vowed that he'd research the subject upon his return to New York. In a book by Irving Richman called *California Under Spain and Mexico,* Holzer found a reference to the way in which the

Spanish conquerors had treated the Indians. Holzer described this treatment as "only slightly less cruel than the way in which Hitler's Nazis treated subjugated people during World War II." During the time of the Spanish conquerors, children were literally thrown to the dogs, and the natives were put to death just for kicks. People were suppressed both politically and spiritually. Holzer speculates that one of the remote missions, a sanctuary for the oppressed peoples of the Spanish lands, may have been on the Aetna Springs Golf Course.

At the beginning of the 1500s there also was a violent difference of opinion in the religious community about how the natives should be treated. The Dominicans, who wore white robes, were in favor of treating them humanely, while the Franciscans, who wore brown robes, considered them less than human and endorsed dealing with them as such. It is entirely possible that the white-robed monks, who seem to have died so tragically, were cut down by the Franciscans because they were sheltering the American Indians.

If you visit the Aetna Springs Golf Course you may be able to photograph these poor tortured souls—but it's my hope that Sybil Leek and Hans Holzer were successful in their effort and that these brothers have found a lasting peace. Still, Aetna Springs is worth the trip for its beauty, and I've found that any place once inhabited by ghosts has a lingering essence of their presence that can be detected by those sensitive to such things.

DIRECTIONS: *From San Francisco, cross the Bay Bridge to Oakland. Continue on 80 North across Carquinez Bridge, then take 29 North to St. Helena. Turn off on road to Angwin. Continue past Angwin and Pope Valley to Aetna Springs.*

—JB

MAGIC PLACES OF OAHU
Downtown Honolulu, Punchbowl Hill, and Nuuanu Valley, Oahu, Hawaii

No area in the United States is more steeped in legendary magic and magicians, haunting and haunted landscapes than Oahu, Hawaii. You don't have to be a professional psychic to be sensitive to the living presence of a mysterious past still vibrant enough to be experienced here, despite this island's vastly overdeveloped coastline. All visitors feel the spell, although they may call it by other names, like "enigmatic beauty" or "tropical enchantment."

Hono means "abundance" and *lulu* means "peace," but there are restless spirits roaming through downtown Honolulu at night, as reported in an article by Burl Burlingham *(Star-Bulletin,* January 8, 1986). This business area has been built right over the old native village of Kou, where a Hawaiian chief's compound of houses and grounds once lay between the ocean and what is now Hotel Street and between Nuuanu Avenue and Alakea Street. It must have been an idyllic location, and some of the most splendid surf for riding rolled into the narrow entrance to the harbor of Kou.

Glen Grant, a teacher of American Studies at Kapiolani Community College and a collector of Hawaiian ghost stories, is quoted in the Burlington article. He says that the spirits of Kou's former residents go looking for their homes in the offices and sidewalks around the intersection of King Street and Nuuanu Avenue.

In my own research into this haunted area, I note that there was a place called Kewalo near Kou's harbor entrance, where the lowest class of servants *(Kauwa)* were put to death by drowning. Whether these poor people were being punished or sacrificed we don't know, but the law pertaining to the practice was picturesquely known as *ke-kai-he-hee,* meaning "the law of sliding the servants under the waves of the sea." It might well be that spirits of these unlucky souls are marching back from their watery graves to old Kou at night. At any rate, older Hawaiians tend to avoid the harbor area after dark, when the ghosts are afoot.

Another place known to be haunted since the turn of the century is the junction of Alakea and Merchant streets, where ghosts the Hawaiians called *wai-lua* would gather nightly, according to legend, to play games and sports such as rolling the flat-sided stone disk known as the *maika* stone. "These ghosts," according to an early book of Honolulu legends, "made night a source of dread to all people." It seems a shame, since the *wai-lua* were obviously out for a good time!

The native Hawaiian religion is called *huna* and its priests *kahunas* or "keepers of the secret." Like many other seemingly playful, cheerful island peoples, the ancient Hawaiians had a dark side to their religious practices. Although the power of *huna* was known to effect marvelous healings and other desirable miracles, there was a frightening element as well. Human sacrifices were offered, and there were many religious laws, called *kapu*, which meant death if broken. However, if a *kapu* breaker could run to a temple sanctuary before being captured, he would be safe from execution and could perform ceremonies of absolution. The largest of these sanctuaries, on the "big island" of Hawaii, was called the "city of refuge" and is now The City of Refuge National Historic Park.

More than a hundred *heiaus*, (temples)—some sanctuaries and some not—are still being discovered on Oahu. One of the most famous was the Pakaka Temple, which stood on the western side of the foot of Fort Street (long before the fort for which the street is named was built). A school for Oahu's priests was located in this *heiau*. The temple was decorated with the heads of human sacrifices.

Inland from Kou, in the Nuuanu Valley, where the Oahu Country Club now stands, is the legendary home of the *E'epa,* Oahu's "little people." They are reminiscent of Europe's elves, which are variously known as gnomes, fairies, leprechauns, or brownies. Like their European counterparts, the *E'epa* were small creatures who performed stupendous tasks at night. It is said that the *E'epa* had the character of human beings but enjoyed the power of a fairy people.

The Manoa Valley was the home of another fabled people, the *Menehune*. This lost tribe of Oahu lived on Punchbowl Hill and were powerful magicians. Like the *E'epa*, the *Menehune* worked all night and completed fantastic works before morning. Punchbowl, just above Honolulu, is the site of a volcanic crater. Some describe this spot as the most spectacular setting in the

Honolulu area. It's also the site of the National Memorial Cemetery of the Pacific, called "hill of sacrifice" by the native Hawaiians. Over twenty thousand servicemen who died in World War II and the Korean War are buried in this cemetery.

Of these fairy workers, the *E'epa* and the *Menehune*, the Hawaiians said, "No task is too difficult. It is the work of one hand." In one legend, the *Menehune* were asked by a queen to build houses for guests, and it was done "like the motion of an eye."

Although there are many gods, goddesses, "ghost-gods," and magical creatures in Hawaiian legends, the *E'epa* and the *Menehune* are of particular interest because they may represent not just the creations of unconscious fantasy but tales based on a prehistoric people of advanced knowledge who actually existed. If they lived and left behind them traces of their life energy, mediums and those with the sensitivity called "far memory" (intuitive or psychic knowledge of ages past) can attempt to perceive this in visiting their fabled haunts.

There is a theory that such sophisticated peoples actually lived in prehistoric civilizations now lost, and that their survivors became the source of so-called fairy stories that are told to children all over the world. This possibility has been proposed by Jean Hunt *(Mensa Bulletin,* October 1989, Number 330), among others.

According to the Hunt article, there is evidence that a small people, under five feet three inches in stature, with long rather than round heads, still existed in Egypt around the time that the pyramids were built. Since they looked different from their neighbors, they may have seemed ugly or odd. Remnants of these "little folk" were also reported among the Minoans, the Phoenicians, in the British Isles, and in North and South America as well as the Hawaiian *Menehune.* The fairy or gnome-like creatures of legend were always wise beyond the ways of ordinary men and able to accomplish what seemed (to those with only primitive knowledge) like miraculously impossible tasks "overnight."

Tales like these are so prevalent in world mythology, it's at least possible that some grain of truth is lurking within them. It's interesting to speculate that the "magical powers" of the *E'epa* and the *Menehune* may simply have been the development of a sophisticated knowledge that was later lost.

Dedicated ghost hunters who visit Hawaii's legendary landscapes may also want to stop at the state capitol, which is rumored to be haunted by the ghost of Queen Liliuokalani, whose statue can be seen on the *makai* (seaward) side of the building. The queen's ghost has been seen walking in the stairway of the building, carrying ceremonial leis on her arms. A few yards away from the statue, in the Iolani Palace grounds, the spirit of a young Hawaiian girl wearing a white dress sometimes shimmers near the fountain at twilight.

DIRECTIONS: *King Street runs north and south through downtown Honolulu and the state capitol area. Heading north, Alakea and Merchant streets both branch off North King Street, as does Nuuanu Avenue.*

Ward Avenue begins at Ala Moana Boulevard, crosses South King Street near the Mission Houses Museum, and ends at Punchbowl Hill, the circular crater of a dead volcano. The graves of the national cemetery are spread across the bottom of the bowl. If you pass through the memorial area to the crater rim, you will see breathtaking views of Honolulu. This is the fabled home of the Menehune.

Highway 61 out of downtown Honolulu will bring you to Nuuanu Valley, which is E'epa country. If you enjoy hiking, the Puu Ohia Trail, two miles long, provides splendid views of Manoa and Nuuanu valleys. To find the trail, follow Tantalus Drive, which starts at the Punchbowl Crater and goes up into the hills above Honolulu. Puu Ohia Trail begins from Tantalus Drive.

—DR

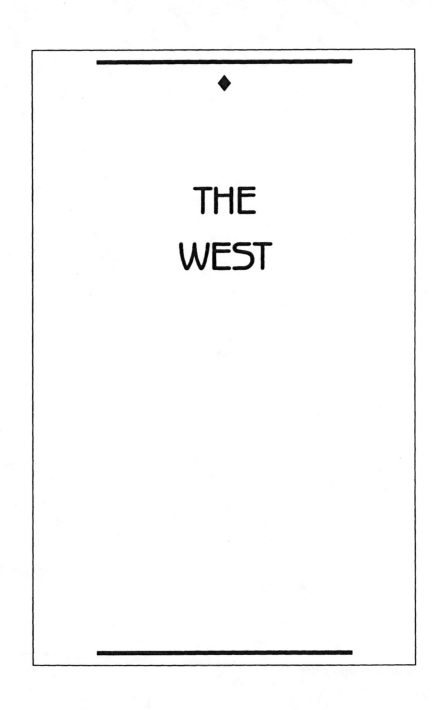

THE
WEST

HAUNTS OF THE HOPI AND NAVAJO NATIONS

Hopi-Navajo Reservation, Arizona

On summer nights in Coal Canyon, on the Hopi-Navajo Reservation, the huge yet graceful apparition of a woman floats above an outcropping of Black Mesa deposits. (Reported in *Arizona Highroads,* July/August 1974.)

Night after night, this persistent ghost appears to be suspended in air above the monumental stone shapes eerily looming in the moonlight. One can see the sinuous turn of her head, the billowing folds of her long dress, and the sweeping motion of her arms, as if she were flying. Sometimes her diaphanous sleeves look more like wings. The Hopis call her Eagle Woman.

You can choose between two explanations for this ghostly figure—or you can, like me, believe that both may be true.

The Hopis say that Eagle Woman was an Oraibi widow of the Bow Clan who lived in the late 1800s. Old Oraibi is an ancient village on the Third Mesa. The Hopis have lived in Oraibi since A.D. 1100, making it the longest-inhabited town in North America.

Although the widow might have taken pride and comfort in her tall, strong sons, she became instead more and more melancholy as the years advanced. She was about forty-five when her depression became unbearable. One day she left her hogan and her family without a word and took the trail up to Coal Canyon. There she rested and meditated throughout the night. The moon came up, huge and full over the wind-sculptured rocks. The woman felt it beckoning to her. She answered the moon's summons by leaping from the high cliff where she had kept her vigil.

It took some time for family members to find her. When her body was finally discovered, it was left where it lay and covered with rocks, the Hopi custom in cases of suicide or accidental death away from home.

The Hopis say it is this widow's spirit that materializes in the canyon today. They believe that one can always see a light in the place where someone has died.

The scientific explanation is less poetic. Phosphorescent vapors rising from the coal deposits in the Black Mesa are said to create this shimmering apparition in midair.

Phosphorescence doesn't totally explain why, if you stay all through the summer night at Coal Canyon, the ghost of Eagle Woman is said to come closer and closer as the hours progress, until you can almost reach out and touch her. But don't reach out too far over the cliff's edge!

Spider Rock and Speaking Rock, two towering columns at the junction of Monument Canyon and Canyon de Chelly, are also the dwelling places of other-worldly creatures, according to Navajo legend (reported in *Desert Magazine,* October 1965). Spider Rock has the sinister reputation of harboring the spirit of a giant spider. Long before such monstrous insects were depicted in films, Navajo children were being frightened by tales of this demon. In traditional Hopi lore, an old ghost woman who lives on Speaking Rock likes to tattle on a naughty youngster to the neighboring spider. The spider then descends from its lair and carries away the offending child. The white color atop the eight-hundred-foot column of Spider Rock is attributed to the accumulation of bleached bones of the small victims.

Canyon de Chelly itself has a magical reputation. It is supposed to be the site of a great power source for clearing the mind and for healing. This renewing force is still felt by visitors, especially psychics, and has lasted through several eras of the red rock canyon's history.

The Anasazi (the "ancient ones") made their home in the canyon for a thousand years, in an interlocked series of dwellings, now called the White House, constructed on a huge shelf under precipitous cliffs. It may very well have been this mysterious early civilization that has left such a strong spiritual imprint on the canyon. Next came the Hopi people, some of whom may have been descendants of the Anasazi, attracted by the power of the place. After the Hopi, in the 1700s, the Navajo sought a home in the canyon. The Navajo originally were a foraging tribe that migrated from Canada. Although not related to so-called Pueblo Indians, the Navajo benefited from the lingering Anasazi influence, which had brought them many major breakthroughs such as weaving, pottery making, and farming, to which they added sheep herding.

The old Anasazi canyon, twenty-six miles long, deep and jagged, seemed like a natural fortress that would prove a strong defense against the Spanish. The Navajo decorated the walls of Canyon de Chelly with beautiful pictographs that can still be seen today. No doubt, Navajo artists hoped these remarkable works had magical properties of protection for the canyon. In 1803, however, the Spanish massacred over a hundred of the resistant natives, but it was left to Kit Carson, acting for the U.S. government, to finish the job in 1863. He employed the very effective "scorched earth" tactic of destroying fields, orchards, and hogans, and confiscating livestock. Then Carson blocked one end of Canyon de Chelly with soldiers and wagons and sent the rest of his troops in through the other end, flushing out and killing the Navajo as they went. The remaining Navajo were force-marched across three hundred miles of New Mexico, many of them dying on the way.

The name *Navajo* was imposed by conquering forces. This nation's name for itself was *Dinneh* or *Dine,* meaning "the People" in the sense of "the real people" or "the human beings." As it happens, there is no *V* in the Navajo alphabet, so the invaders, rather typically, had given them a name impossible for them to pronounce in their native tongue.

In spite of these turbulent episodes, the peace and power of this secluded canyon has resurfaced and remains strong. The psychically gifted will still feel the spiritual emanations of the place, and some have reported seeing visions of the lost Anasazi going about their daily lives in the canyon.

When their reservation was defined in 1868, Canyon de Chelly was given back to the Navajo. Today the Navajo Nation manages this remarkable monument, which they still consider their sacred stronghold, in conjunction with the National Park Service.

DIRECTIONS: *For general information about Navajoland (which includes the Hopi Reservation) write the Navajo Tourism Office, Navajo Nation, P.O. Box 308, Window Rock, Arizona 86515, or call (602) 871-4941.*

To find Coal Canyon, travel State Highway 264 a little more than fourteen miles southwest of Tuba City, en route to Window

Rock, Arizona. Although the canyon may be easily missed, it's within a mile of the highway at that point, and there are signs directing the way to the vantage point.

Canyon de Chelly National Monument is open from April through October. Take U.S. Highway 191, north from Interstate 40 or south from Utah, to the monument's headquarters at Chinle. For advance information about trails and tours, write Superintendent, Canyon de Chelly National Monument, Box 588, Chinle, Arizona 86503, or call (602) 674-5436.

—DR

THE MYSTERY OF THE ANASAZI
Mesa Verde, Colorado, and Chaco Canyon, New Mexico

An enigmatic North American people emerged in the Southwest before the time of Christ's birth, and they continued to flourish there until about A.D. 1500. Later inhabitants of the same region, the Navajo, called these predecessors who were not their ancestors the Anasazi. The term is variously translated as "ancient ones," "ancient enemies," or "the people who have gone away."

The latter translation probably refers to the strange disappearance of the Anasazi in the second century A.D. To archaeologists studying their dwellings, it looked almost as if the Anasazi had walked away for an evening stroll, leaving most of their housewares in their usual places. Although it had taken time and skill to craft the intricate, tightly woven baskets and multicolored pottery, much of it was simply abandoned. Yet there was no evidence that the departure had been a hasty one. Archaeologists say the Anasazi weren't invaded or afflicted with an epidemic. Such catastrophic events would have been apparent from the condition and situation of skeletons found at the various sites.

At a loss to explain this orderly exit, historians have decided that the long drought of A.D. 1276–1299 was the reason for their leaving—although the Anasazi had survived long droughts before. No one really knows where the Anasazi went and why they traveled with so few belongings. Anthropologists theorize that they moved south, intermarried, and were incorporated into other nations. Pottery traditions of the Hopi and Zuni nations can be traced back to the Anasazi.

A second mysterious thing about the Anasazi is that their spirits still haunt the lands that were their home. Many people feel their presence, and some psychics have seen their apparitions.

The Anasazi were part of the golden age of Native Americans in the Southwest, called the Cochise Culture. They are thought to be descendants of migratory tribes who lived by hunting and foraging during prehistoric times. It seems likely that the Anasazi had other ancestors, too, who came to this continent as far back as the Bronze Age, mingling their genes with a population that continued to move southward. The Anasazi were short in stature and had long heads (dolichocephalic) rather than the round heads characteristic of modern man. This distinctive feature, coupled with a height under five feet three inches, has also been found in certain skeletons in ancient Egypt and the British Isles, and among the Minoans and the Phoenicians.

Expert farmers who utilized sophisticated irrigation techniques (not substantially different from those used today), the Anasazi were able to coax two harvests a year from their arid lands—beans, squash, and the all-important corn, some of which has been dated in New Mexico as far back as 1000 B.C. They domesticated dogs and turkeys.

Anasazi jewelry was lavish with turquoise and was exquisitely crafted in designs that are still being copied in southwestern jewelry. Their clothes were made of soft fur or woven cotton fabric. Women cut their hair short, but men wore their locks long among the Anasazi. The family unit was matriarchal.

The Anasazi were also extraordinary architects who built apartment-style dwellings into the sheer faces of formidable cliffs. By grouping rooms together with shared walls and building one on top of another, using ladders for access to different levels, the roof of one apartment became the patio of the one above. One of the most elaborate multitiered dwelling, whose construction was begun about A.D. 900 in Chaco Canyon, has eight hundred rooms in five stories.

Far below these so-called pueblos (from the Spanish word for town or community), on the canyon's floor, were the Anasazi ceremonial buildings. They were round "pit houses" featuring a small hole in the floor that traditional lore among southwestern Native Americans says is a symbolic entrance to the lower world, called a *sipapu*—"Spirit Hole" or "Earth Navel." According to Hopi lore, the Anasazi believed human beings originally came from the earth's center. Perhaps this myth was rooted in an acknowledgment of the earth as mother of all living things.

They must have been an extremely strong and agile people, descending daily to the canyon floor to work the fields and fetch water, or climbing to the cliff tops to hunt. It's not an easy matter to explore the Anasazi apartments today.

These pueblos, located in the Four Corners area of present-day Utah, Colorado, Arizona, and New Mexico, can still be seen today, and many psychics have reported that the sites are haunted by Anasazi spirits. The Four Corners area itself is said to be one of the great spiritual power centers of the world.

Psychometrist Kelly Roberts of Escondido, California, a professional psychic and investigator, shared with us her experience at the Anasazi ruins in Mesa Verde, Colorado.

"Walking through the dwellings at Cliff Palace is like stepping through a time warp. I don't know if everyone experiences what I do clairvoyantly while there. . . . I am able to see some of the comings and goings of [the Anasazi] as if they were right in front of me in this time frame. I have talked to others who have seen the same or experienced the same. . . . I find it interesting that long before I knew [the Anasazi story], I described to numerous people in California the history of these people as I had seen it, or perhaps remembered it. This was three years before my first trip to Colorado. It was only later that I learned pieces of their history here and there from the tour books, confirming what I had already seen through clairvoyance. So I feel very much at home at Mesa Verde.

"The energy there feels extremely powerful, awesome. As if you are sharing in something very sacred, whether you believe in anything religious or not. The energy is very spiritual, healing."

After the Anasazi abandoned Mesa Verde, the Native Americans who lived in that region kept the place a secret. Cliff Palace was not discovered by European Americans until five centuries later. In 1874, members of a U.S. Geological and

Geographical Survey of the Territories expedition came upon the ruins by chance and photographed them. The photo was widely reprinted in the East, but, strangely, no other expeditions were planned at that time. The place was rediscovered in 1881 by the Wetherill family, amateur archaeologists who devoted themselves to this major find for the next eighteen years.

Al Wetherill described his first sight of Cliff Palace as a "cavernlike place in which was situated what seemed like a small ruined city. In the dusk and the silence, the great blue vault hung over me like a mirage. The solemn grandeur of the outlines was breathtaking."

There is some very convincing evidence (assembled by Jean Hunt, president of the Louisiana Mounds Society, in her manuscript *Tracking the Flood Survivors*) that the various long-headed peoples (like the Anasazi) found in ancient history and legend belong to a physical group whose lineage may go back to inhabitants of the lost continent of Atlantis. The later Anasazi decided, for some unknown reason, to alter or hide this feature by strapping their infants to wooden cradle boards that flattened their heads, in an effort to make them appear rounder.

There is a sun temple in Mesa Verde that was obviously of great spiritual significance to the Anasazi. Built in the form of a D, the structure contains a curious emblem. It's a symbol often seen on the walls of pueblos: a sunflower. This one is about two feet in diameter, with a central basin and radials extending outward, etched in sandstone, and surrounded by carefully constructed short walls. The mysterious thing about this partic ular etching is that geologists say it was produced by natural erosion and not by carving. Apparently, it was transported to its present site and given an altarlike surrounding. It's called the Sun Shrine.

There is something haunting and intriguing about the Anasazi history, or the lack of it. It's as if we have gained several pieces of a puzzle but not enough to assemble a complete picture of this North American mystery, although the rise and fall of the archaic nations of South America are quite well documented. Only those who are psychically gifted can reach into the past to know the Anasazi.

DIRECTIONS: *Mesa Verde National Park is located west of Durango, Colorado, on U.S. Highway 160 between the towns of Cortez and Mancos. The park is open year-round during daylight hours.*

From the park entrance to park headquarters is a distance of over 20 miles. A ranger must accompany anyone wishing to explore the cliff dwellings. For further information write Mesa Verde National Park, Colorado 81330 or call (303) 529-4465.

Chaco Culture National Historic Park covers 35,000 acres and contains thirteen major ruins, including Pueblo Bonito, the Anasazi eight-hundred-room cliff dwelling. Chaco is located 54 miles south of Bloomsfield, New Mexico, via State Highway 44 and "unimproved" State Highway 57, which runs north-south through the park. For more information, write Chaco Culture National Historic Park, Star Route 4, Box 6500, Bloomsfield, New Mexico 87413, or call (505) 988-6716.

—DR

THE SHADES OF CHEESMAN PARK
Denver, Colorado

B road expanses of well-kept lawn and stately old trees give Cheesman Park an aura of peace and tranquillity, making it an oasis of quiet refreshment in the bustling city of Denver. But what's that moving in the late afternoon shadows? Is it the ethereal form of a young woman in a plain frock, crooning to herself a song of bygone times? Or is it a tall, bearded ruffian with two pistols in his gun belt who's just stepped out from between leafy branches? And at night, who are those gossamer specters drifting about the moonlit marble steps of the pavilion and spilling out of the park into nearby houses? These are only some of the apparitions that have been reported in and around this pleasant placc.

Beautiful Cheesman Park, in fact, is built upon an old horror, and the place is reputed to be haunted. It seems that these attractive grounds were landscaped over the desecration of the old City Cemetery, a rather infamous chapter in Denver's history. As all ghost researchers soon learn, digging up graves is like opening Pandora's box—no good is going to come out of it. The removal of City Cemetery, however, was more than a simple disturbance of the dead. It was a scandal that rocked City Hall, outraged the citizenry, lured souvenir hunters, and filled the tabloids of the time with juicy stories.

In 1858, William Larimer staked out 320 acres of high ground located east of town (now between 8th and 13th avenues) to be used as a cemetery for the new city of Denver, which was founded as the jumping-off place to mining towns of the central Rockies. Rather ironically, Larimer named this burial ground Mount Prospect. Grave sites on the crest of the hill were to be reserved for the rich and famous; paupers and criminals would be buried at the lower outskirts; tradesmen and other ordinary folk could find their niches somewhere in the middle. Class consciousness died hard in early Denver.

Folklore maintains that the first corpses consigned to Mount Prospect were those of John Stoefel and the victim of his rage. Stoefel, a Hungarian immigrant, had come into town to settle a dispute with his brother-in-law and ended up murdering the man. After a summary trial, Stoefel was dragged away and hanged from a cottonwood tree that once stood where 10th and Wazee streets are now. His body and that of his brother-in-law were hauled to Mount Prospect—the lower section, of course. With grim efficiency, both were buried in the same grave. One imagines them eternally bound together, wrestling out their differences through time.

The name Mount Prospect didn't stick. In its early years, the cemetery was popularly called Ol' Boneyard or Boot Hill or Jack O'Neil's Ranch. There's a colorful story behind the third name.

Jack O'Neil was a bold, handsome gambler who made a reputation for himself in the 1860s. One night he got into a bitter quarrel with a Mormon named Rooker. Old accounts don't give the details, but I'll wager that Jack thought he'd won himself a ranch and Rooker welshed on the bet. Jack suggested that he and Rooker decide the matter privately, man to man, with knives and no witnesses. When Rooker chickened out of this gentlemanly offer, he was scorned and cursed by O'Neil's fellow gamblers with names calculated to give deep offense. A few days later, while the unsuspecting gambler was buying some supplies, Rooker ambushed O'Neil and let him have it with the twin blasts of a double-barreled shotgun. Strangely enough, Denver courts acquitted the Mormon (who happened to be the scion of one of Denver's founding families) of the subsequent murder charge. After the gambler's burial at Mount Prospect, his many pals began referring to the cemetery as Jack O'Neil's Ranch.

Denver soon began to flourish, with vast fortunes being made in silver and real estate. Embarrassed by frontier nicknames like Boot Hill, city officials decided in 1873 to rename the burial ground City Cemetery. Even a new name, however, couldn't change the fact that the place was becoming an eyesore. Lack of interest, care, and water were causing it to revert to its prairie origins, and indeed, prairie dogs ran among tumbledown gravestones, and cattle were allowed to graze on the neglected grass. No wonder affluent families were burying their dead at the newer Riverside or Fairlawn cemeteries instead, leaving City Cemetery to paupers, criminals, transients, and unclaimed smallpox and typhus victims from the local pest house.

Meanwhile, ownership of the cemetery had passed from Larimer to his assistant, a cabinetmaker named John J. Walley. Back in the spring of 1860, the city had hired Walley to build a casket for executed murderer James Gordon. This new business looked like a good deal to Walley, who decided to call himself an undertaker thereafter. Teaming up with Larimer, Walley took over the management of the cemetery—or perhaps mismanagement would be a better term.

With mansions being built left and right in surrounding areas, a lot of pressure was brought to bear on city officials to improve this blot in the midst of a prime residential area. These beleaguered politicos soon found a way to pull a fast one on Walley. Suddenly, someone in the U.S. government discovered the cemetery's land to be part of an old Indian treaty dating before 1860, which made Uncle Sam the real owner. Once the Feds took over in 1890, they immediately sold the cemetery back to the city of Denver for about $200, which was a bargain even then. Getting cut out of the deal didn't seem to bother Walley much; when he died at the age of ninety-four he was the oldest undertaker in the country and proud of it.

During the time Walley owned the cemetery he had divided it into three different sections. While the city portion had deteriorated, the Catholic and Jewish sections continued to be well maintained, so Denver officials returned ownership of the Catholic cemetery, called Mount Calvary, to the Church, and the Hebrew cemetery to Jewish community leaders, who quietly removed their dead and leased the property to the City Water Department.

The following summer City Hall served notice that all interested parties should have their dead removed from City Cemetery and buried elsewhere within ninety days. Some were reburied by concerned family members, but five thousand of the dead were forgotten and unclaimed. In the early spring of 1893 the city made ready to move these remaining bodies.

It happened that Mayor Platt Rogers, who worried about the health hazards of opening all those graves, was out of town on business when ordinances were passed to release funds for this project. With great haste, an undertaker name E. F. McGovern was awarded the contract, which specified that each body would be dug up and placed in a new box made on the site, but the box had to be only three and a half feet long by one foot wide. Upon delivery of the filled minicaskets to Riverside Cemetery, McGovern would be paid $1.90 each, and Riverside would get $5 to put these little boxes in the ground in land this cemetery's management had bought for $1 an acre.

It was typical March weather when McGovern's workmen began the job, just warm enough for the idle, the curious, and a few eager young reporters to watch from the sidelines. At first it went well enough, row after row in orderly progression, but then—whether hurried by a profit-conscious boss, inclement weather, or just feelings of unease—the workmen became more and more careless.

Maryjoy Martin, author of a book about Colorado's ghosts, has written that a certain Madame Cynara stood by watching while the workmen were prying up coffins, repeatedly warning them that they must whisper a prayer or the dead would return. The workmen probably laughed at that crazy old lady with her multiple shawls.

As more and more of the old caskets were dug up, they were smashed open with the backs of shovels. Bodies that had not decayed sufficiently to fit into small boxes were broken into pieces. There were no ceremony, no prayers, no one to say "stop" if the remains that fell out of broken caskets got rather mixed up in the process of being shoveled into those cheap new boxes. Watching with fascination and horror, some onlookers helped themselves to a few souvenirs—a moldering Bible or a greenish piece of jewelry.

According to Maryjoy Martin, one of the workmen, Jim Astor,

felt the spirits of the dead alight upon him, causing him to throw down his cache of brass plates, pried from the original caskets he had looted, and to run for his life. People in surrounding homes reported that apparitions suddenly appeared in their rooms or became visible in mirrors. At night, a low moaning could be heard over the field of opened graves. Perhaps that was only the March wind, but some people claim they can still hear it.

By the time Mayor Rogers got back to town, *The Denver Republican*, no friend of his administration, was running front-page stories about the atrocities being committed at City Cemetery and the general state of corruption in City Hall. At this time, it also came to light that there were certain discrepancies between the number of reburials charged to the city and the actual number of boxes delivered to Riverside. The matter had become a full-blown scandal, and, with the help of the health commissioner, the mayor had the project halted while an investigation ensued. Yawning graves were left unfilled, and the rest of the bodies abandoned. They're still there, somewhere under the surface of the park's placid lawns and gardens.

Plans for the park suffered a setback when silver prices collapsed in 1893, plummeting in four days from $3.20 to $.30 an ounce. It wasn't until the turn of the century that Reinhard Scheutze, a landscape architect from Germany, was hired to draw the plans. The land (with the remaining corpses) was plowed up for seeding and trees, and the place was named Congress Park, because of a federal grant received. In 1907 the old City Cemetery part of the park was renamed for the deceased Walter S. Cheesman, a prominent citizen of Denver. In 1909 Cheesman's family donated money for construction of a marble pavilion dedicated to Cheesman's memory, now the centerpiece of the park. In 1950 the Catholic Church sold its adjacent cemetery, and an orderly removal took place, making way for Denver's Botanic Gardens. Only the land leased to the Water Department is still called Congress Park.

The souls dispossessed to make room for the park apparently have returned—or perhaps they never left. My friend and intrepid researcher Dave Deame, who gathered much of this material while he was in Colorado, visited the park in broad daylight and found it to have a pleasant enough aura, which he attributed to its more recent history of relaxed, peaceful, and fun times. But he also detected an undertone of sad feelings, mixed together with the pleasantness—"like succotash," Dave said. He compared notes with a friend living in Phoenix, who grew up near Cheesman Park and used to roller-skate there but had never known its tragic story. She had garnered the same double impression during the years she lived in Denver. They agreed that there are two distinct wavelengths of emotion in the park; the visitor can tune in to either, depending on the mood he or she brings to the visit.

If you visit Cheesman Park, you may also wish to take a look at Larimer Square, which preserves the elegance of Victorian Denver; the refurbished mansion of Unsinkable Molly Brown; and the nearby Grant-Humphreys Mansion, which is also haunted. In one Halloween séance conducted by local radio station KNUS, a psychic detected five different entities in the mansion, one of whom is probably A. E. Humphreys, a noted marksman who died of a gunshot "accident" while alone on the third floor.

DIRECTIONS: *Cheesman Park is at the center of Denver, not far from the Colorado Heritage Center, the Denver Art Museum, and the Civic Center. The park is between 8th and 13th avenues; the numbered avenues travel east to west. University Boulevard goes through that area, north to south.*

—DR

TALES OF THE LARAMIE GHOST
Ford Laramie National Historic Site, Wyoming

The Allison family had passed down from father to son the story of the enigmatic horsewoman of Fort Laramie. In 1951 Colonel P. W. Allison was interviewed by Superintendent David L. Hieb at Fort Laramie, and a record of their conversation about the ghost was placed in the Wyoming State Archives. I obtained a transcript of this interesting bit of oral history from an archivist researcher at the state offices.

In 1871 young Lieutenant Allison of the 2nd Cavalry, fresh from West Point, arrived at Fort Laramie equipped with a fine thoroughbred mare and a large Russian wolfhound, with whose assistance he hoped to get in some good hunting.

The U.S. military had purchased the fort for $4,000 from the American Fur Company in the late 1840s, when an increasing influx of westward-bound emigrants, topped off by the great Gold Rush, had made a military presence necessary along the Oregon Trail.

Allison soon became attached to a party of other young officers eager to hunt wolves along the hills east of the fort. One afternoon while the hunters were riding out with their dogs, the animals sighted their prey, a family of wolves, and eagerly took off in pursuit. Having a better mount than his companions, Allison soon outdistanced them. Thus he found himself alone when the time came to pick his way down from the hills toward the Oregon Trail to return to the fort.

Unfortunately, Allison's horse went lame, so he had to dismount. He found a stone in one of the mare's shoes and removed it. As he turned to remount, he saw in the far distance someone riding rapidly eastward on the trail. He could see that their paths would soon intersect, so naturally he was quite curious to know who was coming, friend or foe. At first he thought it was a Sioux warrior with a blanket flapping as he rode. But as the figure came closer, he realized that what he was seeing was a young lady wearing a long riding habit of dark green and a hat with a feathered plume. The outfit appeared somewhat old-fashioned, the kind that might have been worn before the Civil War.

She must be a visitor newly arrived to the fort, Allison thought. Apparently she had no comprehension of the dangers she faced in galloping through the hills by herself. He signaled to the attractive girl to stop, intending to warn her against riding out so far alone and to gallantly offer to accompany her back to the fort. But as she came up to the lieutenant, he saw her raise her quirt (riding whip), which glittered brightly in the sun, and whip her great black horse to dash past Allison. She and her mount soon disappeared over a rise of ground.

Allison leaped on his horse and pursued the woman, but as he topped the rise he was amazed to find no one in sight. Dismounting again, he examined the trail and was again surprised to find no tracks. It's hard for us now to imagine, since all our thoroughfares are busy ones, but in the Old West, tracks were the language of the trail, clearly recording information about all who passed that way.

Allison's wolfhound cowered against his legs and whimpered in fear, something the brave animal had never done before, not even when outnumbered by angry wolves.

There was a shout from the ridge to his south, and one of Allison's fellow officers rode hurriedly toward him, laughing and teasing the lieutenant about the lady who had brushed by him so abruptly.

Allison urged his friend to look for the tracks the horsewoman should have left as she passed. The other man was just as astonished as Allison to find there were none.

That night, dining with the other officers and their ladies, Allison first assured himself that none of the women at the fort had gone out riding alone in the afternoon. Although he realized that he might be making himself the butt of some teasing, he told the assembly about the strange encounter.

Before even one joking comment could be made, the commanding officer spoke up. "Well, Allison," the older man said, "you have just seen the Laramie ghost." And he proceeded to relate the ghost's story, one of the fort's legends.

Back in the days when Fort Laramie was just a fur-trading post, the commanding officer said, an administrator (called a factor) of the fur trading company brought his beautiful daughter to the fort.

The girl, educated in Eastern schools, was an accomplished horsewoman, but the factor warned his daughter that she must never go out riding alone. There were many natural dangers in the wild surrounding country, and there was also the possibility that she might be kidnapped by one of the Arapaho, Cheyenne, Crow, or Sioux who hung around the fort. In general, those at the fort enjoyed a peaceful relationship with the Native Americans, because the goods the whites offered to trade for buffalo tongues and skins were items the natives wanted very much: blankets, calico, knives, guns, ammunition, combs, mirrors, glass beads, vermilion paint, and, especially, whiskey. The Native Americans had never learned to make alcohol and were unprepared for its pleasures and problems. Away from the stern authority of the fort, anything could happen if normally friendly natives had received a keg of whiskey in trade. The factor ordered his assistants to keep an eye on the girl to be certain she obeyed his instructions.

From time to time the factor was obliged to ride out with a few of his men to smoke the pipe of peace with some chief whom it would be useful to honor. On one such occasion, his headstrong daughter took the opportunity to mount her favorite horse, a handsome black stallion, and, over the protests of everyone, she raced out of the stockade. Before anyone could pursue her, the girl and her horse were speeding eastward down the Oregon Trail and were soon lost from sight. She never was seen again.

History does not record what severe punishments the factor might have inflicted on those who had allowed his daughter to have her way against his explicit orders. Certainly, everyone was involved in the search, which lasted for weeks. As far as the father was concerned, though, it never ended.

As the years passed, a legend grew among both the traders and the Sioux that every seven years the beautiful girl was seen riding again down the old trail.

Allison listened to his commander's tale with respect, but he wondered about the rider he'd seen. She'd seemed like flesh and blood to him, and the horse, too, was real enough. The young lieutenant determined that he would investigate the story himself. He spoke to many of the Sioux in the area about the factor's daughter and finally found one very old native woman who had been at the fort the day the girl disappeared. He asked her to describe the girl, and the old lady chanted out an unforgettable description of the factor's daughter. She'd been wearing a long, dark-green dress, a feathered hat, and she'd carried a jewel-handled quirt.

Allison was convinced at last that the mysterious horse-woman whose quirt had sparkled in the sun as she whipped her mount was the Laramie ghost.

As time went on Allison buried his encounter with the beautiful horsewoman in his memory until years later, as he traveled by train through Wyoming, he overheard a conversation between two cowboys on the station platform. One of them was talking about how a rancher had just seen the Laramie ghost. Allison wanted to jump down and ask the cowboys for more details, but the train engine started up before he could do so.

There have been many witnesses over the years to this

lifelike apparition. Whoever the beautiful girl was, she is still out there on the Oregon Trail!

Fort Laramie National Historic Site is managed by the National Park Service, which has the responsibility of protecting and restoring it. The fort was the scene of treaties signed with the Sioux, Cheyenne, and other Great Plains nations in 1851 and 1868, and it served as a Pony Express station. Five years after Lieutenant Allison's arrival at Ford Laramie, the fort was used as a base of operations in its last major Indian campaign against Sitting Bull and other rebellious Sioux chiefs. The fort is open year-round: between Memorial Day and Labor Day, from 7:00 A.M. to 7:00 P.M.; the rest of the year from 8:00 A.M. to 4:30 P.M. Twenty-two of the original structures remain, most of which have been restored and furnished.

DIRECTIONS: *In southeast Wyoming, Fort Laramie is situated 3 miles southwest of U.S. Highway 26 between Douglas, to the northwest, and Torrington, to the southeast, near the Nebraska border.*

Traveling this historic highway, you will be following the old Oregon Trail, called the "First Road West." A natural travel route over the prairies and Rocky Mountains, the Oregon Trail was the only east-west road through the Great Plains. Today it is still a major travel route through Wyoming. Besides Fort Laramie, there are a number of other historic sites on this route: trading posts, Pony Express stations, and other military establishments.

—DR

WYOMING'S SHIP OF DEATH
Platte River, Wyoming

Y ou don't want to see this ominous ship rise before your eyes from the mists of the Platte River. It has always been the harbinger of death—not of the death of the person who experiences this horrifying phenomenon—but of someone very close and dear to that witness who's doomed.

The Cheyenne Bureau of Psychological Research collected some engrossing personal accounts regarding the Ship of Death, as reported by Vincent H. Gaddis in the very first issue of *Fate* magazine in 1948. The date of the last encounter recorded by the bureau was November 1903, but there may have been others since that went unrecorded, and—who knows?—the Ship of Death may sail again.

Leon Webber was the first person to report this apocalyptic sighting. It happened six miles southeast of Guernsey, not far from Fort Laramie. One afternoon in early September 1862 Webber was getting ready to return to his summer camp, which was located two miles down the Platte. The first thing he noticed was a gigantic ball of fog that seemed to be riding on top of the river. Excited by such a strange sight, Webber ran closer to the river to get a better view, and Webber's dog, who liked a merry chase, ran with him. But when they came to sit down on the bank, the canine became fearful and hid behind his master's back, whining and whimpering.

The ball of fog rolled nearer. As a youngster might have done, Webber picked up a stone and hurled it at the floating mass. The moment the stone left his hand, the cloud assumed the shape of a sailing ship that Webber realized was a "vessel of an ancient time." The mast and sails sparkled with frost.

Webber heard the sound of heavy timbers dropping somewhere on the ship. Then several sailors appeared and stood in close formation on the deck. After a few moments, they stepped aside to reveal the corpse of a young girl lying on a canvas spread at their feet. She, too, was touched by shimmering frost that glittered brilliantly in the afternoon sun.

The ship veered to Webber's side of the river, so close that he could see the girl's beautiful features. Recognizing the face of Margaret Stanley, his fiancée, Webber cried, "Margy!" and jumped into the water. At the sound of his voice, the entire apparition vanished into nothingness.

Understandably, Webber was so disturbed by this vision that he stayed on the bank of the Platte until long after the sun had set, but he saw nothing more of the spectral ship.

There was no quick way then to get in touch with Margaret. It was a month before Webber was able to visit the Stanley home, and when he arrived, he learned of Margaret's tragic death. He was not surprised to hear that she had passed away on the same afternoon in September when he had seen the Ship of Death.

In the fall of 1887 the Ship of Death rolled out of the mists on the Platte again, near Casper. This time the phantom appeared to Gene Wilson, a cattleman who was rounding up some strays near the river.

Wilson's dog, who was running ahead, began "to raise a terrible rumpus." Wilson tried to bring his horse nearer, to see what was going on, but the animal shied away fearfully and could not be coaxed or commanded to go toward the bank. When Wilson threw the reins over the horse's head and dismounted, the horse snorted and ran away. The cattleman gave chase and caught his mount, securing the reins to a scrub pine. He approached the river on foot.

"I saw something that set my nerves atingle," Wilson wrote later. There on the Platte was a fully rigged sailing vessel, motionless on the swiftly moving river, as if held by a strong anchor. It seemed to be formed of icy mist.

Wilson scrambled down on the bank opposite the ship. He saw nine sailors and a captain on board, and he heard ship sounds, but they seemed to be coming from the other side of the river. His arms folded across his broad chest, the captain gave his crew orders to lower a square of canvas that was attached by its corners to four ropes. The burden of the canvas became visible as it reached the deck —a body covered with a frost-laden piece of sailcloth.

One of the sailors gripped the edge of the sailcloth and drew it back, "disclosing the face of a woman who seemed to be terribly burned," Wilson wrote. "In spite of the frightfully scarred face, I recognized my wife. Overcome with terror, I screamed and covered my eyes.

"When I looked again, the ship had vanished. After a few moments, I rose, mounted my horse, and, with all speed, returned home to relate to my wife what I had seen. Topping a hill a quarter of a mile west of my house, my heart stopped beating, the blood froze in my veins. There in full view, I discovered my home to be in ashes! Spurring my horse to run, I was soon beside the smoldering embers, frantically calling to my wife. . . .

"Receiving no reply . . . I hastened toward the river which ran within a hundred yards of what had been my home, when I came suddenly upon the remains of my wife, burned to death.

My supposition is that, upon discovering her clothing to be on fire, she had run toward the riverbank, hoping to extinguish the flames by plunging herself into the water."

The third report of the spectral ship was registered at the Cheyenne Bureau by Victor Heibe, who did not know about the two similar experiences that had occurred previously.

On the afternoon of November 20, 1903, Heibe was chopping up a fallen tree for firewood on the riverbank near his home at Bessemer Bend. Farther west than the other two occurrences, Bessemer Bend is the site of the first cabin built by a white man in Wyoming.

As he wielded the ax Heibe was thinking of his friend, Thomas Horn. A few months earlier Heibe had testified on behalf of Horn, who stood accused of murder at the criminal court in Cheyenne. Despite the evidence Heibe was able to bring forward, Horn had been found guilty and sentenced to hang.

A short time later the condemned man had escaped jail in the company of another prisoner. That was the last news Heibe had heard about his friend until November 20.

As he paused to light his pipe Heibe noticed that a huge ball of fog had appeared from nowhere on the river. The cloud was advancing in Heibe's direction but moving slower than the river current. For some reason, Heibe glanced at his watch and noted that the time was 3:15.

Before Heibe's amazed eyes, the mass of mist began to form the shape of an ice-covered sailing ship of ancient vintage. There were sailors on the deck, and Heibe could hear voices.

One of the voices said distinctly, "All right, but I am telling you that you are hanging an innocent man."

A second voice replied, "That is not for us to determine. You were tried and convicted of murder. Men, do your duty."

When the ship was about twenty feet from the place on the shore where Heibe stood spellbound, a sheet of canvas was drawn up, revealing a horrible scene. Here is Hcibe's description: "On the forward deck just to the rear of the captain, who faced the bow of the craft, stood a gallows of the 'L' type, from whose crossarm was suspended the body of a man they had hanged. As the body swayed to and fro from the rocking of the ship, it turned so that I gazed directly into its face. It was the blackened face of my dearest friend, he whom I had defended with my testimony in the court at Cheyenne only a few months previously."

As Heibe ran toward the water, shouting, the ship withdrew to the middle of the river and faded from sight. Later Heibe learned that Thomas Horn had been recaptured and hanged in the jailyard at Cheyenne on the afternoon of November 20, at 3:15.

Three times the frost-shrouded ship was sailed down the Platte to bring the news of death. In the annals of parapsychology, receiving such news telepathically is one of the most common extrasensory experiences, and many of these events are well documented. It seems that at the moment of death the spirit cries out to those who care and, freed of the body forever, travels through space-time to be with a friend or loved one once more.

In the case of the Ship of Death, however, something of the Platte River itself has entered into the vision. In many myths, those who have died travel across a river onto that unknown shore, and it seems as if the Platte sometimes takes on the aura of that legend. Interestingly, the three experiences recorded at the Cheyenne Bureau all took place in the fall, when the veil between life and death is said to be at its thinnest.

We wonder—has this grim vision ever appeared again? Will its ice-covered masts be seen at some future time?

DIRECTIONS: *The Platte River runs through southeast Wyoming, from Torrington to Alcova.*

—DR

ROBBER'S CAVE
3245 South 10th Street
Lincoln, Nebraska

When the Europeans first came to Nebraska, the Pawnee Nation had their central seats along the Platte and Loup rivers. High on the summit of Pahuk Bluff was a place that was holy to the Pawnee, and here they met in council. Also located on the sacred bluff was one of their most important villages. Here, too, in 1854 the Pawnee met in peace talks with General John M. Thayer, later governor of Nebraska. Despite any agreement reached then, Pahuk Bluff was selected by the settlers as the ideal site for "Neapolis," the projected capital of Nebraska, by an act of the Territorial Legislature of 1858. The Pawnee were removed to reservations to the south, and their village burned.

In the Pawnee religion, the one god Tirawa was present in all things, in the heavens and everywhere on earth. Lesser deities and magical animals represented the immanence of Tirawa. Young men who aspired to supernatural powers, which were granted by animals to medicine men, met in underground lodges, "spirit caves," because the spirit of Tirawa, being omnipresent, was under the earth as well as upon it. In torchlit caves, one of them known to be a part of Pahuk Bluff, the younger men were initiated into the animal powers and the healing virtues of roots and plants as well. The sound of chanting and the beat of the medicine drums echoed in the spirit caves.

But there were other lodges—five according to legend—whose locations have been lost, or nearly lost, to history. One of these spirit caves, located in the city of Lincoln, was later called Robber's Cave, and it is haunted by sounds of the past. Visitors have reported unexplained voices speaking unintelligibly in a hidden room in the cave. Whether the ghostly voices are Pawnee or arise from later inhabitants of Robber's Cave has not been determined.

If the Great Depression spawned one good thing, it was the Federal Writer's Project, a series of guides to the United States that does not neglect to include tidbits of fascinating folklore. In the *Guide to Nebraska*, the following entry describes Robber's Cave. "The Cave, 11th and High streets . . . is a series of caverns and winding passages in an outcrop of Dakota sandstone. The walls scratched with names, initials, and dates, are streaked with ocherous yellow and hematine reds and browns. In Pawnee legend, it was in the 'Nahurac' spirits cave [the Pawnee name for Robber's Cave] that medicine men held mystic sacred rites, and neophytes were proven and initiated. A snowbound wagon train used its protection; and after the Indian scare of 1862, settlers lived in it all winter."

Even if it weren't haunted, Robber's Cave would be an interesting place to explore. Fourteen different shades of sand-

stone are seen on its walls. Its passageways are 500 feet long,
it has 5,500 square feet of floor area, and it plunges to a depth
of 60 feet if you count the old well within it, formed by the
seepage of ground water that created a massive hole straight
down into darkness.

According to local legend, the cave was a resting place for a
steady stream of runaway slaves heading north on the underground railroad. Then in 1863 the original entrance was destroyed in the process of quarrying stone, when the capstone
was removed. But in 1869, brewers from Wisconsin hired a
laborer to dig out the tunnels in order to store the barrels of
beer underground in the Old World way.

The brewery failed in 1873, and from that time on the cave
became a meeting place for gamblers, horse traders, and
outlaws. The big name in outlaws in those days was Jesse
James, and legend has it that he and his gang visited Robber's
Cave in September 1876. While trying to locate fresh horses
after a fast getaway from a bank robbery in Northfield, Minne-
sota, James used the cave to hide out from his pursuers.

One room in particular is associated with the motley crew of
outlaws who used the cave. If you climb five feet up on a series
of holes chipped into the cave wall, you will reach a narrow
ledge that leads into a vast hidden chamber, which is nearly
square and not as damp as the rest of the cave, having a thick
carpet of dry sand. On one side there is a natural chimney and
a firepit below. The far end of the room has been blocked off
by a wall of brick, sandstone blocks, and concrete. If you put
your ear to this wall, it is said you'll hear the unearthly voices
of Robber's Cave.

In 1906 an unconfirmed story about a treasure box found in
the cave brought so many visitors that its present life as a
tourist attraction was born. Intrepid sightseers and picnickers
had to share the dim recesses of the cave with a host of bats
who'd moved in after the outlaws and gamblers departed. At
times the whole ceiling was a seething mass of fur and fluttering
wings.

Having followed the history of the cave up to the present, we
can see that haunting voices of Robber's Cave have many
possible sources. They could be the Pawnee medicine men and
the magical animals they invoked. Or they could be the voices
of settlers who hid in the cave through a terrified winter. Or
perhaps they are runaway slaves whispering in the dark, or the

spirits of outlaws, one of whom may be guarding a treasure somewhere in the cave.

And there's still one more possibility. The sealed-off passage once led to another series of tunnels that connected to the penitentiary and the State Hospital for the Insane. One last legend tells that inmates used the tunnels as an escape route, until that avenue was finally sealed off forever. Could it be their cries that the visitor hears at the wall?

Robber's Cave may be explored for a modest fee. Its hours are 11:00 A.M. to 6:00 P.M., Sunday through Friday. The cave is closed on Saturdays.

DIRECTIONS: *The Cave is located at 3245 South 10th Street in Lincoln, half a block south of 10th and High streets, on the west (right) side, between Burt's Auto Sales and the Powder Keg Gun Shop. For further information, call (402) 423-3370.*

A DISTRAUGHT MOTHER AT FORT LEAVENWORTH
Leavenworth County, Kansas

I f you were to wander at night through the national cemetery at Fort Leavenworth or the nearby golf course, you might encounter the ghost of Catherine Sutter. You'd be able to recognize her by the old-fashioned calico dress and black shawl she wears and the lantern she carries high above her head. She'd be calling her children, Ethan and Mary. Over the years many people have encountered Catherine. Once she stopped youngsters out for Halloween trick or treat, peering anxiously into each little face. When she saw that these were not the faces of Ethan and Mary, the disappointed mother drifted off to continue her search, as she has for the past 110 years.

Fort Leavenworth is a U.S. military post of some 8,000 acres, situated along the Missouri River, in Leavenworth County,

Kansas, two miles north of the city of Leavenworth. Established in 1827 as an outpost for the protection of travelers on the Santa Fe Trail, it soon proved to be equally beneficial to the thousands of emigrants taking the Oregon Trail. Since 1881 the fort has been the home of the Command and General Staff College of the U.S. Army, where high-ranking officers receive postgraduate training. It is sometimes called "the generals' school."

Leavenworth played a colorful role in our nation's history, from the dangers of westward expansion through the tragedy of the Civil War. Forts are often the scenes of hauntings, so it's not surprising that many strange sightings have been reported in and around one that has figured in as many dramatic events as Leavenworth has. A Kansas-based psychic investigator, Maurice Schwalm, was very helpful to me in researching these occurrences.

It was in 1880 that the Sutter family came to Leavenworth. Hiram and Catherine Sutter, with their two children, were bound for the promising new state of Oregon, and this was to be just a resting place on their long journey. There were hospitable relatives at the fort who hosted the Sutters, and this must have been a pleasant sojourn for the tired family of westward travelers.

One morning shortly after their arrival, the two children were sent outside the compound, which is not walled, to gather wood. Ethan and Mary were gone much longer than they should have been, and their parents began to worry. Soon they and others at the fort set out in search of the lost children. There were no answers to their frantic calls. The sun set, and the parents, carrying lanterns, kept searching all that night. But the children could not be found, not that night nor during any of the succeeding days.

The trip to Oregon was set aside, and the Sutters stayed at the fort, their hopes diminishing as the weather turned colder. But Catherine never ceased hunting for her children. Her black-shawled figure, holding the familiar lantern, was seen each night, regardless of the weather. When winter came, Catherine contracted pneumonia and died. In the spring, Hiram moved to Indiana.

Some time later Ethan and Mary were found living with the Fox Indians. The adoptive parents said they had fished the two children out of the Missouri River and taken the youngsters

home to their own campfire. No one knows how Ethan and
Mary got themselves into the river; perhaps they decided to
build a makeshift raft. The Missouri was known to be one of
the most treacherous and unpredictable of rivers, "too rapid for
oars and too deep for poles."

Once found and identified, the Sutter children were sent to
their father in Indiana. Apparently, Catherine's spirit never
learned of this happy reunion. Instead of resting in peace, she
still roams at night with her lantern, calling her children's
names.

Catherine's story brings up a question that is central to the
matter of hauntings. Does Catherine's spirit return from the
dead? Or did she charge the scenes of her search with such
strong emotions that, even today, those who are sensitive to
this energy will perceive it in the form of an apparition? Which-
ever is the case, those who come in contact with this revenant
are advised to see if they can communicate with her and assure
her that the children are safe.

Although the ghost of Catherine Sutter is the most notorious
of the fort's apparitions, other spirits lurk in its shadows.

Chief Joseph, who, with four hundred of the Nez Percés
nation, had led the U.S. Army a merry chase, finally said, "I
will fight no more forever." Following his surrender Chief Joseph
was confined to Fort Leavenworth, from 1877 to 1878, before
he and his people were "removed" (as they liked to call it then)
to Indian territory. He became quite a celebrity while he was at
Leavenworth, and important visitors never omitted calling upon
the old chief. He held court in captivity with the dignity of
Socrates, and his impression has lingered. The spirits of Chief
Joseph and his warriors are said to prowl in dark corners of the
fort and the cemetery to this day. Whether or not you encounter the chief (whose real name, by the way, was *In-Matuyah-
Lat-Cut*—Thunder Cloud Traveling Over the Mountain) his
portrait can be seen at the Fort Leavenworth Museum.

Built in 1832, the Rookery is the oldest house in Kansas
continually occupied as a residence. It is located on the fort's
Main Parade and is considered one of the points of interest in
touring the fort. According to an article by Shirley Gilfert in the
Kansas Star, October 31, 1983, apparitions seen and heard in
this early dwelling include a chattering old woman, a bad-
tempered girl, and a bushy-haired old man dressed in white
robes who disturbs sleepers in the late hours of the night.

General Douglas MacArthur lived at the Rookery during the early 1900s. One wonders if the general ever heard any of these noisy ghosts.

Many other rumors of ghostly activities have been whispered among the private residences at the fort. Especially well known among these is Father Fred, who likes to appear in or near cheerily burning fireplaces. When the original St. Ignatius Chapel burned in 1875, the young priest perished in the blaze. Some of the chapel's salvaged building material was used to construct a house on the same site, now 632 Thomas Avenue. But Father Fred is not confined to that location; the talk is that the jovial cleric often shows up for parties at other residences and was once captured on Polaroid film during a festive affair. On another occasion a surprised officer's wife found Father Fred at her sewing machine, mending his robe.

The ubiquitous Lady in Black hovers around residences on Summer Place. No one has a clue as to who she is, or was. The lady loves children and has been known to comfort a fussy or fearful child. One resident came upon the Lady in Black in her kitchen, appearing to be washing up the dishes. Of course, the dishes being scrubbed were also from another time frame. (Regrettably, ghosts are rarely of any practical help. For *Haunted Houses, USA,* we investigated one historic house in Connecticut, where a phantom workman had been heard hammering night after night. The restorers finally started leaving a list of chores on the table when they locked up in the evening, but, alas, the ghost proved to be of no assistance at all in this earthly realm.)

Lieutenant Colonel George Custer was court-martialed at Fort Leavenworth in 1867 for shooting soldiers in his command without a trial and giving no medical treatment to those who were merely wounded, not to mention damaging government horses. Although found guilty on all counts, his sentence was most lenient—a year's leave without pay—with the approval of General Grant. His military career relatively unscathed, Custer was able to lead troops into those other battles for which he is now infamous. In 1877 the remains of young Leavenworth officers who were victims of Custer's last crazy stand at Little Big Horn were reinterred at the fort. Custer's ghost is another of the restless phantoms at Leavenworth, said to roam the first floor of the commanding general's residence at One Scott Avenue.

And finally, runaway slaves and Civil War soldiers wander about the cemetery from time to time, and phantom troops have appeared on the Main Parade. Psychically speaking, Fort Leavenworth literally teems with supernatural phenomena!

The Main Parade, where the Rookery is located, is the original center of the post and has been beautifully preserved. The Post Museum holds the largest collection of horse-drawn vehicles in the nation. The museum is open year-round, except major holidays. The hours are Monday through Saturday, 10:00 A.M. to 4:00 P.M.; Sundays, 12 noon to 4:00 P.M.

DIRECTIONS: *Fort Leavenworth is on Highway 73, two miles north of the city of Leavenworth.*

—DR

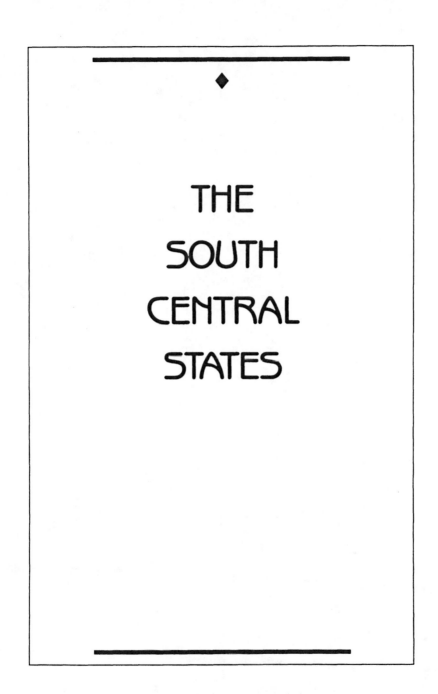

THE
SOUTH
CENTRAL
STATES

THE BRAGG ROAD LIGHT
Saratoga, Hardin County, Texas

The Marfa Lights in Texas (featured in the story on page 66) have been given a great deal of publicity lately (and rightly so), but there are other mysterious lights in the state that haven't received as much attention recently but are equally interesting. Across the state from Marfa in Saratoga, a town just north of Houston, the Bragg Road light has been a source of controversy for years. Although there are many theories about the light, no conclusive data have yet been assembled.

In 1901 a railroad line was established to connect the Gulf, Colorado, and the Santa Fe Railroad with the town of Saratoga. At that time the tiny town of Bragg, named after a confederate general who once had been a railroad engineer, was established along the line by railroad workers and their families. The tiny hamlet flourished until 1934, when the railroad, no longer in need of this route, pulled up the tracks. In less than a year, the entire town of Bragg had disappeared. The buildings were dismantled and the citizens scattered to various points to pursue their lives and other jobs. What's left now, and what the curious will find there, is a sandy road—once the bed for the railroad tracks.

It's on this sandy road that most visitors, at least those brave enough to go there at night, encounter a strange light. When it first appears it's dim and blinking at the end of the road, which is not too frightening. Then as it gets brighter, it's obvious even to those people who are not inclined to believe in the supernatural that this approaching light isn't attached to a car or to anything else that's visible. It's been described as looking like a gasoline lantern swinging back and forth as if someone were carrying it as they walk. But no one is carrying it. It's just there! One reporter who visited Bragg Road wrote that when he saw the light it appeared to be a dull yellow before it changed to an intense white, so bright it was difficult to look at. Next

61

the darn thing turned a bright red, looking hot as coals, then back to white before it flickered a few times and turned off. His report is pretty standard.

There are many theories about what's behind the Bragg Road light. (Just as there are with so many of the stories of spirits.) One of the most often told goes this way: When the railroad was in full swing in Bragg, Jake Murphy, a brakeman who worked the line, lived there with his family. Jake had spent his life on the rails, and he was well acquainted with his job and his responsibilities. On a night when the rains were coming down so hard it was almost impossible to see more than a few inches in front of one's face, the train on which Murphy worked was creeping through the town of Bragg, the whistle blowing to warn anyone who might be in the way, and everyone was paying full attention to his job. As the train chugged along, Murphy, for some reason that's never been established, jumped off the car. Since the train was traveling at a snail's pace, Murphy probably thought he'd have no trouble jumping back on. But just as Murphy's feet hit the ground the train picked up a little speed and he, realizing he'd better get moving, attempted to jump back on board. His boots were covered with mud and the step on the train was wet. Murphy's foot was on the step about a second before it slid and he lost his balance, falling headfirst under the train.

It was a gory mess, and the neighbors kept his wailing wife and children from going to the site. The funny thing was that Murphy's head wasn't found—not on that rainy night when the terrible accident occurred, not any time since. Many people looked, combing through the bushes, but the head had vanished. It's commonly thought by the folks of Saratoga that the light is carried by Murphy. He's walking along swinging his lantern, looking for his head.

Another version of the Bragg Road light goes this way: Because Mexican labor was cheap, the railroad employed several Mexican workers. They weren't treated as well as the Americans by most of the foremen, who considered them second class and fair game for whatever mischief seemed like it might be amusing at any given time. One particular day, one foreman was up to more than mischief. He realized that if the Mexican workers vanished, nobody would really notice. After all, their families were in Mexico and the people around Bragg had no interest in them. He plotted to take their pay on this day and murder them, disposing of the bodies in the nearby swamp. The evil foreman called them into his shack one at a time, supposedly to give them their wages. As each one came through the door, he hit him on the head with a large metal pipe and threw the body behind the door. There were four men, and he dispatched all of them without a single problem. After pocketing the dead men's money, he waited until the middle of the night and carried the bodies one at a time into the swamp, where he thought they'd never be found.

What the foreman didn't know was that one of his men had struck up a friendship with one of the Mexicans, and he missed him at work. This man was rather persistent in his search, and eventually he uncovered the bodies of the dead men. There was a trial and the foreman was found guilty. But that didn't help the Mexicans. Legend has it that the spirits of the four victims walk the track, swinging a light as they search for the money they worked so hard to earn.

Yet another version tells of a man who lived in Bragg and went out with his gun one night in search of food. He didn't know the bogs around the area as well as he'd thought, and soon he was hopelessly lost. When the man failed to return home by morning, a search party was formed, and for two days the local volunteers combed the swamps and bogs looking for the hunter. No trace of him was ever found. Could the light belong to the hunter? Many people think he is still trying to find his way to Bragg and his family.

Blair Pittman, a Houston photographer who frequently takes pictures in the area, was quoted by the *Houston Chronicle* in 1987 as saying he'd seen the light at least twenty times. The first time he was shooting pictures for *National Geographic* magazine when the light appeared. But he's not sure there's anything eerie or mysterious about the light. Pittman said he believes it is a reflection of headlights from route FM770, which is at the end of the road.

In the same article Debbie Collier, a secretary in Saratoga, said that when she was a teenager she and her companions would go about a mile and a half up the road and park. They chose this spot because it was far from civilization and they could turn on the car radio, dance, and play the music as loud as they wanted without disturbing anyone. One night as she and a group of friends were in the car just about to leave and go home, they saw a ball of light glowing in the road right in front of the car. It was about five feet off the ground and about 300 yards in front of the kids. They were quite unnerved and the driver sped up to get out of there quickly. The light seemed to disappear, but as the kids drove off, they looked out the rear window of the automobile and there was the light. It appeared to be chasing them. The teenagers were more than a little frightened and didn't go back to the road for any more evenings of dancing.

Although not too much is heard about the Bragg Road light these days, back in the 1960s it was getting plenty of publicity, and many people visited the area in hopes of catching a glimpse of the unexplained illumination. Francis Abernethy, president of the Texas Folklore Society, wrote, "Light-seers poured onto the road by the hundreds. People of all ages and intellects came to see and test their belief in the supernatural. They shot at it, they chased it, and they tested it with litmus paper and Geiger counters. A preacher harangued the road's multitudes from the top of his car, marking the light as an ill omen of the world's impending doom."

Archer Fullingim, who was publisher and editor of the local *Kountze News,* ended the rush to see the Bragg Road light when he wrote that the luminous balls were gaseous substances arising from the swamps of the surrounding thickets. Those who believed in the story thought him a villain and hated him for printing what he apparently thought was the truth.

In 1989 a Japanese film crew, who had been filming the Marfa lights with amazing success, decided to make a trip to Hardin County to try to get some footage of the Bragg Road light. The county officials greeted them with warmth, offering to do anything they could to make the Japanese film crew's trip both comfortable and profitable. Robb Riggs, cofounder of the Institute of Applied Harmonics, a man who'd researched the Bragg Road light extensively, met with Professor Yoshi-Hiko Ohtsuki, head of the Japanese film crew, and related his findings. Riggs was excited about the visit, asserting, "This gives credibility to what we're doing. We want to establish a data base worldwide so other people can use this information." But the Japanese, Riggs, and the county officials were in for a big disappointment. There were unseasonable, driving rains of such force that it was impossible for the film crew to see down the road, let alone take pictures. The Japanese waited for three days, but the weather persisted in being uncooperative, and in the end they left without any video of the Bragg Road light. (But they did have the key to the city, which was presented to them by the chamber of commerce.)

Riggs's research has led him to believe there are three kinds of mystery lights. Large orange balls, very small lights which he says often look like large red stars, and those in between in size. The latter is the type seen on Bragg Road. They glow more intensely than the other two types, according to Riggs. In an article by Richard Stewart, published in the *Houston Chronicle* in 1989, the author says that Riggs "thinks fluctuations in natural magnetism may cause the lights to be seen more in some areas than others. The geometry of the earth causes these magnetic hotspots to be most commonly distributed along a line near 30 degrees of north latitude. [Both the Marfa and the Bragg Road lights are along this line.] He had no data about light sightings along 30 degrees south latitude but expects the lights to be seen there too."

Whether these lights are a phenomenon that science will one day explain or a visitation from a world beyond remains unknown. There are people who devoutly believe that the Bragg Road light is the work of spirits, and then there are those just as certain there is a scientific explanation.

If you visit with an open mind and experience the light, you're bound to come away having formed your own conclusion.

DIRECTIONS: *Take 105 west out of Beaumont for about 39 miles to Saratoga. At Saratoga, go west onto 770 about two miles to 787. Follow 787 north about 3½ miles to Bragg Road (an eight-mile dirt road). For further information phone the Big Thicket Museum (409) 274-5000.*

—JB

MARFA CELEBRATES ITS
MYSTERIOUS LIGHTS
Marfa, Texas

In October 1987 all of Marfa's 2,440 residents turned out for a parade, a rodeo, and a good old Texas barbecue in honor of its number-one tourist attraction, "ghost lights"—unexplained glowing balls of light that dance over the hills outside town. Town fathers hope to make the Marfa Lights Festival an annual event.

There hasn't been so much excitement in Marfa since Elizabeth Taylor, Rock Hudson, and James Dean were there on location to film the epic *Giant*. The locals remember that James Dean brought his own telescope and mounted it on a fence post in hopes of catching sight of Marfa's ghost lights.

Founded in 1881 as a water stop on the Texas and New Orleans Railroad, Marfa is located about sixty miles from the Mexican border in the rugged desert and mountain terrain of the Big Bend. Today the town is a small ranching community, with Mount Locke and the University of Texas McDonald Observatory just forty miles "down the road."

The earliest recorded encounter with the lights occurred in 1883. A sixteen-year-old cowboy named Robert Ellison was helping to drive a herd of cattle onto what is now known as Mitchell Flat. As evening came on, Ellison and his companions thought they saw Apache campfires flickering in the shadows of the distant Chinati Mountains. When daylight came, the cowboys investigated and found no signs of an encampment.

Since then such sightings have been recorded constantly over the years. Most observers report one or more bright, twinkling lights just below or just above the horizon after dusk. The usual color is greenish-yellow, although blue, white, and red lights have also been reported. Sometimes the lights divide or split into several lights. They may float gracefully or they may zip around fitfully. To one frightened man they appeared at first to be the headlights of an oncoming car. The next thing he knew, a cantaloupe-size ball of light was hovering outside his car window, which was rolled down. Although he drove faster, the light stayed with his car for two miles.

Certain atmospheric conditions seem to summon the lights. Fall and winter, when the Big Bend weather turns frosty, are the best seasons for viewing. Particularly good times are just after a rapidly moving cold front has come through or just after a rainstorm has settled the dust. Sometimes the lights appear near Twin Peaks, and sometimes on the black-brush flats north of the Cuesto Del Burro Mountains.

A Native American legend holds that the lights are the phosphorescent souls of Apache warriors slain through treachery. One local theory suggests that soldiers from nearby Fort Davis slaughtered a party of Apaches, except for the chief, who escaped to the hills. Now the chief's ghost comes down from those hills to wander the desert in search of his companions.

In an article that appeared in the *Houston Chronicle* January 13, 1980, Stan Redding wrote of his own pilgrimage out to the viewing spot, a shoulder off the road in the mountains nine miles east of Marfa. Looking toward the Burro's eastern flank, he saw lights dancing all over the distant flats. "They were blue," he wrote, "shaped like a Chevrolet emblem, and they were zipping all over the tops of stubby black-brush like kids in a playground, bobbing up and down in instances like a basketball being dribbled."

Later Redding talked to a bartender at the Branding Iron bar who said that as a child he'd seen the lights come right up close to his house. He and his friends used to chase the lights and throw rocks at them.

Recently, Yoshi-Hiko Ohtsuki, professor of physics at Waseda University in Tokyo, Japan, came to this country especially to study ghost lights like these. He brought with him a film crew, special photographic equipment, a device that measures radioactivity, a gas-detection instrument, an electric-voltage measuring instrument, and a magnetic-field measuring device. Obviously, this was to be a serious effort!

When Ohtsuki was a thirteen-year-old schoolboy he saw a strange, luminous ball of light drifting over the trees in northern Japan. Ohtsuki determined right then and there that he'd become a scientist to unravel the mystery of this phenomenon.

In March 1989 Ohtsuki saw the mystery lights on moonlit Mitchell Flat southwest of Marfa (Richard Stewart, *Houston Chronicle*, March 26, 1989). "It was very exciting," Ohtsuki said. "We succeeded in capturing a ten-second image of the light on videotape." (This was not the first successful photograph; the lights have been photographed on numerous occasions with 35mm still cameras and with electronic video equipment.) One light was green and remained stationary for about two hours; the other was crescent-shaped and moved toward Marfa.

One possible explanation for the lights, Ohtsuki said, is plasma excitation (*The Marfa Independent*, March 23, 1989). "Plasma in physics is a form of matter composed of electrically charged atomic particles and can be created by heating a gas or by passing an electric current through it." We won't know whether Ohtsuki, with all his sophisticated equipment, has solved the mystery of the lights' origin until he publishes a forthcoming scientific paper on the subject.

Some skeptics brush off the phenomenon as an illusion created by headlights. The fact that the Apaches incorporated the lights into their early legends makes this theory rather doubtful. Perhaps some people have sighted headlights bouncing around the hills and thought they were viewing ghost lights, but there is a great deal of evidence and history to support Marfa's claim to genuine ghost lights.

Whether the mysterious phenomena on Mitchell Flat can ever be explained scientifically, I will always believe that those lights are the ghosts of Apache warriors haunting the mountains and deserts of Texas.

DIRECTIONS: *Marfa is in Presidio County in the southwest corner of Texas, near the Mexican border. There is an official roadside viewing area on Highway 90, nine miles east of Marfa. You probably won't find a sign, because souvenir hunters keep stealing them. For more information, stop at the chamber of commerce in downtown Marfa, next to the city square. A small, helpful book by Dennis Stacy called* The Marfa Lights: A Viewer's Guide *can be obtained from him for $3.00. Write to Box 12434, San Antonio, Texas 78212.*

—DR

THE COTTAGE
Baton Rouge, Louisiana

If ever a building belied its name, it's The Cottage just outside Baton Rouge, for it is not the humble, cozy edifice that the name implies but a magnificent mansion containing twenty-two enormous and elegantly appointed rooms. The Cottage was the heart of a plantation that boasted its own sugar house and cotton gin. This shining domain in the land of Dixie was built in 1825 by Abner Duncan and given to his daughter, Frances, and her bridegroom, Frederick D. Conrad, in honor of their marriage.

The Conrads were high on the social register, and such notables as Jefferson Davis, Henry Clay, President Zachary Taylor, and the Marquis de Lafayette enjoyed the hospitality at The Cottage. The Conrads themselves had an impressive pedigree. Frederick was related to George and Martha Washington. It was a good life for the Conrads. They traveled in lovely carriages pulled by the finest horses. Their home was furnished with imported rosewood furniture, and the young Mrs. Conrad wore beautiful jewels that were the envy of all her friends.

Then the Civil War came and life changed, never to be the same, for the landholders of the South. The Union army took over The Cottage Plantation, the jewels were stolen, the horses put to military use, and the magnificent furniture confiscated by the officers for use in their own homes back north.

After the troops left, The Cottage served a noble purpose as a hospital for victims of yellow fever. This kept it from further looting. Long after the echoes of the last yellow fever victim had faded, the local vandals were afraid to enter The Cottage for fear of contracting the dread disease. Because the plantation stayed more or less intact and didn't meet the fate that so many of the neighboring mansions did, it has attracted a great deal of interest over the years. It was used as the setting for several movies, including the *Burning Candle*, a silent film made in 1917. *Cinerama Holiday* used The Cottage in 1956, and *Band of Angels*, starring the late, great Clark Gable, was also set at The Cottage. So is The Cottage haunted by movie stars? No, it seems that the simpler folk are the ones who find it difficult to leave.

Back in the heyday of the place, nights were often filled with the music of slaves. Anyone who visited during those days could attest to the lighthearted chatter and laughter that came from the slave quarters. The Conrads sometimes asked their slaves to dance, sing, and generally entertain guests at The Cottage. Of course, the slaves complied.

The first ghostly manifestations at The Cottage were of slaves who could be heard on sultry summer nights singing, dancing, and having a high old time. This echo of the past persisted over the years and was enough to attract those interested in the paranormal to The Cottage.

Then in 1940 *The Elk's Magazine* decided to do an article on the plantation. A reporter and a photographer descended on the place to do research for the article and take appropriate pictures. The photographer was zealous, taking pictures of everything in sight. He was very surprised when he developed the film and found in a picture he'd taken that there was a man's face superimposed over the old plantation house. There had been no man there! There were no double exposures! The photographer was no amateur, and he knew he hadn't made a mistake. From showing the picture to people who were familiar with The Cottage and those who had inhabited it, the photographer for *Elk's Magazine* learned that the man in the picture was a Mr. Holt, who had been Frederick Conrad's secretary.

It seems that when the troops occupied the plantation, they had been none too kind. Both Frederick Conrad and Mr. Holt had been held prisoners in the house, an experience so rough that Frederick Conrad died soon after the pair was released. Although Holt survived the ordeal and continued to live at The Cottage for another twenty years, his imprisonment had taken a toll on him, too. His mind was never clear again, and he lived in a continual state of fear.

One of the demons that Holt felt was pursuing him was poverty. He acted in a cunning manner to ward it off by stockpiling whatever he could put his hands on. He hid his old clothes, new clothes, any clothes he could find. He saved part of every meal and stored it away in an old trunk. He abandoned the practice of shaving and was often seen pacing the house at night with his long white beard flowing.

In 1960 The Cottage burned to the ground. There are nothing but ruins where the once stately building stood. But still those people who venture onto the land hear the music and laughter of the slaves, dancing amid the ashes of what once was home to them. As for Mr. Holt, there are those who claim he still can be seen in his nightshirt, pacing back and forth with a worried look on his face. He's still worrying about being poor, not realizing that it can't affect him in his spirit world.

There are many spirits of this type—poor souls who aren't aware they're dead. Psychics have often been instrumental in helping these tortured entities cross over and find peace.

DIRECTIONS: *From Baton Rouge, take Route 61 North for about 25 miles to St. Francisville and The Cottage.*

—JB

THE RELUCTANT BRIDE
Parlange Plantation
False River, New Roads, Louisiana

There's a long double row of trees that creates a path to Parlange Plantation. The ghost of a young girl who died there among the oaks on her wedding day often runs between the rows of trees, her wedding gown flowing behind her, a veil covering her stricken face. The spirit of Julie Vincent de Ternant has never been freed from this earth. She seems to relive the few minutes before her tragic, unnecessary death over and over again.

Parlange was built in 1754 by the Marquis Vincent de Ternant on land he had been granted by the French government. This grand old plantation is still owned and run by descendants of Vincent de Ternant. It is one of the oldest operational, self-supporting plantations in the state.

In 1757, Vincent de Ternant died, leaving the property and all his money to his eldest son, Claude Vincent de Ternant. Claude's first marriage ended tragically with the death of his wife during childbirth. This would have been Claude's first child, and it was a double blow when the attending doctor announced that the tiny infant had also succumbed.

After a year of mourning, Claude Vincent de Ternant remarried. His bride was Virginie, a young, lovely second cousin of Claude's who lived at the plantation. Virginie was only fifteen, and she was physically strong. She bore him four children: Henri, Julie, Maurius, and Marie Virginie. Claude's second wife was not only strong of body, she had a strong will. In addition to that, she was a snob. Anyone who didn't meet her strict code for social acceptance wasn't allowed to hobnob with her children. She vowed that they would receive a superior education and be conversant with the best of manners. This ambitious mother was overbearing and made all decisions for her children. She was sure they'd grow up to be at the center of Baton Rouge society. The fact they all had her uncommonly good looks didn't hurt.

Of course, the children were attended by a nanny whom Virginie selected herself. But it seems this girl was lax in her job, for when Henri was a toddler (before either Maurius or Marie Virginie was born), she became distracted by a suitor one day while she was out walking the children around the plantation. Little Henri was quick, as most children are, and in the time it took Nanny to bestow a furtive kiss on the lips of her would-be lover, Henri had run to investigate a bubbling stream, toppled in headfirst, and summarily drowned. Virginie, pregnant at the time, was almost inconsolable.

When she gave birth to Maurius a few months later, her joy at having another son was enormous. And from that day until his death, Maurius was her unquestionable favorite. She spoiled him, doting on his every new word and gesture and satisfying his every whim. With a childhood like this, it's small wonder that Maurius grew up to be a petulant, self-indulgent, albeit handsome oaf who spent money wildly and drank whiskey with great gusto almost from the time he arose until the time he fell into bed at night. This latter vice proved to be his undoing, and Maurius died an alcoholic at the age of twenty-five.

Virginie now had only her two daughters. She'd always been strict with them—ruling with her iron will. When Maurius died she became even stricter. Marie Virginie proved no problem; she had long since taken her mother's values as her own. But the frail and lovely Julie had a mind of her own. At one of the many social functions in Baton Rouge, Julie met and fell in love with the son of a local plantation owner. You'd think this would have pleased Virginie. To the casual observer it seemed like a match made in heaven, for the young man's pedigree was long and impeccable. But Virginie had always been perverse, and this time she'd made up her mind that both her remaining children would marry French noblemen. Julie balked at this, but her pleadings fell on deaf ears. There was nothing for the young girl to do but sneak out at night and meet her heart's desire. The more they were together, the more in love they became.

One night Virginie went to her daughter's room and found that Julie wasn't in her bed. She searched, but Julie wasn't in the house. But the foxy lady didn't confront her daughter with the information. Instead she waited in the hall, out of sight, the next night. Sure enough, Julie left her room, quietly descended the stairs, and went out the front door into the dark night. Unknown to Julie, her mother was close on her heels. Julie flew into the arms of her beloved, unaware that Virginie was silently watching from a short distance. The next morning Virginie approached Julie, telling her that she knew of her secret meetings, and that from then on there would be a servant assigned to her room every night to make sure that the disobedient girl would never see the young man again.

Julie cried and spent days languishing in bed. She begged her mother to change her mind and let her be with the man she loved. But Virginie wasn't having any of it. Although the servants were partial to Julie—they called her Mam'selle Pom Pom—they didn't dare defy their mistress.

Virginie had her own plans for Julie's future. She had been in touch with the family of a young man of noble birth in France. They were delighted with the prospect of having a beautiful, young, wealthy American daughter-in-law, and so the wedding was planned. Virginie decided it would be the most magnificent wedding ever to take place in the Baton Rouge area. She hired a most expert seamstress, who cut and sewed a splendid bolt of white satin into a breathtakingly beautiful wedding gown—so beautiful, in fact, that many guests failed to notice the unhappy expression on the bride's face. Flowers, which had been picked fresh the morning of the nuptials, graced every possible corner of the mansion. There were so many flowers that one guest was heard to whisper to another that it looked almost like a funeral—a most prophetic remark, as it turned out.

The wedding itself came off without a hitch (no pun intended).

The hundreds of guests oohed and aahed as Julie walked among them to the preacher and the man who would be her husband. She mumbled her vows, a fact most people attributed to her shyness, and stood around after the ceremony greeting guests, thanking them for coming, and trying her best to look happy.

It was a scant hour after the ceremony when Julie realized she couldn't keep up the charade. The reluctant bride looked around her at the smiling people, and then she opened her mouth and screamed. All faces turned toward her as guests exchanged looks of astonishment. Julie screamed again and bolted from the room, running as fast as she could out of the drawing room, out of the house, and down the alley that ran between the two rows of oak trees. The young girl flung herself at the bottom of one of the trees and gave one last scream as the life left her body.

For once Virginie blamed herself for the death of one of her children. She realized too late that she had been wrong in keeping Julie from the man she really loved. The next day the same people who had attended the wedding once again gathered at the plantation. This time their faces were somber, for they had come to bid farewell to Julie. She was buried in her wedding dress on the grounds of the plantation.

Virginie's one remaining child, Marie Virginie, followed her mother's wishes and married a French nobleman. Marie had several children, one of whom was painted by the renowned artist John Singer Sargent. The picture, titled *Madame X,* hangs in the Metropolitan Museum of Art in New York City.

Claude Vincent de Ternant died long before his wife, but then, he was many, many years older than she. Virginie spent much of her time after that in France, visiting her daughter and enjoying the social events in Paris. At one of the many balls she attended she met Charles Parlange. He was a gentleman, a widower, and very handsome. He was quite taken with Virginie. Although she was no longer a girl, she was still a beauty. The pair married and returned to Louisiana. The plantation became known as Parlange, a name that has stuck down through the years.

Virginie never got over the deaths of her three children, but she dedicated the rest of her life to her remaining daughter, her grandchildren, her second husband, and most of all, to making Parlange a showplace. On her frequent trips to Paris she'd buy expensive furniture and have it shipped to her home.

When the Civil War broke out Virginie kept Parlange safe by making it a resting place for the troops, a haven where they could come at any time to enjoy the wonderful food and fine drink that the war had made scarce.

Parlange is still in the family. And Julie still makes her home there—at least sometimes. She's most often seen on a night when the moon is full, making her run down the path between the oaks, probably looking for the lover with whom she could have enjoyed a full and happy life.

DIRECTIONS: *This plantation is about 35 miles north of Baton Rouge. Take I-190 West to Route 1. Follow 1 North for about 5 miles to the plantation.*

—JB

THE HIGH AND LOW GHOSTS OF NATCHEZ

Natchez, Mississippi

Old Natchez of the eighteenth century wore two faces, one aristocratic and the other bawdy. There was the city high on the bluffs, where the Spanish grandees built beautiful homes for their privileged wives, with an architectural elegance whose influence is still felt in that region. And there was Natchez-Under-the-Hill, meaning below the bluffs, on the riverbanks, where saloons, gambling halls, and prostitutes of every color hosted rivermen, backwoodsmen, and outlaws. Mark Twain describes these denizens of the low life as "heavy drinkers, coarse frolickers in moral sties like the Natchez-Under-the-Hill of that day, reckless fellows, everyone, elephantinely jolly, foul-witted, profane, prodigal of their money, . . . fond of barbaric finery, prodigious braggarts . . . and often picturesquely magnanimous." What congress there was between the city on the bluffs and Natchez-Under-the-Hill was stealthy, dangerous, and disease-ridden.

The ghosts of old Natchez come from both the high and the low sides of the city, and stories about them are reported frequently in local newspapers. A particularly intriguing account by Jeanerette Harlow appeared in *The Clarion-Ledger,* October 30, 1969.

In the haze and fog that rises from the Mississippi River, a ghostly brigade of Spanish soldiers is seen from time to time, Harlow wrote, often promenading on the bluffs, still guarding the property of highborn Spanish rulers.

Down in Natchez-Under-the-Hill, near where the Daughters of the American Revolution have placed a marker to denote the beginning of the Natchez Trace, the ghosts of several notorious outlaws haunt the scenes where they so often spent their ill-gotten loot, this same article states. Specifically mentioned are Mason, Murrel, Hare, and the Harpe brothers. The deeds of these outlaws were infamous on the Natchez Trace and their names are still not forgotten.

The Natchez Trace was a series of interrelated paths that existed long before the first Europeans—Hernando de Soto and his men—found and followed them. The Choctaws, Chickasaws, and Natchez natives, merely by taking the possible trails through impenetrable canebrake and thick, moss-hung forests for many years, had created the Trace. This barely beaten path stretched through the wilderness, with many hazardous bodies of water to be forded, between the future sites of Natchez, Mississippi, and Nashville, Tennessee. And every foot was perilous.

But the Natchez Trace was indispensable. Travelers could go south on the currents of the Mississippi, but those currents wouldn't bring them back again—at least, not until the steamboat was invented many years later. The only way north was overland on the Natchez Trace. There were great fortunes to be made for northern merchants who took flatboats crammed with goods to New Orleans. They would sell their wares to eager buyers, break up and sell their flatboats for lumber, fill their saddlebags with money, and start the long trek home. Once on the Natchez Trace, these bold traders could, and frequently did, fall prey to illness, accident, snakes and wild animals, marauding natives, and, of course, highwaymen. Rather than engage in chancy trade, it was much simpler, these outlaws concluded, to accost lonely travelers on the Trace and make off with those saddlebags filled with gold bars and coins. No traveler's checks to keep your money safe in those days!

More prudent merchants would wait until a large group of northbound travelers had assembled—there was some safety in numbers. It was also a wise idea to get on the road before July, when the mosquitoes and black flies would take their toll.

Mississippi, where the Natchez Trace began, was first the province of the Spaniards, who exercised their usual philosophy of holding the most land with the least number of their own countrymen. In California Spain had used the missions for this purpose; here they accomplished the same goal by allowing the French and the English to take over some of the development of the region, while they themselves remained the rulers and controlled the economy.

After the Revolution, a number of Americans who regularly traveled from the States to Spanish territory and back again were suspected of being in the pay of the Spanish. One in particular, a high-ranking military officer who accepted Spanish gold in return for imparting secret information, has been seen as a ghost on the bluffs (also reported in *The Clarion-Ledger*) at the scene of this treasonous act. Perhaps he has his regrets.

Although their tentacles were reaching out so effectively in all directions, the Spanish governors in America were sold out by the Spanish crown—literally, to France. For a time, Napoleon entertained the notion of extending his empire into the New World until large-scale slave uprisings around New Orleans and yellow fever in the West Indies made the project look less glamorous.

The tenure of the cultivated Spanish left its mark on more than the architecture of Natchez. In spirit, too, they are still holding on, ghostly soldiers parading in the mist.

Like the Spaniards, the refined French who ruled the area afterward looked on the American adventurers, with their rough manners and rowdy pleasures, as barbarians. It was when the American flag finally flew over Mississippi, so they said, that Natchez-Under-the-Hill truly became the worst hellhole in the East.

Outlaws on the Trace frequently sought Spanish passports so that when the Mississippi got too hot for them, they could frolic safely in New Orleans for a while. Money, of course, was no problem, and these larcenous individuals lived high when they weren't attacking travelers on the Trace. During the years the outlaws were most active—the end of the eighteenth century and the beginning of the nineteenth—the Trace came to be called the Devil's Backbone.

Joseph Thompson Hare, who was based in New Orleans, worked his thieving way north on the Trace while the Mason gang worked south from Kentucky. Hare was a literate outlaw, kept a diary, and once or twice was known to make a sentimental gesture. For instance, Hare beat one of his henchmen "until he bellowed for help" for dallying with a refined Spanish girl fresh from the convent school. This good-looking member of Hare's gang had a sideline of marrying girls and abandoning them once he got his hands on their dowries.

According to local legend, Hare was not always so gallant; he once punished an unfaithful mistress by ordering his men to bury her alive wearing the jewels he had given her. Her grave is reported to be near the Devil's Punch Bowl, where Hare had one of his camps. In Natchez, they say her ghost appears at night there, offering gold to anyone who will help her.

A native of Philadelphia, Hare had once been an apprentice tailor and never lost his love of dandified clothes. When he wrote in his diary about the incident of his arrest (he was later hanged for the crime) he also noted that he had been caught while buying two coats, one with a crimson silk lining for $35 and the other in the style of an officer for $75.

But when Hare was out on the Trace, he dressed like a woodsman and painted his face with berry juice and bark stains. Impressed with the beauty of the trail, he jotted down in his diary a list of the flowering trees he encountered while robbing a company of luckless travelers. He also noted, "I got twelve or thirteen thousand dollars altogether from the company, all in gold."

One of these victims cried to Hare that he had fought for his money as a privateer but could not fight in the wilderness. Hare was touched and gave the man back a few gold coins and his watch. "He looked as thankful as if I had done him a favor, instead of robbing him," Hare reflected in his journal later.

Hare watched and chronicled long processions of slaves being taken south, "like a troop of wearied pilgrims." The blacks were so slow and tired, so tattered that the whole train had a sad and funereal appearance. He allowed these poignant parades to pass by unchallenged, knowing that when the slavers returned, they would be carrying a lot of money.

Although Hare was reticent about recording actual murders in his journals, he and his men left many a traveler's body for the wolves and buzzards on the Trace. His mistake may have been to spare the life of a cattle dealer while robbing him of a rather small amount of money (by Hare's usual standards). This victim was to be reckoned with; the cattle dealer organized a posse to follow Hare's trail.

While riding rapidly away from this angry pursuit, Hare had a vision. He wrote: "I saw standing right across the road, a beautiful white horse, as white as snow; his ears stood straight forward and his figure was very beautiful. When I approached him, and got within six feet of him, he disappeared in an instant, which made me very uneasy, and made me stop and stay at a house near there, all night." As a result of this case of nerves, Hare was taken in bed by the posse and sent to jail for five years. Upon release he returned to his life of crime.

Years later, while awaiting the gallows for robbing the night mail coach of $16,900, Hare remembered this vision. "I think this white horse was Christ and that he came to warn me of my sins, and to make me fear and repent."

Joseph Thompson Hare is now one of the ghosts of Natchez-Under-the-Hill, where the Trace began. Especially on Halloween night, when the veil between life and death is thinnest, his laugh and the hoofbeats of his horse are heard, which doesn't sound as if he's spending his eternity in repentance.

The capture of Hare did not make the Trace safe for merchants by any means. In 1801 Colonel Joshua Baker, a planter returning from delivering his crops in New Orleans, halted at a small stream and was accosted by four men demanding his money, horses, and traveling utensils. These bandits got $2,300 in cash, but one frightened pack horse took off with some of Baker's money. Later the colonel was able to round up this animal and so retained a part of his profit.

Not many weeks later one of Baker's companions recognized two of the robbers in Natchez, Samuel Mason and his son. Mason had a good record as a patriot and was a well-dressed, fine-looking man, except for one front tooth that grew horizontally and could be covered by his lips only with difficulty. This distinguishing feature gave him what was described as "a wolfish appearance."

The Masons were tried for robbery in Natchez and found guilty, but a fast-talking lawyer got them off with a sentence of thirty-nine lashes and a day in the pillory.

"I shall never forget," one witness of the flogging wrote, "their cries of 'Innocent' at every blow of the cowhide which tore the flesh from their quivering limbs, and until the last lash was given they shrieked the same despairing cry of 'Innocent, Innocent.' "

Despite this heart-rending scene, information from other highwaymen confirmed that Mason and his gang worked the Natchez Trace for its easy pickings. Mason had turned to crime after leading a respectable life for many years. When Mason's daughter, against her father's wishes, married a criminal from Carolina named Kuykendall, Mason pretended to forgive the couple and invited them to a party in honor of their marriage. That evening he killed his new son-in-law, and later, a pursuing officer. Thereafter, he and his son took to the life of the highwayman.

John Swaney, a mail rider, witnessed one such robbery while riding the Trace. One morning at daybreak, as he woke up after a night in the woods, the mail rider heard voices. Hoping the voices were those of returning boatmen, he jumped on his horse and road toward the sounds, emerging on the scene just as a robber with a painted face shouted "Surrender!" to a mounted gentleman, who nonetheless drew his musket. Then, as Swaney watched helplessly, the bandit shot the traveler, who fell forward across his saddle horn. Swaney's horse shied and reared, and the bandit took off into the woods. Further along the Trace, Swaney caught up with the dead man's companions, one of whom was his teenage son. He and his father had come from Carolina carrying gold to buy a plantation. Enlisting the aid of nearby Choctaws, Swaney and the others returned to the scene of the murder. In the meantime the robber had come back, stripped his victim to his underwear, and taken his horse. Perhaps hurried and nervous, he'd failed to find the money belt the Carolina gentleman had worn next to his skin.

The bereaved son carved this inscription above his father's shallow grave:

ROBERT MCALPIN
MURDERED & KILLED
HERE JULY 31

Swaney, the one witness, always claimed this crime was the work of the innocent-crying Masons, whom he had known earlier.

When President Jefferson appointed William C. C. Claiborne governor of Mississippi, the noose tightened around Mason's neck at last. The new governor, conscious of the business being brought to his state by the constant flow of merchants down the river and up the Trace, offered a $2,000 reward for Mason, "dead or alive." There being not so much honor among thieves on the Trace, two other outlaws, posing as respectable citizens, brought in Mason's head in a big lump of blue clay to retard decomposition and claimed the reward. Among those asked to identify the head was the mail rider Swaney, who had his doubts that the right man had been decapitated. Perhaps the telltale "wolf fang" was not in evidence.

In the ensuing discussion, one of the bounty hunters was recognized by someone in the crowd of onlookers as Little Harpe, the younger of the notorious Harpe brothers, Wiley and Micajar. Although the outlaw vigorously denied this allegation, it was soon established beyond doubt. A man named John Bowman from Knoxville stepped forward and testified that Wiley Harpe should have a scar under the left nipple of his breast, because John had cut him there during a fight. Little Harpe's shirt was pulled off, and sure enough, there was the scar!

Little Harpe and his companion, Mays, managed to escape the crowd, but not for long. Shortly afterward, in 1804, they were hanged, and their heads cut off. These grim reminders were stuck on poles along the Trace as a warning to other outlaws.

The Terrible Harpes had turned to crime after betting and losing everything they owned in a horse race. They traveled with two women who always seemed to be pregnant. As Big Harpe lay dying, he said his only regret was that he had dashed out the brains of one of their infants on the wall of a cave that was their hideout. Apparently, he had no such repentant feelings about all the other murders he'd committed. After Big Harpe committed one particularly vicious attack, a furious posse followed and caught up with the Harpes. A man whose wife and child Big Harpe had killed put a bullet in the outlaw's spine. Little Harpe escaped through the woods.

While Big Harpe lay paralyzed on the ground, taking a long

time to die, the impatient avenger began to cut off his head. "You're a goddamned rough butcher," Big Harpe is reported to have said, "but cut on and be damned." The head was nailed to the fork of a tree in Kentucky.

These three decapitated outlaws—Samuel Mason, Micajar Harpe, and Wiley Harpe—are now among the ghosts of the Trace, seen in the place where the trail began, in Natchez.

The last of the four outlaw apparitions is that of John A. Murrell, who was born about the time the Harpes were being decapitated. Murrell was a slave stealer. Like a page out of Somerset Maugham's *Rain,* Murrel's mother had been a woman of ill repute until his preacher father met, saved, and married her. Mom Murrell's redemption lasted only until her husband went on the road with the gospel, which he did for the good of his soul, since he found himself constantly after his wife. When he was home the preacher did his best to keep the woman from walking with swinging hips and other unseemly behavior.

From this inauspicious beginning, John began by robbing his mother's "visitors," and then turned to horse thievery while still a young man. Once, when he was caught, the letters H. T., for Horse Thief, were branded on his thumbs.

Murrell would promise to lead a slave to freedom if the black would allow him to sell and steal him back a few times on the way. When that particular slave became known as part of a scam, Murrell would kill him and find another. Once he disposed of an entire black family—father, mother, and child. From this small beginning, Murrell went on to land piracy. Then in 1835 a man named Stewart reported that Murrell and his gang were planning a massive slave uprising, set for the 4th of July. The large-scale revolt was to begin in Madison County, move through Natchez, and go on to New Orleans. All the white people, except handsome women, were to be killed, leaving the entire South under Murrell and his gang's control.

When Stewart spread the news of this conspiracy, the South went wild with terror. Many people, black and white, lost their lives in the ensuing panic. Armed posses, bloodhounds, lynchings, torture, hasty trials, and executions were the order of the day. Not only suspected conspirators but also abolitionists and gamblers merely traveling through Mississippi were caught and hanged.

Stewart became a hero in the state, but some cooler heads doubted that there ever had been a conspiracy, among them

Governor Claiborne, who called Stewart "a notorious scamp." In 1860 the governor wrote: "The whole story was a fabrication. Murrell was simply a thief and counterfeiter, and Stewart was his subordinate, who, having quarreled with him, devised this plan to avenge and enrich himself. The whole 'plot' and its tragical consequences may now be regarded as one of the most extraordinary and lamentable hallucinations of our times."

Murrell himself somehow escaped the carnage and died in prison ten years later of tuberculosis.

Besides haunting the Trace, the ghost of John Murrell is also connected with the Devil's Punch Bowl, which is reputed to have been his hiding place. There are actually two such "punch bowls," huge sinks in the bluffs, about a mile north of Natchez. Whether Murrell's hideout was in the larger or the smaller of them is still an open question.

Ned Smith, writing in the *Jackson Daily News*, January 15, 1970, described the place and its local legend, hidden gold. "The large punch bowl is one of nature's freaks. No scientist has ever fully explained it, nor has any plausible theory or reason ever been advanced for its presence, but all who view this wonder spot with its weird and sinister beauty feel it has a secret connection with the Mississippi River. . . . [Some people] advance the theory that hidden treasure is buried here in huge containers and much digging for piratical gold has taken place in the basin of 'The Devil's Punch Bowl.' "

A good time to visit Natchez, keeping a sharp eye out for its romantic spirits and its more terrifying ghosts, is early in October, when the Natchez Fall Pilgrimage offers a two-week tour of thirty-two antebellum homes. After the Civil War the fortunes of Natchez took such a plunge that residents were too poor to tear down and rebuild their ruins. Consequently, many of these mansions were patched up, saving them for later restoration. Nowhere is a southern antebellum town more intact today. And by the way, one of the homes on this tour is Magnolia Hall, a haunted house we wrote about in *Haunted Houses, USA*.

A section on the bluff is still known as the Spanish Quarter. The equally historic Natchez-Under-the-Hill is still in the same place, but times change, and today you'll find it a pleasant area of gift shops, antique stores, lounges, and restaurants with a view of the Mississippi River. The Natchez Trace Parkway follows part of the northbound route of the historic Trace with none of its pitfalls. Along the way to Nashville you'll find picnic areas, nature trails, and Indian mounds.

And perhaps on a misty evening in Natchez, one still may glimpse those long-dead Spanish soldiers emerging from the haze on the bluffs or hear on the banks of the river below a horse's hoofbeats and the laugh of the outlaw Hare.

DIRECTIONS: *Within the city of Natchez, Silver, Ferry, and Water streets comprise the area known as Natchez-Under-the-Hill. The Natchez Trace marker erected by the Daughters of the American Revolution can be seen in Bluff Park, which is off Broadway.*

To connect with the Natchez Trace Parkway, you will have to travel north out of Natchez on Highway 61 for thirteen miles. At this writing, the city of Natchez is trying to obtain funding to bring the parkway right into Natchez, just the way it was in the old days.

Over one hundred sections of the original Trace are preserved within the Parkway boundaries. Exhibits along the way are designed to help you learn more about the Trace's colorful history. A comprehensive map showing the locations of exhibits, nature trails, picnic areas, water recreation, campgrounds, and rest rooms is published by the National Park Service.

For information about the Trace, write Superintendent, Rural Route 1, NT-143, Tupelo, Mississippi 38801 or call (601) 842-1572.

For information about Natchez, write the Natchez Convention and Visitor Bureau at 311 Liberty Road, Natchez, Mississippi 39120, or call (601) 446-6345. The map of the Natchez Trace Parkway is available from this bureau.

—DR

THE MYSTERY OF *THE IRON MOUNTAIN*
The Mississippi River from Natchez to Vicksburg

Not all ghosts take the form of apparitions; some ghosts are heard rather than seen. Not just knocks on the wall or footsteps on the stairs, but actual voices speaking distinct words.

Travelers along the river from Natchez to Vicksburg, Mississippi, and especially in the area of St. Joseph, Louisiana, sometimes hear the desperate cries of a French woman who calls out that she is being cruelly attacked by a group of men. This assault isn't happening in our time, however; it's been related to an incident that occurred over a hundred years ago— the disappearance of a steamboat, *The Iron Mountain.*

Steamboats still travel the Mississippi; nowadays they carry passengers who have a nostalgic yen for the romance and luxury of yesteryear. In their heyday, during the mid-1800s, these grand river conveyances were advertised as "flying palaces." But old-time steamboat travel wasn't necessarily as attractive and safe as cruising aboard their modern replicas. Cabin passengers had accommodations fitted up in magnificent style, but the majority of passengers were crowded into rows of berths like chicken cages, where they were unable to move about or stretch. And steamboats were blown up, burned, sunk, or otherwise destroyed at the rate of a hundred or more a year. More lives were lost in river travel annually in the nineteenth century than in crossing the Atlantic. Business was so brisk, however, that the destroyed steamboats were replaced just as rapidly as they exploded or were sunk.

Nearly six hundred steamboats were in operation on the Ohio, the Mississippi, and other interior rivers in 1850. A traveler could go from Philadelphia to New Orleans by way of Pittsburgh on the rivers in nine or ten days for $36. And a great deal of cargo could be moved very cheaply, barring accidents.

The Iron Mountain, which carried both passengers and cargo, was well named. The steamboat was one of the largest of her kind, more than 180 feet long and 35 feet wide, powered by five boilers. She needed every bit of that power, because *The Iron Mountain* regularly towed a string of barges loaded with various goods between New Orleans and Pittsburgh.

In June 1872 she was making one of these routine trips when an extraordinary thing happened. The whole huge bulk of the riverboat simply disappeared. She had just made a stop at Vicksburg and when last seen, rounded the bend on her way north. Anyone standing on the dock at Vicksburg that fine summer day caught the last glimpse of *The Iron Mountain* anyone ever had.

There was a big search and a major investigation, of course. All that was found was the string of barges the steamship had been towing. The tow rope had been cut, not broken or frayed.

There was no sign of debris such as might have been expected if *The Iron Mountain* had floundered and sunk.

If someone hijacked the steamship, what did they do with it? Riverboats constantly passed and repassed each other as they traveled the length of the Mississippi on routes as regular as buses. Captains and crews got to know one another's boats by sight. Yet nobody on any other boat saw *The Iron Mountain* once it rounded that turn out of Vicksburg.

Strangest of all, no trace of any of the passengers or crew was ever found. Surely, if *The Iron Mountain* had exploded or sunk, bodies would have washed ashore somewhere, sometime. But not one of the fifty-four people on that boat ever turned up, dead or alive.

Yet there is one possible piece of evidence, a ghostly one. Dating from that unexplainable disappearance, fishermen and riverboaters near St. Joseph, Louisiana, have often heard a woman's cries coming from the middle of the Mississippi— particularly just north of the city. This strange phenomenon begins with a single piercing scream, followed by words that can be distinguished, and always the same phrases.

"Gaston! Gaston!" she calls. *"Aidez-moi au nom de Dieu. Les hommes me blessent!"* ("Help me in the name of God. The men are hurting me!")

Folklore in the area of Natchez, St. Joseph, and Vicksburg maintains that the voice belongs to a passenger aboard *The Iron Mountain*. The belief is that the boat was hijacked in some mysterious fashion, perhaps dismantled piece by piece and hidden. It would have been necessary, of course, to kill the passengers and crew and bury their bodies, which would explain why none of them washed ashore. One can only imagine the tragic scene suggested by the ghostly voice in the river.

There were river pirates in those days, although the crime was a capital offense. (In fact, the notorious Harpe brothers and Samuel Mason, outlaws who are featured in the story of the Natchez Trace on page 75, tried their hand at river piracy for a time.) Covering all traces of such a crime would have been a monumental undertaking. If *The Iron Mountain* were indeed hijacked, the canny pirates successfully hid their terrible deed— except for that one little detail, a voice crying for help, the testimony of a ghost. The woman's feelings of terror and desperation are imprinted near the place where she was probably brutalized and murdered.

As we have discovered in researching many of these tales of the supernatural, the energy generated by strong emotions is not easily dissipated. Occasionally, it crystallizes a moment in time that replays for generations afterward.

We'll never know for sure what was the fate of *The Iron Mountain,* but if you're in the vicinity of the Mississippi River where it defines the border between Louisiana and Mississippi, you may hear the last words of one of the steamboat's ill-fated passengers.

DIRECTIONS: *Traveling north or south on U.S. Route 65 in Louisiana, take Route 128 East to St. Joseph. It's on the Mississippi River near St. Joseph where the legendary voice has most often been heard. But you can also listen for that voice anywhere on the river between Natchez and Vicksburg if you are traveling in Mississippi.*

—DR

A DECLARATION OF INNOCENCE
The Boyington Oak
Mobile, Alabama

My friends Bob and Alice Bahr moved from Pennsylvania to Mobile, Alabama, a couple of years ago. They've always been skeptics, sort of humoring me and my interest in the paranormal. They're practical people—Bob is a writer and Alice the head librarian at a college. But when they heard about this book they were quick to contact me about the many ghosts in Alabama and offered to research some of them for me. Since the Boyington Oak is right in their home territory, it's the first one they visited. And they told me the story of this mighty oak.

It was November 1833 when Charles Boyington first set foot on Alabama soil. He arrived on a day when everyone's attention was on the event of the night before—the unforgettable night when a shower of meteors, unrivaled for size and glitz, had rained down on Alabama, lighting the sky like a pyrotechnics display on the Fourth of July.

Boyington was an affable enough fellow, and it wasn't long before he had established himself in residence at a boarding-house run by a Mrs. William George. Shortly thereafter he obtained just the job he was looking for—that of a printer. Nathaniel Frost was also a resident at Mrs. George's establishment and he was also a printer—so with those things in common it was natural that the two young men became fast friends. Mrs. George and others who knew the two thought very kindly of Boyington for befriending Nathaniel Frost. Frost not only was introverted and subject to bouts of melancholy that made him a poor companion, he also suffered from tuberculosis. He was too sickly to work fulltime.

Boyington was unswervingly kind to his friend. He accompanied him on walks—often to the graveyard to read tombstones—a pastime they both enjoyed. Frost's penchant for self-pity gave way to Boyington's chatter and his habit of breaking into humorous songs and ditties. He was quite a tonic for the ailing Nathaniel Frost. And Charles Boyington was becoming very popular with the upper crust in Mobile. They loved the poetry he composed, were impressed with the way he played several musical instruments including the harp and the mandolin, and, of course, as has always been the case, a single man was a welcome addition to any party. So it wasn't surprising that though he'd been in Mobile for only a few weeks, Boyington was invited to a posh ball to be held at the Alabama Hotel.

He used a good portion of his savings on the correct clothing for the affair, and he knew he cut a dashing figure when he entered the hotel's ballroom. Looking at the surroundings, his eyes quickly fell on a beautiful young girl with chestnut curls falling to lily-white shoulders. Her shapely body was adorned in an ivory gown that cascaded to the tops of her satin slippers. Boyington felt breathless just watching her. Never, he told himself, had he seen such a lovely vision. But Charles wasn't the only young man taken with her beauty. She was surrounded by admirers, and she danced every dance. Boyington knew he had to meet her—this chance might not come again—so he summoned his courage and cut in on the girl as she danced with one of her suitors. Somehow he managed to keep her to himself the rest of the evening. They danced every dance under the eagle eye of her father, who seemed to become increasingly agitated as the night wore on.

Charles learned that the object of his affection was named Rose—a fitting name, he thought—and that she attended mass at the local Catholic church each morning. Boyington had never spent much time in prayer, but he arose early the next day and was on hand that morning and for many mornings to come to participate in the religious ritual. Rose was always accompanied by Lydia, a member of her father's household staff. But, fortunately for the couple, this servant had a romantic streak and a strong liking for her young mistress and for the fellow who seemed so smitten with Rose. Lydia was only too happy to pass notes between Rose and Charles. Although this minimal communication was frustrating, it was the best the couple could hope for, except on those rare occasions when Rose's father went out of town on business and Lydia could pretend to accompany her charge on a walk or shopping trip. At these times Charles Boyington would meet them and walk hand in hand with his beloved, usually through the Mobile graveyards, since those quiet places didn't seem to attract gossips and busybodies.

Their love deepened and Charles spent his hours away from Rose dreaming of her and the day when they'd be together forever. He lost some of his conviviality and instead of attending social functions spent time in his room writing poetry to Rose. Affairs of this nature are pretty hard to hide from people living under the same roof, and soon Charles was the butt of jokes at the boardinghouse. The other roomers teased him good-naturedly. But the chiding only made Charles angry, for the more he thought about his wish to be with Rose, the more hopeless he felt it was. Rose's father wasn't going to let him marry her unless he had the money to take care of her, and the money he was making, while adequate, wasn't enough to convince this overprotective father that Charles was the right choice for a son-in-law.

Charles Boyington's obsession made him less efficient on his job. The vision of Rose's sweet face seemed to impose itself between him and the print he was supposed to be setting. After several warnings about the quality of his work went unheeded, Charles was fired one day in the spring of 1834. This was the final straw . . . now Rose's father would never allow Charles to court his daughter. Charles did try to improve his position.

Every day he set out looking for employment. But his only skill was that of a printer, and he'd just been fired because of incompetence by the largest printing firm in Mobile.

Nathaniel Frost surprised Charles Boyington by telling him that he, Frost, had money put away in a chest in his room at the boardinghouse. Furthermore, since Boyington had been such a good friend, Frost offered to help him through his depressions and illnesses and pay for Boyington's room and board for as long as it took for Boyington to obtain gainful employment—a magnanimous gesture for the sick man to make to one of the few people who had ever been a friend. You'd think that Charles Boyington would have been grateful, but instead he felt humiliated by this gesture. And he couldn't help wondering just how much money Frost had hidden away in his room. By now Rose had found out about Charles's streak of bad luck and spent as much time as she could (eluding her father) comforting him. She did love Charles—perhaps as much as he loved her.

One day after a particularly grueling stint of job hunting, Charles Boyington returned to the boardinghouse to find his friend Nathaniel whittling a piece of wood. Boyington was struck with the idea of whittling a heart and sending it to his lovely Rose. He asked Frost to teach him how to carve, and the two set out with a piece of wood and a knife to their favorite spot in the Church Street Graveyard, where Nathaniel Frost intended to instruct Charles on the fine points of carving. A few hours later Boyington returned to the boardinghouse alone. Mrs. George was quite concerned about the frail Nathaniel Frost and his whereabouts, but Charles calmed her fears by saying that Nathaniel had chosen to stay behind for a while to enjoy the spring evening.

Charles Boyington seemed a bit distracted as he hurried to his room. Then, just before he left the boardinghouse for what was to be the last time, he handed Mrs. George a package and asked her to have it delivered to Rose. That night a ship named the *James Monroe* left Mobile bound for Montgomery. Among its passengers was Charles Boyington. Mrs. George was disturbed that Boyington hadn't come home during the night, and she was alarmed to find Nathaniel Frost's bed empty the next morning. Sensing that some disaster had befallen him, she summoned the police. The search was a short one. The first place the police looked was the Church Street Graveyard, the cemetery where Frost and Boyington had spent so many happy times, and there, lying beneath a tree with a hideous look of pain on his face and numerous stab wounds in his lifeless body, was Nathaniel Frost. The knife that Nathaniel had used in his skillful carvings was missing.

Circumstantial evidence certainly pointed to Boyington as the murderer, and on Monday, May 12, 1834, the Mobile papers carried an article by John Stocking, Jr., the city's mayor. It said in effect that the body of one Nathaniel Frost had been found in the Church Street Graveyard and that Charles Boyington was suspected of having done the evil deed. Furthermore, the board of aldermen, at the urging of the mayor, had put aside the sum of $250 to be used as a reward for anyone who could catch up with Boyington. The article carried a description of the fugitive. Two hundred fifty dollars sounded tempting to the local riffraff and bounty hunters of Mobile, and by Thursday Boyington had been discovered aboard the *James Monroe*, handcuffed, and returned to Mobile and the county jail. Despite what looked like pretty convincing evidence to the contrary, Boyington staunchly maintained that he was innocent. The month was May, and the trial was set to take place in November. In jail Charles was reunited with his darling Rose. She'd received the little hand-carved heart and wore it on a chain around her neck. Rose was a daily visitor, and she always brought him small gifts of books, flowers she'd picked with her own delicate hands, or succulent fruit from the trees near her father's mansion.

Rose was completely convinced that her Charlie would never commit murder, and she would have continued these pilgrimages to see Boyington, but her father (whom she had successfully avoided) finally found out about the jailhouse trysts. After that Rose was kept under twenty-four-hour surveillance. Charlie wrote to her and composed poems to her, but she was not allowed to answer. In some ways she was as much a prisoner as he.

The trial was a short one. Down to a man, the jury believed Charles Boyington guilty and found him so. He was sentenced on a November day in 1834 to hang by his neck until he was dead. Through the trial and right up until his execution in February of 1835, Charles Boyington swore he was innocent. Even clergymen doing their duty by trying to cleanse his soul and prepare it for the hereafter were unsuccessful in shaking his story. On the day of the execution curious citizens lined the streets, straining for a glimpse of the condemned man as he marched behind his coffin in a parade to the gallows. A minister strode along beside, still trying to get the man to confess, but Charles Boyington said only, "I'm innocent, I'm innocent." He had prepared a speech, which he read to the jeering crowd just before the noose was put around his neck. In it, he again professed his innocence and promised that over the spot where he was buried an oak tree would grow. This, he told his detractors, would be proof that he did not commit this awful crime.

The hanging was a mess. Inexperienced hangmen botched the job badly. Just as they were about to open the trapdoor under Charles Boyington, for some inexplicable reason the sheriff fainted and fell off his horse, who then toppled over. A lady sitting on a nearby log also fainted. During the ensuing excitement, the prisoner tried one last time to save his neck by slipping it out of the noose. But as he was sprinting across the platform, the bumbling officials came to life and dragged him back to his fate. Few mourners followed the casket to its final resting place in the Church Street Graveyard in a corner by the wall. The clergyman mumbled a few words over him, and the people of Mobile got on with their lives, forgetting about Charles Boyington and the murder of his friend Nathaniel Frost. Rose met a young man of whom her father approved, put the carved heart away in a box of souvenirs, and fell in love again.

After a few months had passed, a couple walking through the cemetery noticed a seedling oak pushing its way out of the earth that covered Charlie's body. Word of this spread fast, for the local folk remembered Charlie's words. Many of the townspeople came to look and ponder about whether this really could be a sign that Charles Boyington had been put to death for a murder he didn't commit.

A playground now covers the area that once was a graveyard. The echo of children happily playing fills the air most afternoons. But the oak, now grown tall and strong, is known to all of Mobile as the Boyington Oak. It's a giant oak, and it has withstood storms that have felled many lesser trees. The story still is discussed by a few residents, and tourists to the city sometimes visit the site. Many of those who have stood by the grand old tree on a quiet evening swear that they've heard its branches murmuring plaintively, "I'm innocent, I'm innocent." When my friends the Bahrs visited the spot they claim they didn't hear anything. Maybe the breeze wasn't right, maybe it was the wrong time of day, or maybe their disbelief kept them from being receptive to the mournful cries of Charles Boyington.

DIRECTIONS: *From the intersection of Government and Broad streets in Mobile, go east toward downtown and the bay, to South Bayou Street. Go south on South Bayou for one block to a gravel parking lot on the left. There are many huge live oaks here, but the Boyington Oak is the only one surrounded by wooden posts.*

—JB

THE END OF AN ERA
Bladon Springs Cemetery
Bladon Springs, Alabama

Norman T. Staples, steamboat captain and designer of the steamboat *John T. Staples,* took a gun, put it to his chest, pulled the trigger, and ended his life when he was only forty-four years into it. The year was 1913; the month was January. Norman was interred beside the bodies of his children, James Alfred, Bertha Jaddetta, Mable Claire, and a boy known only as "baby" because he had been stillborn and was never named. They still lie together in the Bladon Springs Cemetery. And Norman's ghost hovers over them, protecting them in death as he never did in life. His suicide wasn't precipitated by grief over the premature deaths of his children but by grief of another kind.

Norman Staples was raised in Alabama on the banks of the Tombigbee River. During his entire childhood he heard tales of the steamboats, watched them come and go on the river, and envisioned the day he'd be a riverboat captain. He didn't mind when the sounds of the riverboat whistles awoke him at night (a common complaint of his family and neighbors). It was a sound dear to his heart.

In the late 1800s, when Norman was growing up, the steamboat was at the height of its popularity. Norman loved to observe life along the river. The wealthy ladies and gentlemen boarding the steamboats for trips up or down the Tombigbee provided fodder for his imagination. On occasion Norman was able to travel with his family on a steamboat. A few times he was even invited to go right up into the pilot house. Those were the high points of his young life and he cherished the memories of them. When it came time for Norman to select his life's work, it was an easy choice. He got a job on a riverboat just as he'd always known he would.

Norman was a fast learner, and he soon knew all the hazards of the Tombigbee. He became a skilled navigator and in no time was offered the position of boat pilot on one of the most luxurious ships on the river. While his entire family was impressed with his accomplishments, it was his sister Mary who helped with his career. She had married a wealthy man named Fred Blees. Fred adored his wife and would do anything he could to impress her and keep her happy. So he listened with a willing ear when Mary asked him if he could possibly provide the financing for her brother to build his own boat. Norman was an expert pilot, Mary told her husband, and she would be ever so grateful if Norman could have his own boat. Not only that, she asserted, blinking her long black eyelashes, it would be a good investment, and Fred was sure to add many dollars to his already vast bank accounts, and . . . Fred, always willing to humor Mary, gave no argument. He loaned the money to Norman with only one stipulation. The ship would be named the *Mary S. Blees* after Norman's sister and Fred's wife.

Mary's confidence in her brother paid off. The *Mary S. Blees* made more money than any other boat in the entire history of steamboating in Mobile. Norman was extremely pleased to be able to pay back the loan in a scant two years. Heady with his first success, Norman designed and had built a second steamboat. This new boat was called the *Mary E. Staples* after Norman's mother. The *Mary E. Staples* joined her sister ship in steaming up and down the river, transporting passengers and goods and making a great deal of money for its owner.

It's time, Norman thought, to design an even greater ship—one that will be the most magnificent ship ever to be seen in Alabama. In 1908 Norman Staples built his dream ship. It was a beauty, easily identifiable even by those people who weren't conversant with the subtle differences between steamboats on the river. A large star hanging on the front of the steamship—twinkling between the twin smokestacks—separated this ship from the others. The ship was a beautiful sight. Norman proudly called it the *James T. Staples* after his father. The impressive vessel was soon known as the *Big Jim*.

Along about the time he was building his first ship, Norman met and married Dora Dahlberg. If Dora expected a loving, attentive husband, she must have been disappointed. Norman was nice enough when he was around, but most of his time and energy were spent either aboard a ship or planning to build a new one. His wife seemed like an accessory to his busy life. Norman must have paid some attention to Dora, however, for just nine months after the nuptials the girl gave birth to their first child, James Alfred. Norman was pleased to have a son, but after the initial strutting and handing out of cigars, the new father paid little attention to the baby. Dora was pregnant again before little James Alfred was six months old. This time it was a little girl whom they called Mable Claire.

Before Dora recovered from the birth (which had been a difficult one) James Alfred was suddenly taken sick, and in a matter of days was dead. Dora and Norman grieved, but Norman had his boats to keep his mind off of the tragedy. After a few months, Dora was again with child. Of course, the couple hoped for a boy to replace the one they'd lost. Each tried to hide their disappointment from the other when Beatrice Alice was born. They thanked God she was healthy. Three more pregnancies produced three more daughters—Bertha Jaddetta, Melanie Dora, and Mary Faye. Between Bertha Jaddetta and Melanie Dora there was a stillborn son, laid to rest beside James Alfred.

Norman and Dora saw even less of each other now. His attention was focused on the growing boat business, and work made it easier to forget about his dead sons. Then, in the winter of 1907, the unthinkable happened. All of the children took sick with the fever. Mable Claire and Bertha Jaddetta succumbed. Instead of making Dora and Norman closer (as one would think) it drove them even further apart. Dora was inconsolable, but in time she rallied for the sake of her remaining daughters. Norman fared better—he had his ships.

Every extra penny that Norman Staples could lay his hands on went into building the *Big Jim*, and at another time it probably would have been a wise investment. But in 1908 the

Birmingham and Gulf Navigation Company had set their sights
on owning and operating all the boats on the river. No trick was
too dirty for them. Norman Staples, who wanted only to run
the best boats on the river, was no match for them. Norman
had just three boats, and the Birmingham and Gulf Navigation
Company had many. They cut rates so low Norman simply
couldn't compete without putting his investments in jeopardy.
But compete he must. Finally Norman was forced to cut his
rates, too, in order to get any business. This only put him in
such financial hot water he almost went bankrupt. As if this
weren't enough, while Norman was struggling to keep his
steamboats running, the railroads came into their own. Compa-
nies that had previously shipped their goods by steamboat now
used the trains that ran beside the river. Norman's dream, the
Big Jim, took so much money to run that it was turning into his
nightmare. He'd weathered the loss of four children quite well,
but the prospect of losing his beloved shipping company took a
large toll on his health.

Norman managed somehow to keep going until December
1912. Shortly after Christmas, his creditors closed the books
on him and took over the *Big Jim*. Nothing had ever caused
Norman such pain. Not only had he lost his ship, but even he
had to admit that the era of the steamboat was drawing to a
close. Norman made it through the new year desperately trying
to figure out what he could do with the rest of his life. On
January 2, 1913, Captain Staples ceased his quest for a new
career by ending his life. His wife and two daughters wept
openly as his body was lowered into a grave near those of his
other children.

The creditors who'd taken the boat away from Norman were
having their troubles, too. No one wanted to crew the *Big Jim*
without Norman Staples, who'd been considered a fair man and
a good friend by those who worked for him. Finally a crew was
assembled, but then several of the ship's firemen claimed they
saw a ghost—not just any ghost but the ghost of Norman
Staples—lurking around the boiler room. It made them uneasy,
so they quit their jobs. Hearing of the story caused most of the
other men to abandon ship, too. What made the tale so creepy
was that all of the men, when questioned individually, related
the same experience. The figure, they said, was shadowy, but
it was definitely the image of Captain Norman Staples. It moved
around the boilers with a purpose, as if it had authority there.

Then the ghost just disappeared—first it was there, then it was gone—in the blink of an eye.

It was with great difficulty that the owners of the ship got another crew together. This time it was made up entirely of blacks who hadn't heard about the ghost. A few hours before the boat was to depart, when the passengers and their luggage were all on board, when the cargo was in place, a strange thing happened. All of the rats that were living in the hold of the ship started to leave. They rushed down the gangplank and scurried off into town. Although there was a considerable effort put forth to keep the black crew from seeing the departing rats, see them they did, and knowing that rats desert only a sinking ship, they left—not pausing even long enough to quit their jobs.

A new crew was put together in a few hours. The passengers were assured that everything was fine. A few of them left the ship, but the majority stayed, allowing the officers to calm their fears. Everyone was uneasy as they tried to laugh off the jinx. As the boat pulled out of Mobile and headed north, people began to relax. The weather was fair though chilly, the boat was running along well, and the ghost of Norman Staples was almost forgotten.

The trip went along uneventfully until they reached Powe's Landing, a port about one hundred miles or so from Mobile. The crew was unloading freight, and many of the passengers were enjoying their noon meal. A young girl walking on deck waved her hand to her father, who was enjoying a smoke at the front of the ship. Just at that moment one of the boilers in the ship's bow let loose, exploding with a roar. The steaming hot water gushed over crew and passengers in the front of the shattered boat.

The young girl's father died instantly. There seemed to be a sea of screaming, writhing humanity begging for help—all suffering terribly. Those in the back of the *Big Jim* were stunned for a second, then they swung into action, rushing to help the injured. But many people were beyond help. The captain, second clerk, and first mate were scalded almost beyond recognition. Just moments after the last victim had been removed from the remains of the *Big Jim*, the ship burst into flames that burned the ropes holding the ship to the pier. The *Big Jim*, fire spurting from its hull, drifted down the Tombigbee River until it was almost in line with the Bladon Springs Cemetery, where the remains of the man who had designed the ship had lain for scarcely a week, then, with a great shudder, it sank to the bottom of the river. Twenty-six people had died on board that day and another twenty-one had been seriously injured.

Of course, a full-scale investigation followed. The ship was hauled up from its watery grave and inspected. The conclusion was that the boilers had malfunctioned. The big question was why? They'd all been inspected in December and found to be in perfect operating order. The rumor that went around (and what most of the people of Mobile and surrounding areas believed) was that Norman Staples had been determined that his enemies would not operate his beloved boat, and that his ghost (the one that so many firemen claimed to have seen) actually tinkered with the boilers, causing one or more of them to explode and kill and injure all those people.

Could this man who was such a worthy captain, respected by those who served on his ships, considered to be very fair and trustworthy, have done this evil deed? It seems unlikely—and yet, this was the man who lived through the deaths of several of his children with very little trouble but was so grieved by the loss of his ship that he took his life.

When the ghost left the ship, it took up residence in the Bladon Springs Cemetery near his grave and those of his offspring. He is with them in death much more than he ever was in life. Those who have seen him tell of the transparent figure of a man holding his head in his hands as he roams among the tombstones. Perhaps he wants to comfort his children, or maybe peace eludes his spirit because of the deaths and injuries he caused that fateful day in 1913.

DIRECTIONS: *Bladon Springs is a very small village that doesn't even have a post office, but, because of its state park, it's marked on all the maps. Take Highway 84 East from the village for about five miles until you cross a bridge. About a half mile farther turn right onto a blacktop road. This is County Road #6. The cemetery is about three miles down the road on the righthand side.*

—JB

A Haunted Highway

Interstate 65, South Alabama

AND

A Mystical Power Center of American Prehistory

Moundville, Alabama

Folks who live in and around Evergreen, Alabama, have noticed a curious phenomenon during the past few years; some call it "spooky." There have been an exceptional number of accidents happening on a nearby lonely forty-mile stretch of Interstate 65, from southern Conecuh County to northern Butler County. Since 1984 there have been 519 accidents on that isolated road, with 208 people injured. Twenty-three people have lost their lives.

The talk is that Alabama engineers made the mistake of constructing the highway over sacred Creek burial grounds. According to local folklore, Interstate 65 is just plain haunted. The spirits of Indians whose bones were disturbed to make way for the interstate are said to be rising up on that often empty length of highway—or in some way exerting a negative influence on those who traverse the road.

The local county sheriff, Edwin Booker, who was interviewed about the inordinate number of accidents (*The Providence Journal*, October 29, 1989), admitted that the statistic was above average. But he believes the figure is high because those forty miles of Interstate 65 are on a straight flat road through featureless forests, which causes drivers to simply lose interest.

When questioned about the accidents the tribal chairman of the Poarch branch of the Creek Indian Reservation in Escambia County, Eddie Tullis, said, "I don't doubt it at all. This whole area, especially Conecuh and Butler counties, once had a major concentration of . . . Creek Indians. We feel assured that a lot of our people's graves were disturbed by the interstate." But Chairman Tullis was loath to attribute the anomaly to ghosts.

"Well, I don't think there are spirits causing these accidents," he added. "I believe in a supreme being. And I believe there has been a lack of respect for the people who have come before us. I think if people consider how the Indians have been mistreated, it would cause them to lose their attention while on the road."

An unusual point of view! Perhaps Chairman Tullis believes there's a negative energy rising in a general way from the mistreatment of his people, and he isn't surprised to learn it evidences itself in a place believed to be the sacred Creek burial grounds.

It's certainly possible that drivers are simply not paying attention when they drive that particular stretch of road. Still, stories of a Creek-haunted highway persist among the local residents. The idea was intriguing enough to stimulate a review of Creek history to see why these hostile vibes may be occurring.

Most of the Creek Indians today live in Oklahoma, but up until the early 1800s they made their home in Alabama and Georgia.

In the late 1700s the Creek Nation was one of the ranking Native American powers. Its friendship was sought because it was strategically located between the new American government and the Spanish government in Louisiana and Florida. When the Creeks were no longer needed as a buffer, however, the relationship changed.

At first there were few conflicts, because Creek villages were located about three hundred miles inland from most white settlements, which were coastal. But from the glowing report sent back to Washington by the first Indian agent (appointed by the secretary of war), who rhapsodized over those inner regions, it was clear that trouble was in the winds. The Creek lands, he wrote, were rich in resources, blessed by a mild, healthful climate, and ideal for cultivation, their natural beauty "only rendered unpleasant by being in possession of the jealous natives."

Unfortunately for the Creeks, their nation was divided. There was a persistent enmity between the upper Creek people, called the Red Sticks, and those located to the south, called the White Sticks.

The White Sticks wanted to learn what they thought was the higher wisdom of the Europeans. They welcomed these strangers to their country and eventually ceded to the whites much land, which was described as "delectable" by the hungry settlers. Many white traders, especially the Scots, married Creek women of the friendly south in order to obtain wealth and political power in the Creek Nation. The subsequent generation of White Stick chiefs included many men whose names and features were European. These leaders lived according to Creek customs, although they often wore European clothes and beards, and they amassed land and property in the ambitious European manner.

One of the wealthiest men in the South, for example, was Alexander McGillivray, whose mother was a Creek woman. McGillivray became the undisputed leader of the Creek and the Seminole nations, despite various tribal animosities, commanding over ten thousand warriors until his death in 1793.

Also of Scot and Creek parentage, William MacIntosh became a great chief among the White Sticks, and helped to create a law among Creeks that forbade the sale of their lands without the consent of all the tribal chiefs. In 1821 MacIntosh, who was in the pay of the Georgia Commission, broke this law himself. He made treaties ceding an additional fifteen million acres of land to the state, with only those Creek chiefs under his personal command agreeing, a mere tenth of the total number. The Creek councils met and passed a sentence of death against MacIntosh. His tribesmen went to his house and carried out the execution.

Meanwhile, the Red Stick Creeks, led by a chief named Menewa, had pursued a less "progressive" path and developed strong anti-American feelings. Aggressive toward the advance of the whites, the Red Sticks became a thorn in the American side, and the cry was that they should be "exterminated."

Andrew Jackson was sent to achieve this objective. With the help of the White Sticks, Jackson defeated and killed most of the Red Stick Creeks in a decisive battle against Menewa's encampment at Horseshoe Bend, Alabama. Sam Houston also fought in this battle, receiving wounds that troubled him for the rest of his life.

With seven gun wounds in his body, Menewa lay unconscious among his fallen warriors. After a time he revived and immediately shot at a passing soldier. The soldier returned fire, sending a bullet through Menewa's jaw, which took several teeth in its path. The chief was left for dead, but when darkness came, Menewa revived a second time and managed to crawl to a canoe and float down the Tallapoosa River to the swampland where the remaining Red Sticks had taken refuge.

Menewa regained his health and lived to continue the fight with the remnants of his clan. His resurrection after such grievous injuries is a prime illustration of the unyielding character of the Creek people. This same will of iron showed in the Red Stick women, who killed their young children in order to fight beside their men. Strong spirits like these are just the kind that often linger at the dramatic scenes of American history.

After the battle of Horseshoe Bend, the Red Sticks were essentially defeated and scattered, and their land was opened to settlement. In 1819 Georgia and Alabama became states, created mainly from Creek and Cherokee lands.

Andrew Jackson became a hero and was made a major general. Later, when he was elected president, he made the Indian Removal Bill his first order of business. This bill directed that all Native Americans east of the Mississippi should be removed from their homes to western lands designated as Indian Territory.

When President Jackson recommended removal in 1829, an aged Creek named Speckled Snake summed up the situation for his tribe as follows:

"Brothers! I have listened to many talks from our great father. When he first came over the wide waters, he was but a little man . . . very little. His legs were cramped by sitting long in his big boat, and he begged for a little land to light his fire on. . . . But when the white man had warmed himself before the Indians' fire and filled himself with their hominy, he became very large. With a step he bestrode the mountains, and his feet covered the plains and the valleys. His hands grasped the eastern and the western sea, and his head rested on the moon. Then he became our great father. He loved his red children, and he said, 'Get a little further, lest I tread on thee. . . .'

"Brothers, I have listened to a great many talks from our great father. But they always began and ended in this—'Get a little further; you are too near me.' "

The federal government passed another law outlawing tribal government. Native American councils had been accustomed to making treaties directly with the federal government. But this new bill effectively turned "the Indian problem" over to the state governments to handle by whatever methods they deemed expedient.

State laws were passed that made it legal for squatters, land speculators, and bootleggers to move in and take over the land. One law, for instance, decreed that only a white American could settle a deceased Native American's estate. Another law forbade a Native American from testifying in court against a white.

Not only the lands of the Red Sticks, but also of those of the pro-American White Sticks were plundered. This included some rich plums—the plantations and property of the wealthiest Creeks, who were of half-European heritage. All Creeks, regardless of position or white ancestry, fled for their lives, hid, and starved. This period of Creek history may have been the beginning of any negative energy now lurking in pockets here and there.

During the 1830s the U.S. Army received standing orders to routinely dig up all burial sites in Alabama and to send the remains and artifacts to Washington, D.C., for analysis. (What would normally be termed grave robbing is called archaeology when scientific interest is aroused.) Recently the Smithsonian Institution agreed to return thousands of Indian bones for reburial.

It was also in the 1830s that some of the impoverished Creeks finally accepted the removal treaty. But they managed to stall, postponing their actual departure from Alabama to the lands in Oklahoma set aside for them by the federal government. After five years of this delay, Jackson's secretary of war issued a command to "inaugurate an operation of war, subdue them and remove them to the west." The Creeks were marshaled for the trip, "the road to disappearance."

Observers were touched or amused by the way the Creeks said good-bye to every tree, rock, and stream of their homeland. "They [the whites] cannot appreciate the feelings of a man who loves his country," wrote Washington Irving, quoting Creek chief Eneah Emathla.

Resistant Creeks were manacled and chained together. Of the 15,000 Creek people who migrated, 3,500 died during the removal.

If this weren't enough to explain a residue of negative energy on Interstate 65 (and probably elsewhere) we must also consider that Creek burial grounds might not have been the only sacred sites that were disturbed by advancing settlement. Long before the Creek Nation flourished in Alabama, these lands were the home of the early Temple Mound Builders of the more complex Mississippian culture.

This prehistoric culture officially dates from about A.D. 700 but may go back to an even earlier time. People of the Mississippian culture were master farmers and craftsmen with a much more complicated social structure than the later Creeks. The Mississippians constructed earthwork temples and elaborate underground tombs with much religious paraphernalia and who knows what spells to protect them. Because their stylized artwork featured symbols of death such as skulls, bones, and weeping eyes, and their sculpture showed representations of human sacrifice, they are sometimes called the Death Cult or the Buzzard Cult.

Mississippians traded and settled far and wide, but one of their most important centers was in what is now called Moundville, Alabama. As their culture declined (for reasons we don't know), remnants of the Mississippians mingled with the Natchez of Louisiana. Elements of the Mississippian culture are found in both Natchez and Creek mythology. By the time of the first European forays into America, all evidence of the Temple Mound Builders was underground, waiting to be found centuries later by archaeologists.

I wonder if, underneath the Creek burial grounds where Interstate 65 was built, there were other, earlier burial sites belonging to the Mississippians. A place that has once been sacred is often adopted for religious practices by later cultures. At any rate, whatever spirits may or may not underlie the problems on Interstate 65, it's only common sense to keep alert and take care when driving across this stretch of highway.

If you'd like to experience the powerful spirit of the Mississippian culture, you may wish to visit Mound State Monument in Moundville. Administered by the University of Alabama, this 320-acre monument is open daily, except on major holidays, from 9:00 A.M. to 4:45 P.M.; an admission fcc is charged. You can explore twenty prehistoric temple mounds, one of which is a large ceremonial earthwork six stories high. This temple was the center of the Mississippian religious life, a gathering place for games, holidays, and sacred rituals. Also on the grounds of the Mound State Monument are a reconstructed village, burial grounds, and a museum of the Mississippian culture. There are picnic tables on the bank of the Black Warrior River, and camping is available.

The State of Alabama guidebook notes: "The mounds are an impressive sight for the Easter Pageant held each year at sunrise on Easter morning." This is a perfect example of the evolution of religious practices at one particular locale over the centuries; here Mississippian rituals have given way to the Christian.

If any place or any inanimate thing (like a rock or a statue) is held sacred over a long period of time, it becomes imbued with the spiritual vibrations (good or evil) that have been directed toward it. Walking into an ancient cathedral, one can sense the holiness of the place where generations have worshipped. And landscapes have their auras, too. Psychics and other sensitive people can feel the sorrow emanating from Civil War battlefields in Tennessee or enjoy the peace and healing of a place like Mesa Verde.

Many of the hauntings and other strange phenomena we have investigated have arisen from the disturbance or desecration of a sacred place. Such is the case with Interstate 65.

DIRECTIONS: *Travel north from Mobile or south from Montgomery on I-65. The "haunted highway" is the section of road between Evergreen and Greenville.*

For Mound State Monument, travel west out of Montgomery on I-80. Turn north onto Highway 69 to Moundville (15 miles south of Tuscaloosa). Continue north of the city on Highway 69 to the Mound State Monument.

　　　　　　　　　　　　　　　　　　　　　　　—DR

A LOVE THAT WOULDN'T DIE

Musgrove Cemetery
Fayette County, Alabama

I shall but love thee better after death.
—ELIZABETH BARRETT BROWNING

Robert Musgrove was born in 1866 to a family who had settled in northern Fayette County after migrating from South Carolina. He had brothers and sisters, aunts and uncles, and cousins living nearby. Robert was a happy, cheerful boy who enjoyed playing with the other youngsters and with the toys kids of that day had. When he was about ten his family took him to visit relatives living in Tuscaloosa. The trip was a hot, unpleasant one, but Robert loved meeting his cousins and getting to know the aunt and uncle he'd heard so much about.

But the high point of the trip for young Robert came when the family took him to the Tuscaloosa train station, where he saw his very first train. Robert was enchanted as he watched the long train chug down the track, steam pouring from the chimney, the wheels creaking as they turned pulling their load. From that moment on Robert knew he was going to spend his life working on a railroad, and he would become an engineer. Unlike most small boys, who change their ambitions as they grow, Robert held fast to the notion of becoming a railroad engineer. In fact, he seemed obsessed with his dream.

The Musgrove clan were a handsome group, especially the men, and Robert seemed to have been endowed with uncommonly good looks even for a Musgrove man. When he was a teenager the girls were wild about him, but though they batted their eyelashes and their giggles sounded like mating calls, Robert's passions didn't direct themselves to girls. His waking thoughts and his dreams at night all centered around one thing—trains. Although Robert said he was sixteen at the time, he had scarcely passed his fifteenth birthday when he ran away from home and took a job on the railroad. Of course, he wasn't an engineer, but he was working near his beloved trains if only in the capacity of waterboy. At first he didn't even ride on the trains. He was busy hauling water to quench the thirst of the crews as they laid tracks. But Robert wasn't discouraged; he knew that if he could come this far at fifteen, he would someday realize his ambition of becoming an engineer. The boy worked long, hard hours—always willingly and with a cheerful smile. And he hung around the trains when he wasn't working, getting tips on how to succeed on the railroads from men who'd made the iron horse their lives. In time Robert became an engineer on the St. Louis and San Francisco Railroad.

His family had long known where Robert had disappeared to years before, and he made frequent visits home. While there he worshipped with his family on Sundays in the Musgrove Chapel, a church his family had built next to the Musgrove Cemetery, where they buried their dead. The Musgroves were a large, loving family. Handsome Robert seemed to have it made—he had the love of a wonderful family and he had done what few of us do—made his fondest dream come true. Since all his energies had gone in that direction, he'd had scant experience with women. After some thought on the matter, he decided it was time for him to do some courting and participate in the pleasures of the flesh. He was, after all, in his thirties.

The train on which he was engineer ran between Memphis, Tennessee, and Amory, Mississippi. Robert soon had ladies waiting for him in both destinations. They loved his good looks, they loved his naïveté, and they loved the fact that he was a railroad engineer. Robert was having a wonderful time in the company of some ladies of questionable character. While he still loved his job and the railroad, he realized he'd been missing some of the greatest experiences of life, and he was doing his best to catch up. Robert might have gone on dallying with the ladies of the evening and dating the girls of Memphis and Amory, but one night when he attended a party in Amory, Robert danced with a young lady named Maude. They'd hardly been around the dance floor once when Robert sensed that this girl was not like the others whose company he'd sought. She was soft-spoken, had large, deep-set brown eyes and long, thick straight hair. She was a real lady, someone Robert would be proud to introduce to his friends and family in Fayette County. By the time the couple had taken their second waltz around the room, Robert had fallen hopelessly in love. "When will I see you again?" Robert implored the young girl as the last strains of music heralded the end of the evening.

"Come to dinner tomorrow," invited Maude, giving Robert the address of her family's home.

"Tomorrow I'll be on my way back to Memphis," Robert lamented, almost hysterical at the thought he might not see this precious girl again. "But I'll be back in town again soon," he added hopefully.

"Come round to see me then," Maude said, smiling sweetly.

For once, Robert didn't enjoy his trip. He kept thinking of the lovely Maude and wondering if a girl that exquisite could really be interested in him. When he returned to Amory, he rented a room in the local hotel, shined his shoes till they were like mirrors, put on his best suit, and went calling on Maude. The young girl had been none too happy since Robert had left, for she, too, had felt the strong attraction between them. The couple continued to see each other whenever Robert came to Amory and soon it was obvious to everyone around them that they were deeply in love. It wasn't six months from the time they'd met that Robert appeared on Maude's doorstep one night—a man with a purpose. He'd purchased an engagement ring, hoping that his lovely Maude would accept his proposal of marriage. He wasn't disappointed. Although, in truth, the diamond wasn't a very large one, Maude declared it the most beautiful ring in the world and Robert the most handsome, wonderful man.

Maude's family were delighted with the engagement. They'd become very fond of the engineer during his many visits. Robert took his fiancée back home to meet his folks. They shared his enthusiasm. She was a lovely girl. Maude busied herself making wedding plans. It would be a wonderful event. Her parents, while not wealthy, were well enough off to give their only daughter a tasteful send-off. What fun Maude had selecting her attendants, finding just the right bolt of cloth for her wedding gown, planning the wedding feast. All through this happy time, there were the visits from Robert on his frequent stops in Amory. Every time the couple was alone, they vowed that they'd love each other always—as engaged people tend to do.

While Robert was on the job he kept telling his fellow workers how much in love he was. He was so happy, so fulfilled, so eager to marry his love, and then—one terrible night as he drove his train from Memphis toward Amory and the girl he loved, something went wrong, someone's signals got crossed. No one knows just exactly how it happened, but as Robert sped along toward Amory another train was speeding along on the same track toward Memphis. The results were disastrous, and Robert was killed instantly.

The railroad sent Robert's remains back to his kin. Since the rails went only as far as Winfield, Robert's family and friends drove a group of horses and wagons to that point to pick up the body and the many grieving friends who had accompanied it and to drive them back to Fayette County. Maude was among the mourners. Although she wore her grief well and did all she could to comfort Robert's family, Maude felt as if she had died herself—at least the part of her that could feel passion had died. It would be buried with Robert. She knew that she would never marry, would never bear babies, would never share a happy home with a man she could call her husband.

The funeral service was held in the Musgrove Chapel, where Musgroves had worshipped for years, and Robert was buried with his people in the Musgrove Cemetery. As the mourners filed silently from the grave, Maude knelt beside it and was heard to whisper, "Robert, I'll never leave you." Maude returned to Amory and lived with her family. She never married. The bloom left her cheeks, and though she tried to be loving and helpful to her parents, she never again had much zest for living. As long as she was able to, Maude made periodic trips to her fiancé's grave, clearing away overgrowth and leaving behind a beautiful bouquet of flowers. It's speculated that she probably whispered, "Robert, I'll never leave you," just as she had on the day of the funeral.

When Maude died Robert's grave began to show signs of neglect. Then one day in 1962, about six months after Maude's demise, as Sunday worshippers left the Musgrove Chapel they noticed a strange, shadowy image on the tall, stately granite marker that Robert's family had erected shortly after his death. Closer inspection brought gasps from the startled parishioners. Right there on the tombstone was the silhouette of a girl kneeling in prayer. It was so distinct that one of the older men in the crowd declared, "That's Maude—Robert's girl. It's been a long time, but I still remember her." A hush fell on the small group. Word spread quickly about the image on Robert Musgrove's tombstone. The curious came, saw, and told other curious people, who came to see the silhouette. The family found the influx of strangers annoying, and so a small contingent of them set about to scrub the image from the marker. It was a waste of soap and elbow grease, for Maude's silhouette was just as clear as the first day it was discovered. Finally a stonemason from Birmingham sandblasted the offending image. With nothing to see, the crowds lost interest and Musgrove Cemetery was once again a peaceful place for the living as well as the dead.

Within a month the outline had returned as plain as before. This time the family skipped the scrubbing and summoned the stonemason immediately. And he did more sandblasting than was absolutely necessary, making sure no vestige of the image remained. But Maude wasn't about to be put off by a few humans. She wasn't going back on the promise she'd made to her sweetheart on the day he was buried—the day she'd murmured "Robert, I'll never leave you." The image returned to the marker, and the family, realizing that it was futile to do otherwise, accepted its presence. Today visitors to the cemetery can see the outline of the grieving girl kneeling in a prayer for her beloved Robert.

Bob and Alice Bahr say this story is frequently told by native Alabamans. And, although they've never visited Musgrove Cemetery, they've spoken with folks who have been there and swear that they've seen the silhouette of Maude on Robert Musgrove's marker.

DIRECTIONS: *From Birmingham, follow I-78 North to Winfield (about 65 miles). Take Route 43 out of Winfield six miles south to Doug Hubbard's Service Station/Store, turn west, and continue to church and cemetery.*

—JB

HAUNTED BATTLEFIELDS OF THE CIVIL WAR

Chickamauga National Military Park and Stones River Battlefield National Park, Tennessee

Dale Kaczmarek, an intrepid ghost hunter and publisher of *Ghost Trackers Newsletter,* recently made a pilgrimage to the scenes of two of the bloodiest battlefields of the Civil War. As Dale explains it, "Wherever massive deaths and violent confrontations are mixed, there is always the possibility that ghosts may roam the area." Dale theorized that sudden, violent death may trap an individual in an earthbound plane of existence, so he decided to "check into the possibilities . . . and do some hunting on my own." What Dale discovered at these two national parks more than justified his thesis. Park rangers have been witness to "Old Green Eyes," the ghost of Chickamauga. At Stones River, too, there are weirdly silent places, ghostly footsteps behind the wary tourist, and an apparition appearing before an astonished ranger's eyes. And that's not all!

The clash at Chickamauga on September 18, 1863, was between General Braxton Bragg's Army of Tennessee and General William Rosecrans's Army of the Cumberland, each army numbering about 65,000. Such was the nature of this particular conflict—mostly fought in heavily wooded areas, with division commanders hampered by missed communications from headquarters—that it all came down to soldier against soldier. As Colonel John T. Wilder of the Federals described Chickamauga, "There was no generalship in it. It was a soldier's fight purely, wherein the only question involved was the question of endurance. The two armies came together like wild beasts, and each fought as long as it could stand up in a knock-down and drag-out encounter. If there had been any high order of generalship displayed, the disasters to both armies might have been less."

Veterans of other battles remarked that the unholy din of so many guns all firing at once was greater at Chickamauga than at any other place. One Alabaman described the fireworks as "one solid unbroken wave of awe-inspiring sound."

When the three days of fighting at Chickamauga were done, the casualties numbered above 35,000. Bragg's army pushed Rosecrans's army all the way back to Chattanooga, where the latter received relief from General Grant. This major victory for the Confederacy almost changed the course of the war. But strangely enough, both generals left the scene of the conflict rather sooner than honor would dictate. It was James Longstreet instead of Bragg and George T. Thomas instead of Rosecrans who saw out the battle to the bitter end.

Bragg was miffed that the plan of battle he'd drawn up had not been followed and removed himself from management of the encounter by retiring to Reed's Bridge. His staff had to convince Bragg that victory had been achieved. At one point, a Confederate private was brought in to verify that the federal forces were retreating so fast they were leaving their wounded behind them.

"Do you know what a retreat looks like?" Bragg asked sharply.

"I ought to, General," the man replied, a remark that was later passed from campfire to campfire. "I've been with you during your whole campaign."

With more reason to do so, Rosecrans also got out before the final rout. Charles Dana, who was there as an observer and liaison with Washington, D.C., saw the general cross himself and realized that the situation must be desperate indeed. "If you care to live any longer, get away from here," Rosecrans advised his staff, and that's exactly what they did. Another observer of this scene wrote, "In later years I used occasionally to meet Rosecrans, and always felt that I could see the shadow of Chickamauga upon his noble face."

Besides the racket of gunfire, Chickamauga had been distinguished by another sound, the wild rebel yell issuing from thousands of throats, over and over again, when the Union forces were in full retreat. If Bragg had been a little closer to the battle, he would have been in no doubt as to which side had won the day.

At Chickamauga, which is now a beautiful scenic park where visitors may take a tour with maps and a tape recording to recreate the battle, Dale Kaczmarek talked to Edward Tinney, the supervisory ranger and chief historian, who was "very helpful in pointing out many instances of unusual happenings, both in the past and present. Perhaps the most bizarre story concerns 'Old Green Eyes.' "

Dale learned that there are two versions of this legend. "One is that a Confederate soldier's head was severed from his body, which was blown to bits from a cannon ball. All that was left to bury was his head and, according to legend, on misty nights it roams the battlefield, moaning pitifully, searching for the body.

"The other legend says that Old Green Eyes roamed the area long before the Civil War and was seen moving among the dead at Snodgrass Hill during a lull in the fighting. One of the bloodiest battles [of Chickamauga] took place on Snodgrass Hill and maybe that has some bearing on the sighting. Many people visiting the park near dusk have heard an agonizing groaning that sends shivers up and down their spines."

Charlie Fisher, another ranger Dale interviewed, added more to the Old Green Eyes story. In the 1970s, Fisher said, two different people wrecked their automobiles against the same tree. Both of them swore they had seen Old Green Eyes just before the crash.

Fisher himself has never seen this legendary vision, but Ed Tinney has seen Old Green Eyes on several occasions, according to Dale. "He saw it one foggy night while walking along one of the trails that wind through the park. He said the shape was humanlike but not human. When he first saw it, it was less than twenty feet away and passed right by him. He described the hair on the 'thing' as long, like a woman's hair, with eyes almost greenish-orange in color. Its teeth were long and pointed like fangs, and it was wearing a cape that seemed to flap in the wind, even though there was no wind. The next thing he knew, it just disappeared right in front of him."

Other eerie things that have been experienced include bushes moving when there is no wind, the sound of distant gunshots, although no hunting is allowed in the park, and a rumble of moaning, as if from many wounded men.

And then there is the apparition of a lovely lady in white who floats above the grounds. "Legend has it," Dale writes, "that she is looking for her lost sweetheart who was killed [at Chickamauga]. To this day she hasn't given up hope of finding him."

After exploring Chickamauga, Dale visited Stones River Battlefield National Park near Murfreesboro, where other rangers and park service employees have had supernatural experiences.

The conflict at Stones River happened before the battle of Chickamauga, around New Year's Day 1863, with the same two generals, Bragg and Rosecrans, in command. This battle, too, was considered a Confederate victory, although casualties were so high and the fall back to Tullahoma and Shelbyville ordered by Bragg made in such wretched weather that there was no great rejoicing among the troops.

One particularly touching episode in the Stones River battle happened after one day's fighting had given way to darkness. On each side, military bands played rousing tunes to keep up the morale of the men. The lines were so close that each could hear the other's music, so the concert soon became a battle of the bands, with a loud rendition of "Dixie" being answered by an even louder "Yankee Doodle," and so on through the night. But then one of the bands struck up the strains of "Home, Sweet Home," and the rival band joined in. Soldiers on both sides began to sing the familiar words, and many of them had to hide their tears. For a brief time all hearts were in harmony at Stones River—at least, until the next morning's opening salvo.

In the tour of Stones River, stops are numbered along the way to help inform tourists of the battle action in each place. "Stop number four is a rocky, wooded area with a number of sinkholes," Dale said. He thought such an area should abound with birds and forest animals, but "when I was there you could not even hear a bird chirp in the trees. The area is totally devoid of life. The temperature was in the nineties; however, when I entered the glade, it was ten to twenty degrees cooler." Other tourists have complained of hearing someone or something following them, even when nothing was there. "I personally felt very strange at stop number four," Dale admits. "The area was a virtual bloodbath, with both sides losing a great many men. Even cows grazing in the immediate area were cut down by incidental gunfire. I felt very paranoid, like I wasn't alone. Like there was a large group of people watching my every move."

Another place where unusual things happen at Stones River is at stop number six. Jeffrey Leathers, a park ranger, camped out there one night with friends. Finding that his canteen needed a refill, Leathers headed for the administration building. As he rounded a bend in the path, he noticed a man standing behind some bushes. At first Leathers thought one of his friends was playing a trick and called for him to come out. Raising one hand, the figure advanced toward Leathers, who now saw that the man was not a fellow camper. Leathers, who always carries a few live rounds in his gun, ordered the man to stop immediately or he would shoot. The figure fell to the ground and simply disappeared before the ranger's eyes. Searching the area later, Leathers could find no footprints, no broken twigs, and certainly no body.

Leathers was at a loss to explain this experience, but Dale writes, "It is my personal theory that this could possibly be a reenactment of a soldier trying to surrender himself as a prisoner but then, before he could, he was shot and killed."

Dale tried infrared photography at both battlefields, but the results didn't yield anything out of the ordinary. "But," Dale says, "that doesn't mean the ghosts of Chickamauga and Stones River no longer roam."

DIRECTIONS: *The headquarters of Chickamauga-Chattanooga National Military Park, which features the Fuller Gun Collection and a slide presentation of the massive battle that took place here, is located on U.S. Highway 27, 10 miles south of Chattanooga. The park is open daily during daylight hours. Admission is free. For further information, call (404) 866-9241.*

Stones River National Battlefield includes 351 acres and a museum. Located just outside Murfreesboro on Highway 41/70, the battlefield is open daily during daylight hours. Admission is free. For further information, call (615) 893-9501.

—DR

GHOSTS OF *THE DISTANT EDEN*
Historic Rugby, Morgan County, Tennessee

For we are about to open a town here—in other words to create
a new center of human life in this strangely beautiful solitude.
—THOMAS HUGHES

In 1880, amid a flurry of publicity on both sides of the Atlantic, Thomas Hughes, the English social reformer and author of *Tom Brown's School Days*, founded his utopian community in America, naming it after the famous school featured in his popular Victorian novel. Rugby, which has been called a last attempt by the English to establish a colony in this country, was ideally situated atop the beautiful Cumberland Plateau of East Tennessee.

A charming village with nine acres of manicured lawns, gravel walks, and flower beds was laid out where the residents could overlook the gorge of the Clear Fork. Hughes's town plan emphasized aesthetic considerations more than most American communities of the time.

Now a historic preservation, Rugby is haunted by its past in manifestations that range from footsteps on stairs and apparitions at the windows to the midnight rumble of horse-drawn carriages across cobblestone roads that no longer exist. Ghost stories and tales of strange goings-on have been related about Rugby for decades. Why this attractive village and not another?

To understand what's going on at Rugby, one might start by looking at the hopeful fervor that led to the colony's conception—in other words, the spirit of the original Rugby that clings so tenaciously to its restoration. The overwhelming characteristic that emerges from historical research is that Rugby was infused with the energy generated from powerful dreams. It was created by one dedicated dreamer—and recreated in our time by another passionate dreamer. Everyone connected with both the original and the restored community has been somehow touched by the magic of these dreams.

Like Charles Dickens, author Thomas Hughes had a strong social conscience. For years he'd worked to better the lot of the English working class. In founding Rugby he was attempting, in part, to solve a problem unique to the younger sons of

116

English gentry. Because of primogeniture, the custom by which a titled family's entire holdings were inherited by the oldest son, any other sons were excluded from sharing in the wealth of the estate. Although these young men (humorously referred to by Thomas Hughes as "our Will Wimbles") were expected to keep up a social front, class pressure kept them from entering any but a few professions. The younger son of a duke or earl would be disgraced if he dabbled in trade. The law, the church, or the military were the only acceptable fields, and these were crowded.

But in the new and freer society of America, Hughes hoped these young men's energies and abilities could be directed to manual trades and agricultural endeavors. Although he scorned Marxist communism and was an outspoken critic of government socialism, Hughes designed his colony's government along Christian Socialist lines—a more voluntary system. Settlers would be engaged in a cooperative venture where manual labor and individual initiative would work for the good of all. The single church (now restored and part of the Rugby tour) was designed to be used by members of different denominations.

By 1884, about four hundred fifty colonists were in residence at Rugby, which Hughes called his "new Jerusalem" and "the city of the future."

As a colony hewn out of the wilderness, Rugby was unusually civilized. Although skilled craftsmen and farming families from the area were also invited to join the community, the settlement's tone was undeniably upper-class British. Bowling greens, bridle paths, ornamental gardens, and roads with English names like Farringdon and Longcott were laid out by the gentlemen agrarians with a loving dedication that might have gone to crops and trades. Lawn-tennis grounds were installed; Rugby's tennis team would become one of the first in America. Everything stopped for afternoon tea, and the colonists dressed for that occasion, as well as for dinner. The late arrival of *London Punch* was considered to be a calamity and running out of Worcestershire sauce a disaster.

A lovely library was one of the first buildings to be erected, and the Hughes aura of noble cause inspired publishers of the day to stock it without charge. Every one of the seven thousand volumes is still in place, one of the most complete Victorian collections in existence, called by some a "Rip Van Winkle library."

No county fairs or corn-husking bees at Rugby! Musical, dramatic, tennis, and other clubs were formed, and balls and entertainments were held regularly, many of them at the newly constructed Tabard Inn, named for the inn in Chaucer's *Canterbury Tales* and containing an actual banister from that ancient hostelry.

Like so many other social experiments, Rugby succumbed to the inevitable adversities faced by pioneer communities. Drought, fires, typhoid, and broken promises for a railroad line to that inaccessible wilderness each took a toll. The colony's first step into industry, a tomato-canning factory, failed because the tomato crop was so poor, and a pottery business also proved unprofitable. A decade after its auspicious beginning, most of the colonists had gone off to greener pastures. Rugby began to fall into decay.

Hughes died in 1896, having lost $35,000 of his own money in the Rugby venture.

One of the first weird happenings at Rugby concerned a couple named Davis, managers of the old Tabard Inn. Because thirteen was an unlucky number, most guests wanted to avoid Room 13, and the Davises resided there themselves. But it seems the number may have been most unlucky for them, because Mr. Davis arose early one morning, obviously from the wrong side of bed, and slit his wife's throat. Then he tried to end his own life with poison. Either the poison failed or he became impatient, because following this attempt, he shot himself instead.

A few years later Tabard Inn burned to the ground. The colonists were able to save some of the furniture, however, especially from Room 13, the last part of the inn to be consumed. (The banister from Chaucer's Tabard Inn was also spared.) As the fire reached the scene of the Davis family tragedy, witnesses heard terrible human moans rising from the flames.

Some of the furniture taken from Room 13 that fateful night was moved into Newbury House, Rugby's present-day country inn. Coincidentally, on two occasions guests at Newbury have awakened to find the ghost of a man bending over their beds.

Before Rugby could have a present-day life, however, it had to be recognized as a historic treasure and rescued from neglect and decay. This story, too, is an unusual one. The person who rescued Rugby from oblivion was Brian Stagg, who was only sixteen years old in 1964 when he first began lobbying the Tennessee Historical Commission (and everyone else who might be interested) for help with the project. His energy, enthusiasm, and passion for preserving the twenty Victorian structures of Rugby were contagious; Brian Stagg had the ability to inspire others with his personal dream.

For a very long time, however, the preservation committee, with Brian Stagg as executive director, operated more on that dream than on substance, but he never gave up. It's extraordinary how much Rugby, then only a ruin of its former self, meant to him, almost as if he'd been part of it in another life.

"I can just picture it as if I had been there," he wrote in those early years (reported by Patricia L. Hudson in *Americana*, April 1988) "the town pump, the Tabard Inn, Uffington House with its beautiful gardens and original furnishings restored—it would all be so wonderful. Rugby is so important to me, and I hope that I may someday do something to keep its memory alive." Stagg authored a book about Rugby titled *The Distant Eden*, and went to live in Roslyn, a two-story Rugby house built in 1886.

During his residence at Roslyn, Brian Stagg became aware of a supernatural presence in the house. At first it was through strange little happenings. Whenever Brian went into the garden to work, for instance, the door would lock itself. As time went on, Brian would be awakened by the sound of footsteps in the hall, and most startling of all, he began to see the figure of a lady in Victorian dress pacing that hall and crying.

Another witness, a visitor to Roslyn named Sarah Bonner, saw the same melancholy apparition, distinguished by her hawkish features. Brian and Sarah pored over the old photographs of former residents, and sure enough, they found a woman with the same features and wearing the same dress as the apparition they'd both seen. The Victorian lady's name was Sophie Tyson, and she'd once lived at Roslyn with her mother and brother Jesse, whose spirit was also restless, as the following story illustrates.

The ghostly carriage has been heard by several witnesses. Once when Roslyn was vacant, a former Rugby resident, Mickey Worthington, was exploring the house with friends when they heard the clatter of horses on the drive and saw the apparition of a black tally-ho carriage with four dark horses and a ghostly driver at the reins. The carriage thundered into the driveway, circled the front of the house, then raced off through the impenetrable woods.

Later, archaeologists surveying the original colony found a former road, High Street, now completely overgrown, on the same route the phantom carriage had taken.

The same carriage was heard (but not seen) by Rugbeian Michael Alley, who could distinguish the sounds of iron wheels, horses' hooves, the slap of reins, and the creak of the step when someone alighted at Roslyn's door. Further research uncovered the fact that Jesse Tyson used to drive guests to his mother's parties in a four-horse tally-ho carriage, and he was considered to be quite a daredevil driver, fond of giving the ladies a breathtaking ride.

On another occasion, Michael, Brian, and two friends, one a reporter from Nashville, were in an upstairs bedroom, looking out the window for the deer that could often be seen crossing the lawn at night. As Michael tells the story, he was standing at the window when suddenly he heard terrified shrieks from the two visitors. Everyone rushed for the door in a mad scramble to escape the room. Later Brian and the two men explained to Michael, who'd had his back turned during the incident, that the apparition of a tall man who wore a black shroud and gave off a luminous glow had hovered over the bed.

During those shoestring years of struggle to save Rugby, Brian became very ill and had to be hospitalized. This didn't prevent the IRS from hitting Rugby with a $10,000 penalty for some supposed error in the preservation's paperwork. Paying the penalty would have meant financial ruin for Rugby, and the government would have seized its historic properties. By the time this problem was straightened out, Brian Stagg, after months of ill health, died at the tragically young age of twenty-eight.

Brian's sister Barbara Stagg took over as executive director of Rugby, a position she still holds. She has the able assistance of her husband, John Gilliat, a great-grandson of an original Rugby colonist.

On the first night after Barbara Stagg accepted these new responsibilities, the building containing all Brian's painstaking records burned to the ground. Arson was suspected, but nothing could be proved.

Eventually the preservation prospered with the aid of many helpful grants and donations. The important structures of the village have been rebuilt and refurbished, and Rugby is attracting an increasing number of visitors each year. Its future looks bright.

The dream of Rugby, like a veritable phoenix arising from the ashes, apparently never dies, and phantoms of its heyday linger also, in the homes, the public buildings, and the roads once peopled by Victorian gentry.

In an article in the *Knoxville News-Sentinel,* December 5, 1976, Willard Yarbrough wrote, "There is a 'something' in Rugby, sensed by this writer during many visits here over the years, that is both mystic and unexplainable. . . . Perhaps as one modern Rugbeian explained . . . 'the past has come alive, one cannot live here without feeling it.' "

Thomas Hughes had the Kingstone Lisle house built for himself, but he never occupied it, probably because his English wife and children would have none of this noble experiment in the new world. Hughes's mother, however, did move to Rugby, and he visited her whenever he made one of his frequent trips to oversee the well-being of his colony. His unused residence, now one of the stops on the guided tour, is the home of a snoring ghost, who also kicks off the bedcovers of the neatly made bed from time to time.

Wrote one resident of the Kingstone Lisle house, "We like to dawdle at our breakfast and tea here [in the kitchen] while watching the wild birds feeding at the cafeteria just outside the south window and on dreary days listen to our ghost snore—or groan—depending on which way one's imagination works—in the rafters over the dining room. No, it isn't the plumbing, or the wind, or electrical appliances, all of which have been thoroughly checked by experts. Just a peaceful shade who comes to catch up on the sleep he must have lost along his way. Or perhaps he just likes it here. At any rate, we have come to accept him as our own personal ghost of Kingstone Lisle and miss him when he is off on business elsewhere."

Another spirit presence is felt in the Thomas Hughes Free Public Library, still containing its marvelous collection and even the slips that Rugbeian borrowers signed. This revenant is thought to be that of the German librarian of early Rugby, a fussy and fastidious man who would not allow any one of the seven thousand volumes in his care to be taken out by a colonist until the book was properly cataloged. As Brian Stagg wrote, "Even the visitor not prone to poetic sentiment should feel

Rugby's spell. If he will visit the library . . . and wait for twilight's approach, he might sense, lingering in the air, the presence of a melancholy yet benevolent spirit that refuses to let go of the glory that was Rugby."

And of course, there is the rumble of that ghostly carriage, rushing through the night—from nowhere to nowhere.

DIRECTIONS: *Historic Rugby is located on State Scenic Highway 52, about 125 miles northeast of Nashville, 70 miles northwest of Knoxville.*

Rugby is open for tours February 1 through December 31, and by appointment in January. Tour hours Monday to Saturday are 10:00 AM to 4:30 PM, noon to 4:30 PM on Sunday. Fees are nominal, group rates available. Lodging at the Newbury House and Pioneer Cottage is available year-round; the Harrow Road Cafe is open daily except for major holidays. For information/ reservations, call (615) 628-2441 or 628-2430 or write Historic Rugby, Inc., P.O. Box 8, Rugby, Tennessee 37733.

For ghost hunters, the best time to visit Rugby is during the Annual Rugby Pilgrimage early in August when several of the Victorian homes that are now private residences are also open for touring. Check with the management for exact dates of the Pilgrimage.

Nearby, over a hundred miles of hiking trails, seasonal rafting and canoeing on remote rivers, hunting, fishing, and camping are available in the Big South Fork National River and Recreation Area, Frozen Head and Pickett State Parks, and the Obed Wild and Scenic River Area.

—DR

KATE, the BELL WITCH
Adams, Tennessee

Kate, the Bell Witch of Adams, Tennessee, was one of the most malevolent and "worldly" spirits we've encountered in our research. Most ghosts pursue some mysterious objective without reference to the present time, as if unaware that they are manifesting in the world of the living. A ghost will be heard treading the same thirteen stairs or be seen walking the same moonlit path, sometimes for generations, with never so much as a nod to the flesh-and-blood residents of those places.

But Kate was different! She seemed conscious of herself as a spirit and purposeful in her harassment, constantly interacting with the haunted Bell family, tormenting the children, and probably causing the death of the father, John Bell, apparently by the quite physical means of poison. If that weren't enough, Kate also chatted learnedly with visitors, behaved mischievously toward the neighbors, and even got drunk and bawdy. Possibly in a repentant frame of mind, she sometimes attended two church services on the same Sunday. All in all, it's a story I find quite uncharacteristic and puzzling.

The Bell Witch is "the most documented story of the supernatural in all of American history," according to Don Wick, Director of Information at the Tennessee Department of Tourist Development, who wrote a series of articles on the subject for the *Tennessee Traveler*. Incidents have continued to occur right up to the present time, and the town of Adams has become famous because of Kate's presence. If you go there today, you'll find monuments and markers to commemorate the Bell Witch, and you might even see the figure of a girl said to materialize on U.S. Highway 41. Some motorists have thought they'd struck her, only to find, after jumping out of the car in panic and horror, that the body they expected to be under their wheels had vanished. At night, strange lights are sometimes seen moving over the old Bell place; those who have tried to chase them down say the lights will disappear, then come up in another place.

In 1804 John Bell bought a thousand-acre farm on the Red River in Robertson County, now the town of Adams. He built a fine one-and-a-half-story log home with six rooms and a porch across the entire front of the residence. Still, the house wasn't any *too* big, since he and his wife Lucy had been blessed with nine children.

The trouble began about 1817 with a series of strange noises outside the house. The Bells thought natural causes could explain these occurrences, but matters soon went far beyond that possibility when the noises moved into the house.

At first the gnawing, scratching, scraping, and bumping happened at night in the bedroom where four of the Bell brothers slept, but these eerie sounds would cease as soon as they jumped out of bed and lit a candle. Of course, when the candle was snuffed, the disturbance would begin again.

When the entity began moving from room to room, it sounded like a large dog clawing at the door or chains dragging across the floor. Sometimes there was a crash, as if a chair had fallen over, or the sound of someone gurgling and choking. An unseen hand would snatch the blankets off the children's beds. Later that same hand pulled their hair cruelly enough to make them cry out in pain. One daughter, Elizabeth, was slapped so hard that both her cheeks turned bright red.

No one in the Bell household was getting much sleep anymore. Word got around; neighbors and even strangers visited the farm, some to see for themselves what was going on and some in an effort to help. Impromptu séances took place, with visitors asking questions that could be answered by number. And they were answered, correctly, with a series of sharp raps. Lights were glimpsed flitting through the Bell yard; chunks of wood or stone were thrown at the Bells and their guests.

What had happened so far seems to have been a rather classic case of a poltergeist, the "noisy ghost" that sometimes manifests in a home where there is an emotionally disturbed child. With nine children in the family, the odds are in favor of that possibility. But then something outside the realm of the poltergeist occurred—the entity began to speak!

It was a woman's voice, a whisper at first but soon distinct enough to be heard clearly. When asked, "Who are you?" the voice gave conflicting answers. At one time it claimed to be a spirit whose eternal rest had been disturbed; another time it was an Indian maiden's spirit; still again, an immigrant who'd buried a treasure on the premises, that she wanted Elizabeth to have. The latter persona described the hiding place in detail—near a spring on the banks of Red River—but when the Bells rushed to dig up Elizabeth's legacy, they found nothing but rocks. A mocking laugh was heard in the trees.

Finally the entity identified herself as "Old Kate Batts Witch." As it happened, there had been a Kate in the neighborhood, one of those eccentric old ladies whom country people will call a "witch," and John Bell had quarreled with her in earlier years. This makes me think that *something* was operating through one or more of the Bell children, consciously or unconsciously. One is reminded of the possessed children in

Henry James's story "The Turn of the Screw." "Old Kate Batts Witch" seems like a youngster's description. At any rate, from then on this entity was called the Bell Witch by everyone in the county, and so it is known to this day.

The Bells became celebrities of sorts. Visitors were trooping to the Bell farm to hold conversations with this witch, who would discourse most learnedly on philosophical and religious matters, proving a nice point with the appropriate biblical quote. About this time, Kate would often attend both the Methodist and Baptist church services of a Sunday, and mimic both the sermons later at home in the voices of the two preachers. During this same period Kate seems to have been hitting the bottle, cursing in a slurred voice, and keeping the family up at night with bawdy songs.

As if life were in danger of getting dull around the farm, Kate introduced some friends to the Bells and their visitors, spirits she called Blackdog, Mathematics, Cypocryphy, and Jerusalem. Each new spirit had its own voice. Blackdog spoke harshly in an unrefined but feminine voice, Mathematics and Cypocryphy conversed in more well-bred female tones, and Jerusalem talked like a boy. These new characters came and went, but Kate was a permanent fixture in the Bell home.

When Kate wished to torment someone, she usually picked on Elizabeth, whose cheeks she had slapped early on. The slaps continued, along with pinpricks and other mean tricks, like unlacing Elizabeth's shoes and hurling them across the room. There was no peace for the girl. Even when Elizabeth slept at a friend's house, Kate would show up there, too, to prod and poke her victim. Becoming afraid that the witch would kill their daughter, the Bells allowed two girlfriends to stay with her at night, and at these ongoing slumber parties, the young ladies were witnesses to fresh assaults.

The Bell Witch made other neighborhood calls. William Porter, a young bachelor who lived alone, was host to one of these visits one cold winter night while he was in bed. Suddenly he heard Kate's voice telling him she'd come to spend the night with him and keep him warm. Then he felt her get into bed beside him. Quietly, he stole out of bed, picked up the blanket-wrapped form beside him, and tried to carry it to the fireplace, with the intention of hurling it into the flames. But the bundle in his arms got heavier and heavier and began to smell devilishly bad. As he told the story later, he just had to drop Kate and run out of the house for air.

The Bell Witch's fame continued to spread far and wide. At one time General Andrew Jackson decided to visit the Bells, bringing with him a company of his men, one of whom claimed to be a "witch layer." As Jackson and his party neared the farm, their wagon wheels locked. The whole of that strong company couldn't get those wheels to budge an inch! "By the eternal, boys," the general declared, "it *is* the witch!" At that very moment, they heard Kate laugh and say she would allow them to move on and would see them later that night. Undeterred, the brave general pushed on, and that evening sat in the Bell parlor waiting for Kate to manifest.

The witch layer sat there, too, holding a gun loaded with a silver bullet (a weapon more usually associated with the pursuit of a werewolf). Footsteps were heard and Kate's taunting voice telling this unfortunate man that the gun would not fire. He tried to fire it twice, but it seemed to be jammed. With a crash his chair was overturned, and he began to dance around the room, howling in pain because, he said, the witch had him by the nose and was pinching it fearfully. Finally he was able to run from the house, his hasty departure causing much merriment among General Jackson and his men.

When Elizabeth fell in love with a young fellow named Joshua Gardner, Kate became quite virulent about this romance and vowed to break it up. No one knew why she opposed the union, unless it was just part of her continued antipathy toward Elizabeth.

The second constant victim of the witch was John Bell, patriarch of the clan, and here the spirit became truly malevolent and threatened to kill him. He began to have attacks during which his tongue would swell up, making him unable to talk or eat. The witch laughed and continued to curse and menace the man. The attacks grew more frequent and more serious.

On the morning of December 20, 1820, just three years after the first appearance of this entity, John Bell slipped into a coma. The family sent for a doctor. Meanwhile, John Jr. ran for the medicine that had previously been prescribed for his father. The bottle was missing, and in its place was a small vial of dark liquid. "I've got him this time," the witch's voice rejoiced viciously. "He'll never get up from that bed again." Kate claimed to have given John Bell a big dose of whatever was contained in the vial. One member of the family poked a straw into the dark liquid, then drew the straw through the family cat's mouth. Immediately, the pet went into convulsions and died. John Bell died the following day.

At his funeral, Kate could be heard singing drunkenly as they lowered John Bell into the grave. His tombstone disappeared in 1951 and was replaced with another in 1957. The story goes that the original marker was stolen by pranksters, who threw it away when their car mysteriously began to malfunction.

Kate haunted the Bells less and less after the death of John Bell. It looked as though the future might hold the hope of happiness for Elizabeth and Joshua after all. Then, just after Easter in 1821, the final blow came one day when the couple went fishing with a group of young people. Joshua's fishing pole was snatched away by some kind of monster fish, and Kate's voice encircled the couple, intoning these words over and over again, "Please, Betsy Bell, don't have Joshua Gardner." The fish thrashed to the surface and dragging Joshua's pole. It certainly looked like an evil omen. At this point Elizabeth became afraid and returned her lover's engagement ring. He accepted it, too, and soon moved out of the county. Perhaps John Bell's sad fate had an influence over Gardner.

Elizabeth eventually married Richard Powell, who had been one of her teachers. Apparently, this match met with no disapproval from Kate, who announced that she would be leaving the family, for seven years anyway—a kind of "sabbatical." Elizabeth and her new husband also moved away—to a more peaceful life, one imagines. Elizabeth died in 1890, at the age of eighty-six.

True to her word, Kate returned in 1828, but by then much had changed at the farm. Most of the children had moved away. Only Richard, Joel, and their mother still lived in their log home. Kate made her presence felt, as she had in the innocent beginnings of the affair, with scratchings and gnawings and snatching off bedcovers.

Strangely enough, the one member of the family whom Kate seemed to like and protect was Lucy Bell, John's wife. Kate would give the mother of the Bells helpful advice, relay news of Lucy's family back in North Carolina, and sing to Lucy when she wasn't feeling well. Once when Lucy was ill and didn't feel like eating, several neighborhood women who were visiting the sick woman saw hazelnuts materialize out of thin air and drop into Lucy's hands. When Lucy still didn't eat, the witch asked why, and Lucy explained that she didn't have a nutcracker. Suddenly the nuts began to pop and crack themselves open. After Lucy died, later in 1828, little was heard from Kate for many years. The Bell farm was divided among the children, but, understandably, none of them wanted to live in the family home. In later years it fell into disrepair and was torn down. The log house's location is marked by a large tree today.

Although the Bell Witch seemed to be at rest after Lucy's death, Joel Bell encountered a further manifestation in 1852, as did his son in 1861. A few supernatural events have occurred to Carney Bell, one of the modern descendants, a partner in the Austin and Bell Funeral Home. Carney Bell claims that an adventure with the witch in 1975 enabled him to find a grave he'd been searching for, that of his great-great-grandfather Joel Egbert Bell. The marker was found in a neighbor's field, completely overgrown and invisible, but the Bell Witch had led him to it while he was rabbit hunting.

Most of today's manifestations have occurred around a cave on part of what used to be the Bell Farm, this portion now the property of W. M. Eden. A dark-haired woman has been seen floating through the cave, sounds of dragging chains have been heard, and one young lad had the cap snatched off his head.

There's no doubt about it . . . the Bell Witch is still lurking about in Adams. As you travel that way, watch out for a girl in white who suddenly materializes in front of your car. That will be Kate, up to her old tricks.

The Tennessee Historical Commission has placed a historical marker on U.S. Highway 41, in the heart of "Bell Country." On the sign is printed a brief account of the haunting of the Bells. Nearby is a tall stone monument to the Bell family.

DIRECTIONS: *The town of Adams is north of Nashville on U.S. Highway 41, near the Kentucky border.*

—DR

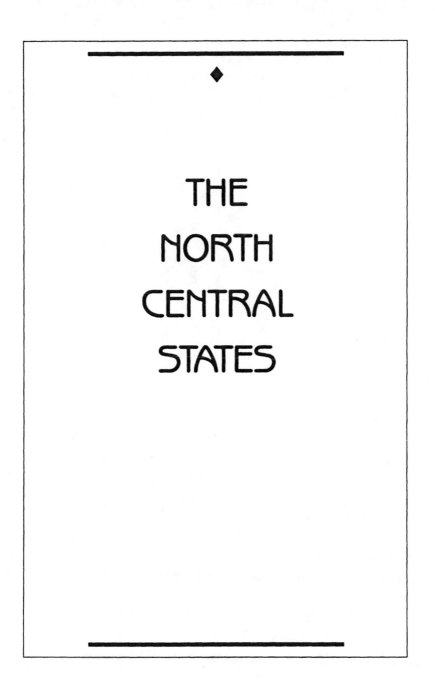

THE
NORTH
CENTRAL
STATES

THE NEOSHO SPOOK LIGHT
Hornet, Missouri

I f you've yet to see a specter, hear ghostly footsteps, or even
feel the presence of something unearthly in any of the
haunted places you've visited, don't give up. Here in the
midst of the scenic beauty of the Ozarks you are practically
guaranteed a glimpse of a genuine metaphysical mystery—the
Neosho Spook Light. Almost everyone who parks on Devil's
Promenade in the evening and waits there patiently for a while
will be granted this deliciously chilling experience. And you
won't be alone. Tourists and natives alike frequent the place
(popularly known as "Spooksville"), located in the village of
Hornet, near Joplin, Missouri, although not as many as in the
old days, when the Spook Light Museum was open. At that
time, the record was 271 visitors in one night, although the
average was 20 to 125, said Garland Middleton when he was
interviewed by Joannie Kidder (*The Joplin Globe*, November 29,
1981). Middleton was the curator and owner of the little
museum, which has been closed since he died.

Middleton probably saw the light more often than anybody
else. He said that sometimes it was the size of a golf ball and
sometimes it was so bright a person couldn't look at it.

Others describe it as beginning in a faint blue haze, then
becoming a pinpoint of light that grows into a glowing orange
ball dancing down the road, varying in intensity, but usually
about equal to a 100-watt light bulb. It is visible from any point
along two miles of Devil's Promenade.

Occasionally the fiery orb gets so close it seems as if one
could reach out and grasp it. But if one walks toward it with the
intention of touching it, the light recedes as if to avoid contact—
or it simply fades away, only to reappear in another location,
perhaps perching in a treetop. Paradoxically, a few witnesses
with no desire to get close to the ghost light have had the
gaseous globe actually enter their cars, causing them to jump

out and run away. Yet photographers who have waited hours to capture the light on film have succeeded in photographing it only at a distance. In these photos the light looks like a small moon hovering over the road.

One woman tells the story of coming home from a school carnival at Quapaw, Oklahoma, when the light decided to "hitch-hike" a ride on the bus. It perched on the rear window, and everyone screamed. So intense was the light that the driver was temporarily blinded and had to stop the bus. As soon as he did that, the light skipped away.

The Neosho light has another fascinating trick. Sometimes it splits into two balls, which caper away separately, bouncing over the rolling mountains. If this is a spirit light, is it one ghost or two?

When this phenomenon first appeared to residents in the 1880s, it created quite a panic in the Joplin area, scaring cattle and causing dogs to howl. Some nervous residents even moved away. Among these refugees was an American Indian couple who blamed the deaths of their two daughters on the ghostly manifestation.

The Ozarks area is rich in colorful folklore and local legends, and the Neosho light has given rise to many intriguing tales.

The most prevalent legend about the ghost light comes from the lore of the Quapaw Indian Nation. A beautiful Quapaw maiden, daughter of the chief, fell in love with a young man from another tribe. When the young man asked the father for the maiden's hand in marriage, the chief put the bride price so high that it could not possibly be met. Being very much in love, the couple decided to run away, but their escape was discovered before they were out of Quapaw territory. The chief sent his fiercest, fastest warriors after the fleeing lovers. Soon it became clear to the couple that they would not be able to outdistance their pursuers. Inevitably the young man would be brought back and tortured and the maiden would have to watch. To prevent this, the lovers decided to leap off a high cliff overlooking Spring River, and they died there together. The Neosho light is thought to be the manifestation of their spirits.

The Quapaw have another story about the light that is even older. In this tale, a man and his wife got into a heated argument, and somehow the husband ended up losing his head, either by the woman's magic or by her employing more physical means, such as his ax. At any rate, the light is the man's spirit, still searching for his head.

The next most popular legend about the light has a similar twist, but it comes from the Civil War era, and there are many who swear this is the true one. Between the battles of Pea Ridge and Carthage, a small detachment of soldiers was ordered to burn some mills south of Joplin, but they were captured by those defending the area. (None of the reports specifies which was the Union and which the Confederate force.) Among those captured was a tough old sergeant who was known for his cruelty to prisoners taken from the defenders' troop. Although technically he was now a prisoner of war, the defenders couldn't wait to execute this man, and even an on-the-spot firing squad wasn't punishment enough. Instead, they tied the cruel man to a tree stump and shot him with a canon. The sergeant was decapitated, and the executioners went in search of his head for a trophy, but it seemed to have vanished. According to this legend, the ghost of the sergeant is also searching for his head, with a lantern—the Neosho light. The light did make its first recorded appearance after the Civil War, although some similar kind of light figured in earlier stories told around the campfires of the Quapaw.

Still another legend tells of a miner whose two children were kidnapped by a marauding band of Native Americans. Although he never saw his little ones again, the spirit of the miner still sets off after dark with a lantern to find them, just as he did in life. In other versions of this tale, it's the miner who was lost and his daughter who searches for him with a lantern. The way the light bobs along down the road, it does look as if an invisible person were walking with a lantern in his hand, the light swinging to and fro with each step. In earlier times some folks used to call the light a jack-o'-lantern.

One poignant legend says the Neosho Spook Light marks the place where the Cherokee—exhausted, diseased, and hungry near the end of the forced march known as the Trail of Tears—were forced to sell their women into slavery in 1836.

Dale Kaczmarek, president of the Ghost Researchers Society based in Illinois, investigated the Neosho light in 1982 and 1983. In his article about the phenomenon (*Ghost Trackers Newsletter,* July 1983) he referred to all of these legends and added two more. "The one legend that I find highly interesting," he wrote, "is the one concerning the farmer who was captured by Indians and beheaded. The legend goes on to say that the light seen by so many people is the lantern of a farmer still looking for his head. This is the standard theory behind ghost lights throughout the United States. There are numerous examples of ghost lights appearing soon after some poor unfortunate person lost his head in some bizarre accident.

"I personally know of several ghost lights which this theory is connected to. Joe Baldwin's light, which haunts the Maco train station in North Carolina, the Brown Mountain lights also in North Carolina, the light near Gurdon, Arkansas, and even the Maple Lake ghost light located in Willow Springs, Illinois . . .

"There is still another possibility for the light. Back when they were laying and carving out the Spook Light road, the contractors supposedly cut right through sacred Indian burial grounds and desecrated many graves. In fact, some skeletons were actually unearthed and strewn about. Perhaps those disturbed are now haunting this section of the road in anger."

With all the eerie tales generated in Hornet, it's not surprising to learn that there's been an important UFO sighting in the area, too. In January 1967 law enforcement officers and weather observers from Pittsburg (Kansas), Baxter Springs, and Joplin reported two unidentified flying objects, saucer-shaped and huge, moving at a low altitude against the prevailing wind, heading for the Spooksville community. The mayor of Carthage, Missouri, managed to get a photograph of one of the UFOs, and a visitor from White Plains, New York, took two successful shots of the object. The UFOs appeared to land at Spooksville, and then take off again. A search of the area for evidence of that landing yielded a mysterious ridged metal disk more than a yard in diameter.

In 1942 a group of students from the University of Missouri made a field trip to the site and camped there for two weeks, trying by various experiments to solve the mystery of the Neosho Spook Light. At the end of this sojourn, they admitted they were baffled, but some of their methods had been less than scientific; they'd occupied a portion of their time shooting at the light with high-powered rifles.

Shooting at the light has always been a popular sport among teenagers in times past. One man remembers from his youth that the light seemed to jump from side to side as if dodging the bullets. He and his friends felt that they never hit their target.

In 1946 the Army Corps of Engineers tackled the Spook

Light, trying to prove that the phenomenon was caused by minerals in the ground or headlights refracting from another road. The engineers tested caves, mineral deposits, and nearby streams. They also set up signal lights and played around with them for several weeks. Their report concluded that the phenomenon was "a mysterious light of unknown origin."

In 1955 science students from Shawnee Mission, Kansas, High School conducted experiments on Devil's Promenade, but they, too, could not solve the mystery.

Various scientists have labeled the light a will-of-the-wisp, which is a gaseous light that rises from decomposing organic matter. This theory doesn't take into account the fact that whereas burning gases caused by decaying organic matter wear themselves out eventually when the causative material finishes decomposing, the Neosho light has been glowing now for a century. Nor has anyone who's actually gone there to look located likely minerals on the site.

One scientific researcher, Dr. George W. Ward, worked out a very plausible explanation of the refraction, or bending-of-light, theory, tying the Neosho light, which is known to appear best after rain, in to a relative humidity and temperature that would produce the correct density of atmosphere for the phenomenon to take place. Light refracted from a car's headlights on a road at a sufficient distance away from Devil's Promenade would appear as one light, this investigator explained in a letter to Bob Loftin, reprinted in Loftin's book, *Spooksville's Ghostlights*.

Another proponent of the refraction theory, Richard O'Neill, a Springfield astronomer, also did tests that proved to his satisfaction that lights from a highway on the Oklahoma side could be seen where the Spook Light appears. (reported in an article by Joan Gilbert and Jacki Gray, *Missouri Life*, December 1984).

Apparently Ward and O'Neill ignored or overlooked the fact that the first reports of the Neosho lights predated automobiles and highways, airports and airplanes. A scientific theory that doesn't cover all the known data is only another shot in the dark.

As a bona fide ghost researcher, Dale Kaczmarek's personal observations of the light vividly bring the experience to light. "In 1982, around Labor Day weekend, I traveled to Joplin to conduct my own investigations and firsthand observations of the

Spook Light. We literally chased this light up and down the road from dusk to dawn but could never catch it. I did get several excellent photographs of the light and saw it through 10/50 power binoculars.

"We observed it best after 3:00 A.M. when the traffic had died down and we were the only ones on the road. When I caught it in the binocular field, it was a few feet above the ground and near a barn. At first I thought the barn was on fire or perhaps someone had a bonfire raging nearby. I was soon to discover that this was not the case. We were approximately seventy-five to one hundred yards away and were in for a shock. The light appeared to be a diamond-shaped object with a golden hue and a hollow center. You could actually see the trees and bushes right through it. It stayed in that area for about sixty seconds and then dropped behind a hill. The area where the light was a second ago still glowed with some kind of luminosity or phosphorescence . . . [and] twinkled with energy.

"After it came back up and went down for the third time, we waited for it to reappear again. It didn't materialize, so we crept up the hill with my car, hoping to see where it had gone. Before we got to the top of the hill, it suddenly appeared right in the middle of the road about sixty to seventy-five yards away. Again it did the same disappearing act, and when it didn't reappear after the third time, we slowly approached the summit. When we got to the top, the light was already about a mile and a half away over the treetops. . . . Elapsed time, about one minute. It displays incredible speed and cunning. It seems to know when someone is getting too close. The light also seems to react to light, sound, and movement, as this next encounter will indicate.

"That same weekend I personally interviewed more than a dozen witnesses who supplied me with a most interesting story.

"There were between ten to fifteen people observing the light when it suddenly appeared about thirty feet away from them in the middle of the road. They said the light was about the size of a basketball, orange-yellow in color, throbbing and slowly rolling along the ground. [Doesn't this sound like a moving jack-o'-lantern?] They were not frightened but awestruck and extremely quiet, because they didn't want to spook it (no pun intended). Suddenly some cars behind them began to crunch the gravel in the road, trying to get a better view. The light rose up about ten feet above the ground, split into two sections, and shot into the woods in both directions at once. The light was apparently reacting to the sound of the gravel and, sensing that too many people were surrounding it, panicked and disappeared. . . ."

And finally Dale adds, "I recently showed these photographs [taken on Dale's second trip] to a psychic, Pat Shenberg, former president of the Illinois Society for Psychic Research and a clairvoyant associate of mine. She says, 'the light isn't a light but a doorway to another dimension.' She says that I was in great danger. Who knows, everyone might be."

DIRECTIONS: *Drive west from Joplin on Interstate 44, take the last exit before the toll gate at the Oklahoma state line, then go south on State Line Road (a gravel road) for four miles. State Line Road intersects with an unmarked road known by the picturesque name of Devil's Promenade; when you see the old museum located on that road, turn the car and park at the top of one of the hills. The Neosho Spook Light may be seen on Devil's Promenade most nights, especially after a rainfall.*

—DR

A PAIR OF CHICAGO GHOSTS
Graceland Cemetery and
Resurrection Cemetery
Chicago, Illinois

Graceland Cemetery, an old, old Chicago burial ground that received its charter in February 1861 is haunted, according to Norman Basile, guide to Chicago's ghostly haunts. Perhaps some of the psychic energy comes from people who've been moved there from other Chicago cemeteries. Or maybe Graceland just has more than its share of restless spirits.

Inez Clarke is one of those souls that seem to have difficulty staying put in Graceland. Inez was an only child—the adored daughter of a well-to-do family who had waited many years for the birth of their lovely daughter. When the blessed event occurred in 1873, their joy knew no bounds. Nothing was too good for little Inez, and everything possible was done to protect her and insure her health and happiness. However, as too many parents have sadly found, no child can be completely protected from the perils of life. Inez was the victim of many of the childhood diseases that plagued the world in the 1800s. When she was just seven years old, her life was snuffed out by a high fever that accompanied one of these ailments.

The Clarkes were inconsolable. And though the funeral for Inez was impressive it wasn't enough. The Clarkes needed to do more to express their love. They wanted to—they needed to—do something unusual to commemorate the life of the child who had meant so much to them. Finally the Clarkes came up with an idea. They commissioned an artist to carve a life-size replica of their daughter out of stone. They showed him one of Inez's prettiest and favorite dresses and asked him to carve the little girl wearing the dress. The Clarkes were pleased with the result and had it placed over Inez's grave with a glass dome over the statue to protect it from the elements.

Visitors at Graceland have seen the statue of Inez with real tears rolling down her cheeks. Norman Basile says that one night a security guard at the cemetery was making his rounds checking to see that everything in the cemetery was in order. He came to the grave of Inez Clarke and, much to his amazement, found that the glass case was empty. Not a man to trifle with ghosts, the guard sprinted away from the cemetery, leaving behind his keys, his guard dog, and the gates to the cemetery not only unlocked but wide open. When he returned cautiously the next day, the statue of Inez was back in its glass case in perfect condition.

This isn't the only instance when the statue of the little girl has escaped from her glass case. Many people have reported seeing the empty case, and the likeness of Inez wandering around among the other tombstones in the cemetery. On really stormy nights, when thunder and lightning assault the area, the statue often disappears. Perhaps like so many children, Inez is simply afraid of the thunder.

Graceland is also host to one Ludwig Wolff, whose mortal remains reside in a large monument built into the side of a hill. Ludwig had left instructions that upon his death he was not to be put into a small hole in the ground but instead should be placed in Graceland in a room with a monument. Wolff's room is twenty feet wide, thirty feet long, and twelve feet high. It would seem that would be plenty large enough for most spirits. But Ludwig Wolff doesn't seem content with his surroundings. On any night when the moon is full, passersby have heard a pitiful howling coming from the monument. Those with stout hearts who aren't afraid and decide to investigate where the noise is coming from have reported they've found a green-eyed ghost running up and down the hill by the monument. Whatever peace Ludwig Wolff hoped to attain by being interred in this large room seems to have eluded him. The poor man has an uneasy rest.

In still a different section of Graceland Cemetery, there is another, more modest monument. This one stands over the remains of Dexter Graves, who died in Chicago in 1844. The monument is in the form of a hooded figure of death. Through the years it has worn to an eerie green patina. The face of this statue, however, has retained its coal-black color, and when visitors look into that face they say it's like looking into the face of death. Many people have experienced a cold chill running right through their bodies when they look at the face of the figure guarding Dexter Graves's body. A close look at the monument reveals a plaque reading "Eternal Silence." No one knows or remembers what kind of man Dexter Graves was in life, but there is a consensus that his tomb is menacing.

Resurrection Cemetery holds the mortal remains (at least most of the time) of Mary Bregavy, a pretty Polish girl with a lust for life. (Many people think that Mary Bregavy is the Resurrection Mary who is so well known to Chicagoans. Other people are sure Resurrection Mary is Mary Duranski.) Like most girls, blond, blue-eyed Mary loved to dance, so she was happy to be invited to go dancing by a beau she liked a lot. She selected just the right gown and was quite pleased with the way she looked when her date picked her up on March 10, 1934. Mary was twenty-two years old at the time. Little did she know this would be her last dance. Mary said good-bye to her family and hello to the other couple waiting in the car, anticipating a happy night of frivolity. They headed for the O'Henry Ballroom, which, according to Norman Basile, is now the Willowbrook Ballroom.

The dance was a huge success as far as Mary was concerned. She was growing fond of the young man who escorted her, and it was obvious to Mary that he returned her affection. Perhaps this was the one she'd been waiting for. The ride home started out with the four young people excitedly exchanging stories about the evening and the other dancers, many of whom they knew. Mary's friend was driving quite fast, and they all found it exhilarating until he lost control and the car jumped the curb, striking one of the huge I-beams holding up the elevated train tracks.

Although the impact was mighty, the three friends who were with Mary that night sustained only minor injuries. As they pulled themselves from the car, feeling lucky to be alive, they looked around for Mary. To their horror her twisted, lifeless body lay on the sidewalk. Mary had been thrown through the window as the car careened into the I-beam.

Mary's grieving family had her buried in Resurrection Cemetery. She was laid out in one of her favorite dresses, and the dancing shoes she'd worn that fateful evening were on her feet. Mary remained in her grave in peace for the next five years. Then one snowy January night in 1939 a Chicago cabdriver, driving the streets looking for a fare, was hailed on Archer Street by a strikingly lovely girl dressed in a white gown and black patent-leather dancing shoes.

The cabbie was surprised that the girl was out on such a night without a coat. But Chicago cab drivers are used to bizarre behavior, so he just shook his head and pulled over to the curb to pick up the girl. Instead of climbing into the back seat as most passengers do, the young lady opened the front door and jumped in beside the driver. She seemed quite agitated as she told the cabdriver she needed to get home quickly. The girl instructed him to drive north on Archer Avenue. As they drove along, the man attempted to make conversation with the girl, but all he could get from her were jumbled, incoherent answers. The only intelligible remark that came from her mutterings was "The snow came early this year!"—a fact that seemed to distress her.

As the cabbie was deciding that maybe this fare had had too many drinks, she screamed at him, "Here, stop here!" She pointed past the cabbie to a small shack. He pulled to the curb, looking for a second in the direction she indicated. When he turned around, the girl had vanished. He swore that the car door never opened—she just evaporated into the air. The cab was in front of Resurrection Cemetery.

Since that time Resurrection Mary has been a frequent sight hitchhiking along Archer Avenue.

And her dancing prowess hasn't gone to waste. Several young men claim they've picked up a beautiful lady in a long white dress and black patent-leather shoes hitchhiking on Chicago streets. All of them have sensed something "other-worldly" about her. In most cases she expresses a desire to go dancing, and the gentlemen comply. All of them report that when they danced with the girl she gave off a cold feeling that chilled them to the bone. She always told the men the way to drive her home—down Archer Avenue. On passing Resurrection Cemetery, the girl gave a blood-curdling scream and jumped from the car, running through the gates of the cemetery and fading into the stillness of the night.

One night in 1977 a motorist passing Resurrection Cemetery saw a girl in a long white dress inside the closed cemetery gates. She looked distressed as she held on to the bars of the gates. Thinking she must have inadvertently been locked in when the cemetery closed for the night and not wanting to scare her further by approaching her, the motorist drove to the nearest police station and reported the incident. The police thanked him for his concern and drove to Resurrection Cemetery with the intention of freeing the girl. When they drove up no one was at the gate. Shining a light into the cemetery one of the officers called out, "Is anyone there?" There was silence. He called out again: "Don't be afraid, we're here to help you." Again, no reply. At that point the beam from the officer's flashlight fell on the bars of the gate. Two of those heavy iron bars had been spread apart, and on each of them what appeared to be a handprint was embedded.

Resurrection Mary still appears from time to time, enticing motorists to pick her up and take her out for a night on the town.

DIRECTIONS: *To get to Graceland Cemetery take Lake Shore Drive North. Exit at Irving Park Road. Go west to Clark Street. The cemetery is right there. To reach Resurrection Cemetery, take I-294 to 95th Street. Go west to Roberts Road. Take Roberts Road north to Archer Avenue, where you'll find the main entrance to the cemetery.*

—JB

THE ACTIVITY AT BACHELOR'S GROVE CEMETERY

Chicago, Illinois

Norman Basile, Chicago psychic and guide to haunted Chicago, calls Bachelor's Grove Cemetery "probably the most ghost-infested cemetery in the Chicago area and maybe in the world." And although Norman has conducted countless tours of the haunted spots in his native Chicago and has visited other places throughout the world where psychic phenomena have been reported, he avows, "I've never encountered an area where there is so much condensed activity. I've experienced phenomena at Bachelor's Grove at all seasons of the year. In my many visits there, I have to say I've found 'other-world phenomena' 100 percent of the time whether I've been there alone, with other investigators, or while conducting a tour. It's my favorite spot to take tours, because the likelihood that members of the party will experience something out of the ordinary is enormous."

This cemetery has been vandalized, brutalized, and neglected, so it's small wonder that the spirits of those people buried there rise up in protest against their treatment. There used to be a road leading into the cemetery, but years of disuse have encouraged weeds and bushes to grow over it. The sign that once adorned the cemetery's entrance was taken long ago by vandals. Today a road runs around the cemetery, which is set about three-quarters of a mile back in a forest preserve. Norman Basile says, "As you walk down the path toward the cemetery it starts to feel cold—so cold it's almost like stepping into a deep freeze. This change in temperature is especially noticeable on hot, humid summer days."

Many people walking through the cemetery have spotted a neat white farmhouse complete with a picket fence and a warm, inviting light shining from inside. But as they've hurried toward the welcoming cottage it has vanished, leaving them confused and often frightened.

Although Norman Basile has not encountered it, he says that many visitors to the cemetery report seeing a blue light bouncing from tombstone to tombstone. In 1983 Norman was approaching the cemetery when he felt there was something abnormal around the trees by the cemetery's entrance. He quickly pulled out his camera and shot a picture. Although there was nothing visible to the naked eye, Basile claims, "When I looked at the picture there was a bluish mist with a face in the middle of it. Since then I've experienced many things. I've heard strange voices, felt something touching me, and seen one tree blowing in a wind that didn't touch the other trees—though they stood close by."

One night in 1984 Norman Basile and a friend of his who was skeptical about psychic phenomena decided to spend the night at the cemetery. Although the friend didn't expect to find anything, he went along with Norman's wish to carry camera equipment and special microphones. The pair arrived at the cemetery at about 10:00 P.M. and walked around looking for anything unusual. By midnight nothing had happened and the friend was feeling quite smug and a bit sorry for Basile. Then for some reason the pair of ghost hunters were standing with their backs to each other when Basile's friend exclaimed, "Oh my God! Look what's standing over there by the trees!"

Basile turned quickly, but not quickly enough, for he saw nothing. The shaken skeptic described a man in his forties, wearing a hat and suit. The entire apparition had been in yellow. As the duo pondered what the figure could have represented, red streaks of light started darting around the cemetery. Then one tree started to shake violently. Norman's friend needed no more convincing. He picked up half of the gear and ran toward the car. All thoughts of camping out for the night were forgotten.

Basile was more concerned for his friend; he believes the ghosts are friendly. He says the spirits are "very confused or frightened . . . far more frightened of people than people are of them." He thinks they're walking about in limbo, wondering why people can't see them. On the many rolls of film he has taken at Bachelor's Grove Cemetery, Basile has found faces superimposed on tombstones, people walking down a path of the cemetery (people who weren't there), filmy blue mists, and strange lights with no earthly source.

Other visitors to the cemetery have seen spectral cars going in or out of the cemetery. The cars go only so far and then they vanish into thin air, to be seen another day by another visitor.

Some people claim that they have even hit these cars and that the cars have disintegrated upon impact, leaving no trace.

One sad ghost that inhabits Bachelor's Grove is known as Mrs. Rogers. She's manifest as a white, filmy figure that floats around the cemetery, clutching a baby in her arms. There's an urgency in her manner as she wanders about searching through the tombstones for a lost treasure or person. Most people think that this is the spirit of a lady who was buried in Bachelor's Grove Cemetery next to the grave of her infant.

In 1983 Norman Basile took his family on a tour of the cemetery. They separated and wandered about. Suddenly Norman's mother summoned the family to join her quickly. As they gathered at a tombstone, all of them saw what Mrs. Basile had spotted. There in the middle of the tombstone was an apparition that looked like a face deeply embedded in the stone. As the family looked on in amazement, the face slowly vanished. Norman has visited the cemetery many times since that outing with his family, and on most occasions he has stood in front of that same tombstone, but nothing out of the ordinary has ever happened again.

Norman is something of a celebrity in the Chicago area, and on one occasion Chicago's Channel 32 asked him to do a program on the supernatural in Bachelor's Grove Cemetery. The TV crew wasn't taking any chances of missing a misty setting, so they brought along a fog machine. Norman was supposed to walk through the mist toward the cameras. Very dramatic! But the unseen powers that exist in the cemetery weren't impressed with this hoax. Every time the mist machine put down a fog, a wind would come up and blow it away before Norman had a chance to walk through it. Although the crew changed the position of the mist, the wind shifted to take it away every time. Finally the TV people were successful, and Norman was immortalized on film walking through the mist.

While Norman feels that most of the spirits in Bachelor's Grove Cemetery are friendly, the neighboring animals don't seem to share his opinion. The woods around the cemetery teem with wildlife, but no squirrel, bird, chipmunk, or other animal is ever seen within the barbed-wire fence surrounding the land where so many restless souls reside.

Why is this cemetery such a troubled spot? Basile can find many reasons. It's an old cemetery. Though the land was deeded as a cemetery in 1864, there is some evidence that people were buried there as far back as 1832. Norman thinks the burial grounds could hold victims from the Black Hawk War.

Vandals have worked viciously to destroy the cemetery, and many of the smaller markers and tombstones have been stolen. Others, too large to move, have been pushed over or desecrated in some other way. The fence around the cemetery has been cut, and there are large holes in it. Gangs of hoodlums party in the midst of the remaining graves—drinking and singing irreverent songs that dishonor the dead souls. Many graves have been dug up and, in some cases, coffins have been left sticking out of the ground. Devil worshippers and members of black-magic cults hold meetings there, carving their symbols in the tombstones. Many people who were murdered in the hectic, lawless days of 1920s Chicago ended up in Bachelor's Grove Cemetery. No doubt all of this negative activity has disturbed the peace of the souls who considered this their final resting place.

No wonder Norman Basile calls Bachelor's Grove Cemetery the most ghost-infested cemetery in Chicago if not the world.

DIRECTIONS: *Take I-294 South to Cicero Avenue, then continue south to the Midlothian Turnpike. Go west on the Midlothian Turnpike to Rubio Woods. The cemetery is across the street.*

—JB

THE LEGEND OF ROGUES' HOLLOW
Doylestown, Ohio

The passage of time has returned Rogues' Hollow to the way it must have been in the old days, a lush green tumble of trees and bushes, called by the Chippewa *Nibrara,* meaning "beautiful valley." Later it was named Peacock Hollow because of the rainbow iridescence of its coal—rich veins under the surface of the land, waiting to be delved into.

In the latter half of the nineteenth century, fifty-one coal mines tunneled beneath the farms of this small valley south of Doylestown. As an important coal producer for steel mills and industrial plants, Doylestown became the most prosperous area in northeastern Ohio. In its heyday, the rip-roaring 1860s and '70s, the Hollow became a microcosm of the American industrial saga. Many of the miners who came there to work had emigrated from Wales and had brought with them a rich tradition of supernatural beliefs.

After the mines came a few mills and a lot of saloons—seven of them in this two-mile area! Each of these establishments had its own unique style, but Walsh's Saloon was the coach stop and also sported a "springy" dance floor, built with support beams spaced farther apart than conventional floors so that the boards would bend under the dancers' feet; workers could dance (and drink) all night without tiring. It was probably because of the saloons that the place came to be called Rogues' Hollow.

This unsavory era gave rise to a number of eerie legends. Restless spirits in the old mine shafts, a mill haunted by the ghost of a workman crushed under its wheel, the devil galloping along the old Clinton-Doylestown Road on a headless horse, phantom workers plying picks and shovels—these are some of the stories bound up in the history of the mines and the mills.

It's rumored that Jesse James once hid out in Rogues' Hollow. Abandoned mine shafts made safe hiding places, but they were wet, cold, and full of the bodies of rats who had wandered too far into the unventilated depths and died. Still, they were useful places for hiding moonshine equipment or for stamping out counterfeit silver dollars from big sheets of metal sent to the Hollow in boxes. To explain the sounds of industry within the operation of the steam boiler that ran the ventilating fan, the counterfeiters would give out the story that they were opening up that mine again.

Many of these intriguing tales are told in a book by Russell W. Frey, *The History and Legends of Rogues' Hollow,* and the Rogues' Hollow Historical Society was organized to discover and preserve more of the Hollow's colorful history. Cal Holden of the society was especially helpful to me in explaining various points of Rogues' Hollow history.

Coal mining was a dirty, dangerous job, and only rugged men could survive in those early mines. If they weren't tough enough to begin with, they hardened fast after a few months stooped over in a narrow shaft lighted only by small oil-burning lamps in their hats, swinging a pick to break up the coal. As soon as a boy could carry a bucket (about age eleven) he was pulled out of school to work in the mines. Youngsters may have had an advantage there, not having gained their full height. Most of the tunnels were only four feet high; one was so low that the delvers called it Pinch Gut Mine.

Each miner worked his own "room" in a mine and fixed his own explosives to loosen the coal. The blasts were set off at the day's end so that the foul air could clear overnight. But the shafts were foul anyway, ventilated only by a steam-driven fan blowing through a square wooden "pipe."

Miners made from $1 to $1.50 a day, paid by the amount of coal, about 45 to 50 cents a ton. On payday, with "hard cash," meaning silver dollars, tucked in their boots for safekeeping, these strong, boisterous workmen headed for the saloons. Cleaned up a bit, now able to walk upright and look at the sky, they were inclined to swagger and boast; their humor was rough-and-tumble, and they were out for a good time. Some of them wouldn't go back to work until their money ran out. That didn't take long, what with the drinking, gambling, brawling, and thievery that took place in Rogues' Hollow. When a drunken miner woke up in the morning with his boots off, he knew at once that he'd been robbed of his remaining dollars.

When there was no more money for liquor, some of the miners took to waylaying farmers driving their wagons to and from Doylestown, demanding money for a "set-up." One dollar would buy a four-gallon keg of beer, called a bummely, to keep the party going for a while. Maybe this was good-natured in the beginning, but later it turned ugly.

In one incident, when a farmer refused to be "held up" for a dollar, which, after all, was a day's pay, his wagon was over-turned and he was dragged out. The miners dug a hole and threw the farmer in it. Two of them stood on the man while the others buried him in the dirt. Nearly asphyxiated, the farmer was rescued by a neighbor who'd heard the commotion.

Prudent travelers began to take the long way around to Doylestown in order to avoid the Hollow. Mothers would frighten naughty children with threats to drop them off there. A newcomer's life was worth no more than the amount of pay in his pocket.

The owners of the mines and the mills lived a completely different life, of course, as pillars of the church or philanthropists or reformers. Some of their wives and daughters saw nothing of the sordid side of life in the Hollow, and their female descendants were inclined to maintain that it wasn't a nasty place at all, whereas males who'd heard stories told by their grandfathers were likely to say that every terrible thing folks had heard was true.

The saloon with the worst reputation, owned by Billy Gallager and called the Devil's Den, was built on stilts in the side of a slope. Right beside it, also on stilts, was the house where a woman and her two daughters resided; the three of them made their living entertaining miners. Upstanding citizens complained, and Pete Angfang, owner of the local grist mill, persuaded some of the Rogues' Hollow beer-drinking habitués to pull this house of ill repute off its stilts. The mob made quite a party of it, drinking and laughing; the ladies, quite sensibly, moved to another state.

About this time, two ghosts made their appearance in the Hollow.

There was a great spreading tree with a huge branch that overhung Clinton Road east of the Hollow. Horseback riders and wagon drivers had to duck when they rode that way. The story goes that, following an ice storm, the branch was heavy-laden and hanging lower than usual. A big brute of a horse galloping at full speed ran into the branch headfirst and was killed. Afterward, travelers on that road began to see the apparition of a headless horse near the "Ghost Oak Tree" on dark nights. Then Micky Walsh, son of Mike Walsh the saloon-keeper, encountered the apparition of the devil with eyes like balls of fire sitting on the same overhanging branch. It must have been a sobering sight. Micky sat there in a daze for quite some time, then turned his team around and took another road home. His friends, of course, laughed at this tale, naturally assuming Micky's devil had been of the bottled variety.

The next time Micky saw the devil on the Clinton-Doylestown Road, however, he wasn't alone. A group of friends was with him and told the story for many years afterward. Right beside the fabled oak was the devil, seated this time *on* the headless horse. Suddenly there was a large cloud of dust, the sound of hoofbeats, and horse and rider disappeared into the night.

The second ghost manifested at the local woolen mill, owned by Samuel Chidester. Chidester was a deeply religious Presbyterian, so much so that he would allow no meals to be cooked on the Sabbath. His family and employees had to dine on the cold food left over from Saturday. When the family had guests, the main entertainment during the evening was the singing of hymns. Chidester's stepdaughter Sarah was the Hollow's angel of mercy, always ready to attend any sick person in the area and quite knowledgeable about home remedies.

A saloonkeeper named Mrs. Ducey, the only owner who kept her establishment open on Sundays (which did not sit well with more pious folk), fell ill with fever and couldn't keep even a teaspoon of water down. The doctor gave her up for dead, and no one was willing to tend her except Sarah. This noble young woman spent three days and nights nursing the saloon owner back to health with prayer and spoonfuls of whey. Mrs. Ducey went back to setting up drinks and lived until 1901.

Legend tells that a young man making repairs on the Chidester mill's water wheel while it was being turned by a powerful thrust of water lost his footing and was crushed to death. Apparently the young man's spirit felt it had unfinished business with this world, because his ghost was known to appear, sometimes headless, in the mill every night and was seen by many witnesses.

Headless ghosts usually appear for a specific reason, as omens or avengers, W. K. McNeil says in his book *Ghost Stories of the American South*. Here in Rogues' Hollow, where both a headless millworker and a headless horse have been seen, these specters perhaps testify to the sad lot of nineteenth-century laborers.

After the mill had been shut down and boarded up, a bunch of young boys, including Walter Collier (whose grandfather "Boss" Bill Collier had run Silver Creek Mine, the Hollow's biggest layout) and William Angfang, decided to sneak into the mill. They found a small hole near the water wheel, which was not running at the time, and slowly squeezed through, one at a time. What a dark and spooky place it was! A sign on the wall which read "No Trust" (meaning "no credit") did nothing to relieve their apprehension.

As they fearfully explored the gloomy interior, they began to hear noises that grew louder and louder. Suddenly there was the apparition of a young man standing before them. One of the boys shrieked, "Gosh! It's the ghost!" With that, they all ran for their lives, hurtling through that small entry hole as if it were greased.

A few days after the Chidester house was sold in 1948, it burned to the ground. Folks said it was the Chidester Mill ghost who did it, theorizing that the ghost didn't want any newcomers in his haunts.

Deborah Chidester, Samuel's granddaughter, always maintained that there was no Chidester ghost. But adding to the lore of the Hollow in another way, Debbie remembered being presented with the gift of a beautiful cup and saucer in 1890 when she was ten years old, rather surprisingly, by a woman named Mrs. Ducey.

Besides these two apparitions, the shadowy forms of miners have sometimes been seen on moonlit nights around the old mine entrances. If you sit quietly and listen, you may still hear the rhythmic sound of their picks and shovels, the squeak of pulleys, or the crunch of mules pulling wagons of coal out of the mines. The miners who put so much of their life's blood into this Hollow surely are still there in spirit!

DIRECTIONS: *Take Clinton Street south out of Doylestown Square, and it will take you directly into the Hollow. Once there, you can follow Hametown Road, which winds along the creek through the Hollow. It's a pretty wooded area now; almost nothing is left of the tough, brawling days of the coal mines. All the mines were filled in; few buildings remain. Two of the more substantial saloons were remodeled into private residences; the rest were torn down.*

—DR

THE
SOUTHEAST

JOSEFFA AND OTHER CURIOUS GHOSTS

Useppa Island, Florida

It's a subtropical island with lush vegetation and the sparkling Caribbean Sea washes over its white sandy beaches. It looks like paradise, but to the defiant girl standing there beside a crude shack so many years ago, it was hell. She had lost count of the terrifying days and nights she'd spent there—twenty-five, thirty, maybe more, maybe less.

She'd fled to the interior of the island only to be dragged back by rough hands, and her attempt to swim away from the place had resulted in having her hands bound together. She would have been beaten, but José Gaspar, her captor, had left instructions not to mar her beauty. To be sure, she was mistreated, but the guards dared not strike her or violate her for fear of their lives—she was Gaspar's property.

Joseffa had been shopping at the wharf in Havana when Gaspar had spotted her. She was young, beautiful, and innocent yet sensual, and he wanted her. He didn't speak to her or convey his desire for her in any way. He simply ordered two members of his crew to kidnap the girl.

That night, when Gaspar set sail for Florida, Joseffa was aboard, locked securely in a cabin below deck. There she remained until they reached Isle de las Captivas (Captiva Island). Captiva was frequented by Gaspar and other pirates and used as a place to exchange and plunder and hold slaves and prisoners, and to store supplies, and house their women.

Gaspar had assumed that Joseffa would soften during the days in confinement at sea and accept her new situation as his mistress, as other women before her had. But she remained defiant, cursing him whenever he approached her. With other worries and other women, the notorious pirate laughed at her belligerence and sent her to an uninhabited island to reconsider

153

her position. She would either give herself freely to him or be turned over to his drunken crew. The choice weighed heavily upon her during the long, tormenting hours of her captivity on the island. The logical choice was to be ravaged by one beast rather than by more than a hundred monsters, but she couldn't bring herself to seriously consider intimacy with such a vile cutthroat.

Joseffa prayed for deliverance, hoped for rescue, and day-dreamed of being saved by her father or the handsome naval officer she'd seen on two occasions in Havana. "It's possible," she told herself. "He's in the military, and the navy is always chasing after pirates. He could come to these islands in search of Gaspar and the other murderers. Father must know who took me. I'm sure he demanded that the authorities find me."

As the weeks passed, the continued strain of her confine-ment, the interminable fear, and the hatred she'd developed toward Gaspar, progressively affected her mind. Her daydreams became hallucinations peopled with accusers rather than com-forters. Her father appeared with arms crossed, shaking his head in negation. "It's the way you carry yourself, you seduce men; you are no longer my innocent little Joseffa."

Joseffa's mother would appear in the corner of the shack in her usual chair, head bent over her sewing, sobbing, "God is punishing you, if you had gone to mass regularly, this wouldn't have happened."

Even the kindly priest, Father Cirilo, lacked consolation. "God has allowed this terrible thing to happen, therefore, it must be His will, my child. Repent and ask the Blessed Savior to forgive you before it's too late," he'd implore.

Joseffa searched her life and soul for some awful sin; but she could not find one. Maybe she hadn't sinned; maybe she was part of some divine scheme. She'd heard of saints who'd been persecuted and had endured torture for the glory of God. This must be the case, she thought. "God wants me to suffer for His glory."

At other times the despicable figure of Gaspar would emerge to taunt and threaten her. Blood was smeared on his hands, and he had a horrible grin as he reached out to grab her. "Have you made your choice, my pretty thing? Pleasure with me, or pleasure for my crew?" Joseffa would retreat to a corner of the shack, and the mirage of the ghoulish form would disappear laughing.

As the mental anguish continued, a new reality developed in Joseffa's mind. Gaspar was demonic; he was the epitome of evil, and God had chosen her to destroy him. "That's why I'm here," she thought, "to kill him for the glory of God." In her confused but dedicated mind, Joseffa searched for a way to carry out her righteous purpose. Although the ruffians who guarded her were armed and their women used knives to prepare meals, they were cautious in her presence and provided no opportunity for Joseffa to snatch a weapon. The only articles she was allowed to keep were a wooden spoon and a bowl. The thought came to her that the handle of the spoon could be fashioned into a dagger if she could only turn the rounded end into a point. While looking around for something that would help her accomplish her goal, Joseffa found a broken shell. The girl spent many hours scraping the handle of the spoon into the desired shape, but the wood was too soft to hold the point when she tested it on the earth floor of the shack.

It was while Joseffa was trying to figure out another method of freeing herself that Gaspar returned for her. She stood by the shack with her shoulders proudly squared, watching the group of men exit the sailing craft and walk up the beach. Gaspar's brig was anchored at Captiva, still loaded with the spoils of his most recent conquest. Gaspar's lust for Joseffa had prompted him to remain on Captiva only one night. He'd spent it with the Frenchwoman Claudine, but the image of the beautiful Joseffa kept distracting him. He'd blamed Claudine for his inability and cuffed her for her failings. Even so, he knew deep within himself the cause of the problem and cursed his weakness for being taken with the girl.

Once on the island with Joseffa, he swaggered up to the shack and confronted her. The girl's jailers backed away in respect for their leader, and the six men who had accompanied him from the boat held back a few steps. José Gaspar stood with his feet spread apart, white knuckles gripping the cutlass hanging from his shoulder. The anger with himself had turned to rage toward Joseffa. "Well," he roared. Gaspar kept his fierce mask, but he was dumbfounded by her appearance, for Joseffa was wild-eyed, her cheeks appeared sunken, her face was covered with dirt, her hair was stringy and her clothes tattered and filthy.

Joseffa answered him, "Well, what?" She saw only a demonic

fiend before her. The hate within her heart blinded her to details. He was the prince of darkness—Lucifer.

In a voice that only slightly reflected his shock, Gaspar said, "I gave you a choice when I sent you to this island, as you well know!"

"Ah, yes," the girl hissed. "I have made my choice. You are a putrid pig, and I would rather sleep with a dog!"

Gaspar didn't hesitate; he calmly drew his sword and, with less than a full swing, severed Joseffa's head from her body.

Through the years, visitors to Useppa (a colloquialism for Joseffa) Island have reported seeing a headless woman near the shore. Pirates, or at least figures with large knives or swords, have also been observed, as have naked American Indians. The latter is not surprising, for archaeologists estimate that the island was inhabited as early as 3500 B.C. (That's about two thousand years before Stonehenge was built and four hundred years before the first Egyptian dynasty was established.)

Juan Ponce de León is credited with discovering Florida in 1513. However, Florida is shown on the earliest known map of the New World—published in 1502. By the early 1820s the Spanish were raiding the west coast of Florida for slaves. The areas surrounding what is now Fort Myers and Tampa were then inhabited by the Calusa (Caloosa) Indians, a warring tribe who learned early not to trust white men. And the white men (Spanish) also quickly learned that the Calusas were fierce fighters. But these Native Americans were no match for the treachery, steel weapons, and diseases of the white men, and they were wiped out within a few generations of their first encounter with the Spanish.

Just as the Calusas had replaced earlier inhabitants of the Lee Islands off the coast where the present Fort Myers stands, the Calusas themselves were succeeded by an assortment of unruly privateers and pirates who hid out there until the 1820s. With such a long and often sinister past, it's no wonder that Useppa Island and other islands in the group are haunted.

DIRECTIONS: *Useppa Island is now owned and operated as a private club by Gar Beckstead. The accommodations include the Collier Inn (built in the early 1920s by publisher Barron Collier) and guest cottages that reflect the architecture of that period. Nonmember visitors are welcome for up to a week. Day trips are available from Captiva Island (nine miles south of Useppa) on South Seas*

The *Equator,* where Robert Louis Stevenson's ghost appears annually. (Photograph by James and Ardeth Bolin.)

The Cathedral Mausoleum, Hollywood Memorial Park, Los Angeles, California. (Courtesy of Hollywood Memorial Park.)

Cliff Palace, Mesa Verde, Colorado. (Courtesy of Kelly Roberts.)

Fort Laramie, Wyoming, as it appeared in 1853. (Sketch by Piercy, courtesy of Fort Laramie National Historic Site.)

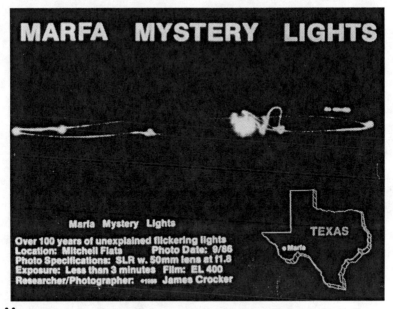

Marfa Lights, Texas. (Courtesy of Marfa Chamber of Commerce.)

Old Natchez Trace, Mississippi. (Courtesy of the Natchez Convention and Visitors Bureau.)

The Boyington Oak. (Photograph by Robert Bahr.)

Wilder Brigade Monument, Chickamauga Battlefield, Tennessee. (Courtesy of Chickamauga National Military Park.)

Michael Alley stands in front of Roslyn, one of many haunted structures in Rugby Village, Tennessee. (Courtesy of the Tennessee Department of Tourist Development.)

John Bell's grave, Adams, Tennessee. (Courtesy of the Tennessee Department of Tourist Development.)

Portrait of John Bell, Jr..
(Courtesy of the
Tennessee Department of
Tourist Development.)

JOHN BELL JR.

Bell Witch historical marker, U.S. Highway 41, Adams, Tennessee. (Courtesy of the Tennessee Department of Tourist Development.)

Neosho Spook Light, Hornet, Missouri. (Photograph by Dale Kaczmarek, Ghost Research Society.)

Chidester Mill, Rogues' Hollow, Doylestown, Ohio. (Courtesy of Chippewa–Rogues' Hollow Historical Society.)

Entrance to
Bonaventure Cemetery.
(Photograph courtesy
of City of Savannah
Cemetery
Department.)

Belle Grove as it looks today. (Photograph courtesy of Belle
Grove.)

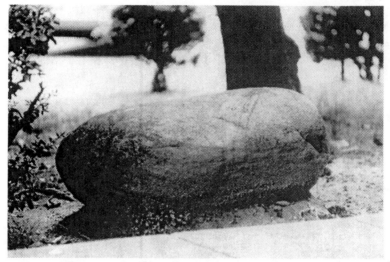

Moll Dyer's Rock. (Photograph by Lynda Andrus.)

Fiddler's Bridge. (Photograph by Don Bingham.)

Composite sketch of the Pennsylvania Bigfoot. (Charles M. Hanna, PASU artist.)

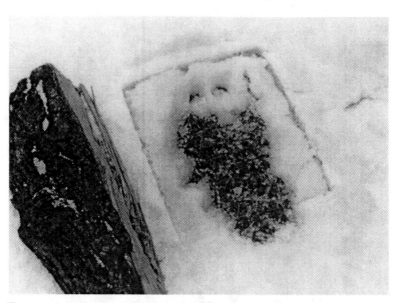

Track of the Pennsylvania Bigfoot. (Courtesy of Stan Gordon, president of PASU.)

Beautiful view from Ringwood Manor. (Photograph by Elbertus Prol, curator, Ringwood Manor.)

Peaceful-looking road in the Pine Barrens. (Photograph by Don Bingham.)

Ringwood Manor. (Photograph by Elbertus Prol, curator, Ringwood Manor.)

Mercy L. Brown's grave, Exeter, Rhode Island. (Photograph by Dolores Riccio.)

Hepzibah's Shop, House of Seven Gables, Salem, Massachusetts. (Photograph by Dolores Riccio.)

The Ropes Mansion, Salem, Massachusetts. (Photograph by Dolores Riccio.)

Megalithic monument at sunset, America's Stonehenge, New Hampshire. (Photograph by Jim Knusch.)

The Sacrificial Table, America's Stonehenge, New Hampshire. (Photograph by Robert E. Stone.)

Plantation's the Silver Lady, *a 150-passenger excursion boat. Or you can sail your own boat to Useppa's marina if the boat is less than 100 feet long.*

For reservations and information on the Silver Lady, *call South Seas Plantation at (813) 472-5111, extension 3329, or (800) 282-3402. To reach South Seas Plantation, take Route 869 from Fort Myers Beach to Sanibel Island and continue to the tip of Captiva Island. To contact the Useppa Island Club, call (813) 283-1061.*

—JB

THE ATONEMENT
Highway 49
Andersonville, Georgia

War is dreadful, whatever its inducement, and civil war is the most atrocious of all, with nation, community, and family divided to kill and maim their own. The self-inflicted carnage committed during the American Civil War was horrendous. Out of a population of thirty-two million, four million soldiers took part in the four-year war, resulting in 618,000 deaths. Of that number, 13,000 soldiers died within the last fourteen months of the war, in a twenty-six-acre stockade at Andersonville, Georgia. That's about one-quarter of the 49,485 men who were imprisoned there. They lived in squalor, with no protection from the summer heat, winter cold, and penetrating rain. They died from dysentery, exposure, polluted water, hunger, and various diseases.

Andersonville was a hellhole, and strong emotions such as fear, pain, and misery saturated the camp. So there should be no surprise that apparitions and other eerie occurrences have been experienced in the area by numerous people over the years. I am relating one particular experience, reported by Kathryn Tucker Windham, because there were two reliable eyewitnesses to the phenomenon.

The hour was late, nearly midnight, and a December chill was in the air. Mrs. Louise Campbell was at the wheel of her car with her friends Mr. and Mrs. Norman Gerritsen beside her in the front seat. They were traveling on Highway 49, returning north from a meeting in Americus. Mrs. Campbell would drop the Gerritsens off at their home in Oglethorpe and drive on alone to her own home in Perry.

The road was familiar, for she drove it often, and she recognized each of the little communities, churches, stores, gas stations, and farmhouses that bordered the route as they progressed northward. They had just passed the Andersonville National Cemetery on the right when she saw a lone figure standing beside the road. He was dressed in a full-length military overcoat with its collar turned up to overlap the military cap on his head. Due to the speed of the car, the figure remained in her view for only a brief second, but she was overcome with an uncanny feeling. Instinctively she knew the figure was unnatural and braked the car. Her feeling and action preceded her thoughts. "Did you see . . ."

"Yes, the man in a strange uniform," Mr. Gerritsen interrupted. "I surely did."

Gerritsen was already looking back over his shoulder in an effort to see the figure again. He was on the same side of the vehicle as the figure and had gotten a better look than Mrs. Campbell.

"Go back," he urged, while peering into the shadows.

Mrs. Campbell was already in the process of turning the car around. Within a few minutes they were back at the site where they had seen the figure.

Nothing!

They drove on past the cemetery, thinking the man had walked in that direction, but there was no sign of him.

"Where do you suppose he's gone?" Mrs. Gerritsen asked, verbalizing the thoughts of the other two. She had not seen the strange figure herself but was eager to see what she had missed.

Her husband shook his head. "I don't know. Doesn't make sense. There's no place for him to have gone in that short time—it's only been a couple of minutes since we saw him. I know he didn't cross the road, because I was looking back. We didn't pass him on the way back to the spot, and he couldn't have climbed over the tall fence of the cemetery because that long coat of his would have snagged on the barbed wire that runs around the top."

"Ah, then you saw the coat, too?" Mrs. Campbell asked.

"Yes, indeed," Mr. Gerritsen confirmed. "An overcoat that I would say was very definitely military in style. And an old-style military cap that I'd say was of Civil War vintage. I couldn't make out the color . . . might have been gray, or maybe blue." Gerritsen frowned. "Say, you don't suppose it was . . ."

"A ghost," Mrs. Campbell interjected. "Yes, it must have been a ghost, that's the only explanation. He—or it—was standing there one minute and gone the next, vanished into thin air. That's what ghosts do, isn't it? And we both saw him."

"You're right," Gerritsen replied. "It must have been a ghost, we both saw the same figure—from slightly different angles, so it couldn't have just been our imaginations playing tricks with us."

"There's no question in my mind," Mrs. Gerritsen stated. "You must have seen a ghost, but whose? Oh, how I wish I'd seen it, maybe I would have seen something neither of you saw—you know, some little detail. But who do you think the ghost was?"

"That's a really interesting question," her husband answered. "From what I gather, this is the kind of place where ghosts appear. You know, cemeteries and battlefields—places like that. With the history of Andersonville, and the look of the figure we saw, I'd say it was a Civil War soldier who died here."

"I'm sure you're right," Mrs. Campbell said. "I've never seen a ghost before or know much about them, but sometime or other I think I've read or heard of Andersonville being haunted. I frankly never gave it much thought. Never had cause to."

During the following days, a great deal of thought was given to the incident. Just about everyone who heard their story agreed it must have been a ghost that they saw, and the consensus was that it was a Union soldier, considering their high death toll at the camp.

One friend, a student of both history and hauntings, ventured the guess that the figure they saw was Confederate Captain Henry Wirz, the medical officer in charge of the inner prison from April 12, 1864, to May 7, 1865. The immediate response was, "Why a Johnny Reb when there were so many more Yankees? Certainly the odds are in favor of a northern boy."

"Well," the friend explained, "many spirits return to this

dimension after death in order to correct wrongs or clear their reputations. Captain Wirz is the only person that I'm aware of who fits the bill. We all know he was unjustly held responsible for circumstances not of his making and beyond his control. I'd say he has a sizable wrong to correct!"

Dr. Henry Wirz immigrated to the United States after earning his medical degree in Paris and Berlin. He had lost the use of his right arm as the result of a wound received in the Battle of Seven Pines. Apparently it was because of his handicap that he was given the assignment at Andersonville's Camp Sumter.

Captain Wirz, with his family, lived in a house in the village of Andersonville, at some distance from the camp. It was here that federal officers appeared, a few weeks after General Lee's surrender, to escort the doctor to General J. H. Wilson's headquarters in Macon.

The officers were most gracious and respectful, and Mrs. Wirz invited them to share the family's meager meal, which they did. They assured the doctor that the matter was routine; the general required an official report on the activities of the prison, that was all. So with no concern, Captain Wirz left his family, expecting to return in a few hours.

The meeting with General Wilson lasted about two hours, in which time Wirz handed over his records of the prison and answered questions concerning the camp. With no apparent reason to detain the captain any further, the general dismissed him with, "Return to your family, Captain."

After the cordial farewell, Wirz left the military headquarters and went to the Macon railway station to await a train for Andersonville. He learned the wait would be several hours—in the aftermath of the war, confusion and delay were the norm rather than the exception. Weary from the day's travel and interrogation, the doctor made himself as comfortable as possible on a bench to consider his postwar options for employment. His damaged arm throbbed, but he had learned to live with the constant pain.

After two or more hours, a federal officer approached Wirz and announced that he was under arrest. The captain was returned under guard to the military headquarters. From there he was transferred to the old Capital Prison in Washington on May 10, 1865.

"Why are you doing this?" the bewildered Wirz asked. "General Wilson found no fault in my behavior or my records." "New information has come to our attention," was the answer. But the circumstances suggest otherwise.

When the public learned of the horrible conditions and high number of deaths at the Andersonville prison, the northern press fed the flames of indignation until Washington felt the heat.

"We demand vindication for the monstrous crimes committed at Andersonville. Somebody is responsible for 13,000 unnecessary deaths, and no conscionable person can rest until the guilty are brought to justice."

A typical editorial stated in part that Lincoln had just been assassinated and northern extremists were calling for blood. The simplest solution was to placate the public by holding Captain Wirz responsible for the tragedy at Andersonville Prison. He was charged with carrying out a Confederate conspiracy to "injure the health and to destroy the lives by subjecting to great torture and suffering" thousands of Union prisoners and the intentional murder of eleven unnamed federal soldiers.

The eleven Union soldiers who were deliberately "murdered" may have included six members of the Andersonville Raiders, a gang of prisoners who initiated a reign of terror inside the camp and were hanged by prison officials.

During the three and a half months Wirz awaited trial, the press had a field day. He was depicted as the personification of evil, a stupid, uneducated oaf who lacked a single trace of humanity, a deviate who must have enjoyed the terrible suffering he caused. He was their sacrificial lamb, and all the guilt of four years of slaughter were heaped upon him. He was public enemy number one, the most hated man alive. For every one who mumbled, "May God have mercy on his soul," a thousand screamed, "There's no divine redemption for Wirz, he'll burn in the pit for eternity."

On August 25, 1865, the trial began. Attorneys and witnesses for the federal government presented their evidence—figures, records, documents, letters, written orders, and testimony by former prisoners and Union officers who had surveyed the camp, following Lee's surrender. However, the most damaging evidence came from the testimony of one young man.

Felix de la Baume, who said he was a nephew of the Revolutionary War hero General Lafayette, spent several hours on the stand vividly describing the defendant's cruel treatment of the prisoners and his total disregard for the conditions at Andersonville.

Baumer's eyewitness account of the captain's inhumane activities at the camp made good newspaper copy, and it also sealed Wirz's fate. It overshadowed the doctor's defense in which it was shown that the Andersonville prison camp was a hellhole before Wirz arrived, and that he had tried as best he could to improve the food and conditions. That in reality, the Confederate guards had had about the same percentage of deaths, because they ate the same food and drank the same water. Barracks had been planned but never built because of the lack of supplies and manpower. Wirz had even arranged for a camp delegation to go to Washington in order to plead with Union officials to reinstate the prisoner exchange program.

Wirz was found guilty and sentenced to be hanged. He was offered clemency and possibly a pardon if he would support the claim of a Confederate conspiracy by signing statements that would implicate Jefferson Davis. He refused, not out of loyalty to Davis, but "because there was no conspiracy."

In 1956 a bronze placard was posted at Andersonville by the Georgia Historical Commission, which reads:

CAPTAIN HENRY WIRZ

1823–1865

Captain Henry Wirz, under the immediate command of Brigadier-General John H. Winder, C.S.A., absent on sick leave, August 1864, commanded the inner prison at Camp Sumter, April 12, 1864, to May 7, 1865. To the best of his ability he tried to obtain food and medicine for federal prisoners and permitted some to go to Washington in a futile attempt to get prisoners exchanged. He was tried for failure to provide food and medicines for Federals imprisoned here—though his guards ate the same food—and mortality was as high among Confederate guards as among prisoners. Of the captain, Eliza Frances Andrews, Georgia writer, said, "Had he been an angel from heaven, he could not have changed the pitiful tale of privation and hunger unless he had possessed the power to repeat the miracle of the loaves and fish." Refusing to implicate others, he gave his life for the South on November 10, 1865.

Henry Wirz was hanged. He was the only Confederate officer to be convicted and executed for war crimes.

On the day of his death, Wirz wrote to a friend, "Please help my poor family, my dear wife and children. War, cruelest war, has swept everything from me, and today my wife and children are beggars. My life is demanded as an atonement. I am willing to give it, and after a while I will be judged differently from what I am now."

And Baume? After being rewarded with a position in the Interior Department for his testimony, it was learned that he was a deserter from the Union Army and was not related to Lafayette.

Now, I'm a dyed-in-the-wool Yankee from Massachusetts, but Henry Wirz has my sympathy—posthumously—and I certainly judge him "differently." I don't know if it was the captain's ghost Mrs. Campbell and Mr. Gerritsen saw, but the captain's spirit surely has cause to be restive, and I, for one, wish him peace and honor.

DIRECTIONS: *From Columbus, take I-185 South to U.S. 280. Take 280 West to Route 26. Travel 26 West to Route 228, then 228 West to Route 49. Go south on 49 for about one mile.*

—JB

THE PERFECT HOST
Bonaventure
Savannah, Georgia

It was an unusual sight! Perhaps "bizarre sight" is a more accurate phrase to describe the scene. Imagine a very large, stately brick house on a knoll overlooking the Wilmington River, a few miles from the heart of Savannah. The great plantation house had been completed in the late 1750s, and Bonaventure was as majestic as it was massive. The brick had been imported from England, as were many of its fine furnishings. Wealth was apparent, not only in the house itself, but in the enormous gardens that surrounded the structure and spilled over the banks of the Wilmington. It was picture perfect, the result of careful planning and faultless execution.

On this particular mild November evening, a large banquet table was set on the back garden terrace, a few yards from the house. General Josiah Tattnall sat at the head of the table and his wife at the far end, with perhaps fifty guests seated between them. It was a pre-Thanksgiving dinner party with hams, turkeys, wild duck, fish, oysters, and a variety of vegetables, breads, and sweets. Fine porcelain china, crystal glassware, and elegant silver flatware adorned the table. Servants quickly refilled the goblets and attentively served the guests from the seemingly endless procession of epicurean delights.

The setting was striking, the food sumptuous, and the fellowship sterling. Yet, within the breasts of several of the women, there was apprehension. They giggled and bravely exchanged gossip with their neighbors, but they found it increasingly more difficult to appear calm and composed, to enter into the spirit of celebration as the men had. How could one be jovial while dining by the light of a burning house with its priceless contents going up in smoke?

As the great house continued to incinerate within its brick shell, toasts were offered to Bonaventure and its rich heritage. The evening's finale came with the last toast, "May the joy of this occasion never end." Following the host's lead, the guests all shattered their glasses against the oak trees' trunks.

They say Nero fiddled while Rome burned because he was mad. What about Josiah Tattnall, Jr., and his wife; were they mad also, or just fatalists accepting the inevitable with grace and good humor? Probably the latter, for there is nothing in history to suggest that the general had any form of mental weakness or infirmity.

Bonaventure ("good fortune") was built by Josiah Tattnall, Jr.'s grandfather, Colonel Mulryne, shortly after he moved his family to Savannah from Charleston. No expense was spared in the construction, for Colonel Mulryne was a very wealthy man and Bonaventure was the fulfillment of a cherished dream. The great house would not only symbolize Mulryne's wealth and status in the Colonies and provide the colonel with creature comforts in his latter years but be the birthplace and regal abode for his descendants. Although the colonel intended to live there himself, Bonaventure was primarily a wedding gift for his daughter, Mary. She was the center of his life, and her happiness was paramount as far as he was concerned. He wanted only the very best for her, and Bonaventure was the very best.

When the Mulrynes lived in Charleston, they were close to the equally prominent family of Tattnall, and, although there were many young men interested in Mary, it was Josiah Tattnall the colonel favored. So when Josiah followed Mary to Savannah and asked for her hand in marriage, John Mulryne was delighted. Not only were the two young people in love but Josiah had the qualities Mulryne wanted in a son-in-law: good family, wealth, influence, ambition, and values that included the fear of God and loyalty to the King.

Once the bond of marriage between Mary and Josiah was certain, the colonel initiated a plan he had conceived while building the mansion. Bonaventure was everything he had hoped it would be, but after all, giving a house as a wedding gift was not that unusual. No, he wanted to give the apple of his eye something unique, something personal, and something—hopefully—eternal. What he had in mind would be all those things, plus. It would also forever link Bonaventure with the proud name of Mulryne after he was gone and his heirs bore the name of Tattnall.

While Mary was busy with the details of her wedding, the colonel supervised the completion of the terraced gardens and extensive landscaping he had designed, including her special wedding gift.

Surrounding the great house, hundreds of live-oak trees were planted in the pattern of a monogram with the initials M and T entwined. Mary of course saw the trees being planted, and knew she was to receive a special wedding gift but was unaware of the connection. So she was truly surprised on her wedding day when her father announced what her special gift was.

"This is it, my dear," the colonel proudly whispered to Mary. "A gift to mark the union of our family with the family of your husband. These trees will grow stronger and more beautiful as the years go by, just as I know your marriage will."

"They are lovely, Father," Mary responded with amazement. "I couldn't imagine what your special gift would be, and now I can't imagine anything that could possibly be as grand and wonderful as this."

The sun shined brightly on Bonaventure and the live oaks

continued to flourish, as did Mary and Josiah's marriage. Mary gave birth to two sons, Josiah Jr. and John. Josiah Sr. successfully managed the plantation, and John Mulryne enjoyed having two grandsons.

Then dark clouds appeared. Georgia and the other colonies became ripe with discontent. Higher taxes, protests, talk of revolution, skirmishes, and finally, war came.

Early on, Georgia was about equally divided between loyalists and patriots, but the patriots gained in support and power and were able to place the royal governor, James Wright, under house arrest in Savannah on January 18, 1776. He had agreed to remain there and not contact the British. However, motivated by loyalty to Britain, or perhaps fear for his life as a consequence of the growing resentment toward loyalists, Wright escaped from his captors a few weeks later and made his way to Bonaventure.

Colonel Mulryne had been instrumental in Wright's escape and was willing to go to any length to see that the governor, a symbol and representative of his monarch, remained free. So in the early hours of February 12th, the two friends were rowed out to the British ship *Scarborough,* anchored just outside Savannah's harbor.

Governor Wright was provided passage to Nova Scotia, where he awaited the return of British control of Savannah in 1779. John Mulryne chose exile in the Bahamas and was transported to Nassau, where he later died.

Josiah Tattnall was just as staunch a Tory as his father-in-law and was undoubtedly involved in their escape. He offered no apology for his loyalty to the King. They were British subjects and to take up arms against the crown was treason, an act he could not condone let alone support. However, he would not bear arms against his neighbors, not because of cowardice but because they were his friends. Nonetheless, his loyalty to George III was well known, and feelings against loyalists became so inflamed and ugly that Tattnall decided it best to move his family to the safety of England.

On the morning of their departure Tattnall was in his study, busy sorting papers, when Josiah Jr., his oldest son, entered the room. He stood straight, with all the dignity he could muster, and solemnly declared, "I am not going to England with you and Mother! Georgia is my home. I am an American, and I shall stay and fight with the patriots for freedom."

The senior Josiah was dumbfounded. He had no idea that his son felt that way. "Josiah, you are only twelve years old; you don't understand what you are saying," he said, after regaining his composure.

"Yes I do, Father. I want to join the patriots and help gain justice and freedom for Georgia," young Josiah retorted. He still stood bone straight, like a soldier, but his voice revealed the strain of confronting his father.

Josiah Tattnall frowned. "You don't know what you're talking about, son. You've heard a lot of lies and distortions by the local rowdies—young men who have been led to believe war is a game, and they're champing at the bit to share in the fun. Let me tell you that insurrection will not solve the problems. To the contrary, it will create a disaster. We need authority, law, and order—without the king, Georgia and other colonies will disintegrate; there will be anarchy."

"But, Father . . ." the boy tried to rebut.

"Not another word. I will hear no more talk of treason. This family is loyal to King George, and you will be loyal to him. This family is going to England, and you are going with us. There will be no more discussion. Go to your room now, and await our departure this evening!"

Tattnall summoned a servant and ordered the boy's bedroom door locked behind him. There was no time to pursue a runaway child with all the last-minute details to be done, and there were many because the family might remain in England for two or three years. He was certain that the antagonists would abandon their stance, if not by reason, then by superior force, within that time, but he was a pragmatic man and was prepared to keep the family abroad for as long as necessary to insure their safety.

As Tattnall returned to the work at hand, he assured himself that his son would quickly lose interest in the revolution. After all, it was just a passing fancy, a childish whim that would be forgotten in a few hours as the excitement of their voyage to England took over.

But that was not the case. When Josiah Jr.'s door was unlocked that evening, the family was met with a still-defiant boy who shouted, "I will not go to England."

The boy had to be dragged to the boat landing and secured in the small boat that was to take them out to the England-bound ship at the harbor's entrance.

During the confusion of loading the family and their possessions aboard the ship, Josiah Jr. jumped overboard and began
swimming back to Savannah.

One of the sailors witnessed his action and dove in after him,
managing to retrieve him before he drowned or made it to
shore. The headstrong boy was locked in his cabin until the ship
was well out to sea.

Once the family was established in England, it was assumed
that Josiah Jr. had given up his misplaced ambition and was
preoccupied with his new life. But this did not happen. He still
longed for Bonaventure, the familiar countryside, and his friends
back in Georgia. Although he was wise enough to conceal the
desire of his heart and mind, he followed the news of the
American war with keen interest. He was, to his thinking, a
prisoner in a hostile country. In his imagination he was there,
with other patriots, fighting the noble fight against the tyranny
of King George.

For over five long years, Josiah Jr. kept his fervor hidden. By
the end of that time he was a student at Eton, and he could wait
no longer; the time had come when he must have a showdown
with his father.

"I have reached the age of accountability. I am no longer a
child, I know what I want," he told his father. "I must return to
Georgia and fight with the patriots. Please give me your
permission, and if possible, your blessing, to do this."

Tattnall could hardly believe his ears; hadn't this issue died
and been buried long ago? As the words sank into his under-
standing, anger rose to the surface.

"You want my permission to turn your back on your family
and country. You want my blessing to become a traitor to your
king. What is wrong with you?" Tattnall yelled in exasperation.
"Your mother and I have given you everything possible, and this
is how you would reward us. The answer is no! Once and for
all, give up this nonsense, return to Eton, and pursue an
honorable life."

For Josiah the honorable life lay to the west, and within a few
weeks he was back in Georgia as a patriot fighting under the
command of General Nathaniel Greene.

Following the Tattnalls' departure for England, the patriots
had confiscated Bonaventure. However, with an heir to the
property fighting for independence, much of the estate, including the great house, was returned to Josiah Tattnall, Jr.

Once peace was restored, Josiah Jr. returned to Bonaventure with his bride. The house and gardens needed some work, but the stand of live oaks his grandfather had planted for his mother were much larger and more impressive than they had been in his childhood.

Josiah exercised the same strength and tenacity in restoring Bonaventure and building a fortune as he had in returning to Georgia and fighting for liberty. He was prominent in organizing the state government of Georgia, was promoted to the rank of brigadier general of the First Brigade of the Georgia Militia, was a member of the Georgia legislature, served in the U.S. Congress, and was governor of Georgia shortly before his death.

As a prominent member of Savannah's social circle, the general and his wife were accustomed to entertaining at Bonaventure with large parties, dinners, and balls. Guests either came inland by carriage, or by boat on the Wilmington River. This was true even for the pre-Thanksgiving dinner that November, for it was very mild that year in Georgia and the chill of winter was not felt until almost Christmas.

So on that fateful evening, the carriages and boats arrived at the front steps or boat landing to discharge their holiday-spirited passengers. As the guests began to gather, Mrs. Tattnall ordered logs to be lit in the wide fireplaces of the downstairs social rooms. Her husband pointed out that there was no sign of a chill in the air, but she explained, "It gives the house a festive look and feel, dear."

The guests had been seated around the banquet table in the large dining room adjacent to the beautiful gardens at the rear of the house. The first course was being served when the butler entered the room and swiftly approached the general. He whispered something, and the host excused himself and hurriedly followed the servant out of the room.

Mrs. Tattnall was puzzled by the activity but surmised that some minor accident had probably occurred in the kitchen or wine locker.

In a few minutes the general returned. "Ladies and gentlemen—my friends," he said calmly. "I am sorry to inconvenience you, but there will be a slight interruption in our meal.

"If you will please rise and follow me onto the garden terrace, the servants will move our chairs and the table outside, where we will continue our dinner."

All eyes were upon Tattnall; breathing had stopped for the moment. In a calm voice he announced, "Bonaventure is on fire and will be destroyed within a short time!"

The general signaled his wife, and together they quietly led their guests outdoors. The massive table followed in the hands of husky servants. It was later reported that not so much as a drop of water was spilled during the move.

A servant asked the general if lamps should be lit. "No need," was the answer. "Bonaventure will provide more than adequate light for the occasion."

After over two hundred years, the live oaks are still there. But the motif of entwined initials is blurred beyond recognition. The formal gardens have reverted to the wild, their manicured order and symmetry overwhelmed by time. Bonaventure, the great manor house, is now only a fable passed on from one generation to the next. It began in the mind of John Mulryne, and it now exists only in the minds of those of us who have the imagination to see it.

Near the former site of the great hall, under the protection of the old oaks in Bonaventure cemetery, is the family plot of the American Tattnalls. Josiah Tattnall, Jr., his wife, and four of their children are buried there.

People passing this site in the still of the night report that they have heard the sounds of that last dinner party, with its laughter and clatter of dinnerware—ending with the shattering of crystal glasses. It seems the general's last wish, "May the joy of this occasion never end," came true.

DIRECTIONS: *From Savannah, follow Bonaventure Road to the Bonaventure Cemetery. For more information call the Savannah Visitors' Center, (912) 233-6651.*

—JB

THE STORY OF LIZARD MAN
Scape Ore Swamp
Bishopville, South Carolina

This story was first reported in the *Houston Chronicle* on July 31, 1988, and analyzed by Ron Schaffner, editor of *Creature Chronicles* in the January 1, 1989, issue. The setting of this happening, Scape Ore Swamp, used to go by the thought-provoking name "Escaped Whore Swamp." Now, with a moniker like that, all sorts of unusual things must have taken place there. Looking into the swamp's history, I found some interesting items.

When the American troops moved through Carolina during the Revolution, British military men fled into this swamp to avert capture.

Sometime in the 1800s a certain lady of the evening seemed to have enchanted many of the Lee County ladies' husbands. This raised the ire of the philanderers' wives—and it seemed there were quite a number of them. So angered were these ladies that they banded together and set out to drive the offending prostitute from the area. Seeing them coming, the girl sprinted off in an effort to save her lovely hide. With the wives gaining on her, she ran into the swamp and was never seen or heard from again. Over the years, local residents have reported spotting air bubbles rising from the swamp—bursting with a loud pop. It's as if someone were at the bottom of the swamp holding her breath. Could it be the girl from the 1800s?

Lee Truesdale, the Lee County sheriff, claims he has had a great many reports of inexplicable happenings in the swamp over the last few years. One early morning in June 1988, Chris Davis, a seventeen-year-old who worked the late shift at the local McDonald's, was driving home by the swamp. Suddenly one of his tires went flat. The boy changed the tire. As he was putting the jack back in the trunk he heard a loud noise coming from the swamp. The report Davis gave the news series went like this: "I looked back and saw something running across the field toward me. It was about twenty-five yards away and all red eyes glowing. I ran into the car and as I locked it, the thing grabbed the door handle. I could see it from the neck down. It

171

had three big fingers, long black nails, and green, rough skin. It was strong and angry. I looked in my mirror and saw a blur of green running. I could see his toes, and then he jumped on the roof of my car. I thought I heard a grunt, and then I could see his fingers through the windshield, where they curled around the roof. I sped up and swerved until I shook the creature off."

A shaken Davis reached home, ran in, and told his father. Together they went to inspect the car for damage. The first thing they found was that the side mirror had been terribly twisted. When Chris Davis's father looked at the roof of the car, he found deep scratches penetrating the paint and even denting the metal.

Mr. Davis called the police. When they questioned Chris, he described the creature. It was seven feet tall, had red eyes, skin like a lizard, and scales like a snake. Although the police were polite, they had their doubts about the kid. But on checking his reputation, they found he'd never been in trouble, wasn't considered untruthful or fanciful, and those who knew him thought he was a clean-cut, honest, all-American boy.

Chris Davis became somewhat of a celebrity over this sighting. As he told and retold the story some of the details changed. For instance, while he first said the creature had scales, he later said the creature was caked with mud. According to Ron Schaffner, Davis was taken under the wing of a local talent agent who had him doing tours, selling autographs, and making media appearances.

Not to be left out of what looked like a money-maker, the merchants had T-shirts made up with "Lizard Man" printed on them. The media was in high gear. One radio station in Columbia offered one million dollars to anyone who could capture the Lizard Man. While these things do make a circus out of what was in truth a frightening event for a teenage boy, I don't think they in any way detract from the credibility of the event, and Chris isn't the only one to claim to have seen a strange creature in Scape Ore Swamp.

On July 14, 1988, Tom and Mary Way parked their car along Route 15 and went for a walk. When they came back the hood ornament on their 1976 Ford LTD was pulled from the socket, and much of the remaining chrome trim was hanging off the car. There were hunks of fur sticking to the chrome. Suspecting that the Lizard Man had struck again, the Ways tooled quickly to the police department to report the incident.

The wildlife officials analyzed the fur and announced that in their opinion it came from a cat or a fox. Bill Moore of the Lee County Sheriff's Office thought it could have been from dogs and claimed that some types of dogs could destroy a car. But most folks were convinced that it was indeed Lizard Man off on another spree of destruction.

On July 24, about three in the morning, Rodney Nolf and Shane Stokes were driving along Highway 15 with their girlfriends. Just as they got to the intersection of Interstate 20, a seven-foot apparition with glowing eyes darted in front of the car. The men wanted to pursue it into the swamp, but their dates nixed the idea, so instead they headed for the sheriff's office.

Two law enforcement officers were dispatched to investigate the sighting—Wayne Atkinson, a deputy from Lee County, and Mike Hodges, one of South Carolina's state troopers. The first thing they found were several forty-gallon trash cans crumpled up with the contents spilled all over the swamp. Then they noticed that the tops of several trees had been broken off at a height of about eight feet from the ground. But most curious of all were the footsteps, which measured fourteen by seven inches. The police eventually took three plaster casts of these footprints, but before that happened, about two inches of rain fell on the tracks, possibly changing them considerably. The three-toed impressions were immediately dubbed hoaxes by the South Carolina Marine and Resources Agency, which claimed that the tracks were too perfect and didn't correspond to the tracks of any known animal or even with Bigfoot's prints.

By now the Lizard Man was big news, and everybody wanted to get into the act. On August 5th there was another sighting. A pilot stationed at Shaw Air Force Base appeared, apparently shaken, at the sheriff's office. He informed Sheriff Truesdale that he had just shot, but only wounded, a green, scaly monster with red eyes. Although he thought his aim was good when he'd shot the .357 Magnum, Orr said he'd only gotten the monster in the neck. However, he claimed there were some bloody scales lying on the ground where the creature was shot. He offered these to Truesdale as evidence of his story.

Truesdale proved smarter than Orr had bargained for. He recognized that the supposed scales were actually the remains of a fish. Caught, Orr did the smart thing and confessed he'd only been trying to "keep the legend of Lizard Man alive." But

Truesdale was not amused and charged Orr with carrying a firearm without a license.

People are widely divided on what caused the attacks in Scape Ore Swamp. Many of them pooh-pooh the possibility of any strange being inhabiting the area—others are just as convinced that the Lizard Man is alive and well and living in the swamp. But one fact remains clear—something has happened on several occasions on Route 15 and to date no one has come up with an acceptable explanation.

DIRECTIONS: *From Columbia take I-20 East to Highway 15. Go north a mile to Bishopville.*

—JB

THE CRAB BOY
Huntington Beach State Park
Murrells Inlet, South Carolina

Of all the spirits who haven't found peace, I think those of children are the saddest. This tale of a boy whose childhood was cut short is one that's often told by South Carolinians.

Many people who walk along the shore in Huntington Beach State Park late in the afternoon are startled by a plaintive call of "Help me! Help me!" After looking around and finding no one in sight most folks continue on their way, chalking the experience up to an active imagination, or thinking it's just the wind. A few people have even called the police. But no one has ever found the source of this cry for help, and they never will. The small cry doesn't come from someone in this world. The frightened pleas are those of the ghost of a youngster known to the people of South Carolina as the Crab Boy, and he's been dead for many years. You might say he was a victim of the Depression of the 1930s.

Bryan was the boy's first name—no one knows his last

name—but everyone seems to know that he came from a large, poor family. In 1930 Bryan's father lost his job and was unable to support his seven children. Bryan was ten at the time, and he had three older sisters and three younger brothers. The family, which had always been a happy one, took to quarreling when the lack of money made food and other essentials scarce. Bryan's father, frustrated by what must have seemed an impossible situation, started drinking, using what little money was available. He just wasn't able to face the trusting looks of his children, knowing he couldn't provide them with the sustenance needed to grow strong bodies. Every day that went by, he took on a little more guilt and that guilt made him drink even more.

Bryan's mother felt all alone in her efforts to care for her brood. Although her husband was there in body, he was more like another child than a partner. But Bryan's father did get up early in the mornings and go searching through the trash and garbage from the homes around the area for tidbits of food on which his family could survive. By then he was drunk most of the time. One morning, when he was returning home from foraging through the garbage, he stumbled out into the street right into the path of a car. The man was mortally wounded, but he lingered on in the hospital for about two days before his spirit departed his body, leaving behind his widow, his seven children, and the medical bills from his unfortunate accident.

After that, Bryan's family didn't even have the half-spoiled food that had been keeping them going. Desperate for a way to feed her children, Bryan's mother took to walking the beach accompanied by her crew of little ones, digging for clams and looking for any other edibles that might have washed ashore. One of the things she discovered was that the marshes in the area were full of stone crabs. Her joy was boundless. Each day the family went to the beach and combed through the marshes for the little critters. Bryan's mother learned to make a wonderful crab stew with the sweet meat and a little milk she got from the neighborhood grocer who was kind enough to extend her a bit of credit. She created crab cakes and biscuits as well as crab stew. On special days Bryan's mother served her family crab with scrambled eggs. The children must have been mighty sick of crabmeat, but not one of them ever complained.

Bryan was the oldest boy, so he was often sent to the marshes by himself to hunt around, sticking his hands down in the water and pulling out enough crabs to feed the family for a day. He always did his crabbing at low tide and within an hour he was back home with the crabs his sisters and mother would prepare to assuage the family appetite. One day Bryan walked to the marshes as usual and proceeded to put his hand in the water, feeling around for the crabs, putting them in the mesh sack he always used to haul them home. Bryan's sack was almost full when he put his hand into the water and felt something grab at it. The boy was scared and quickly pulled back his hand. After a moment he decided what he'd felt was probably just a bit of marsh grass. He had stuck his hand back into the water, feeling around for the crabs, when something firmly grabbed his hand. This time he found that he couldn't withdraw it from the crab hole. The something that had hold of him was pulling him down. Bryan struggled but the giant crab proved to be tenacious and held on to Bryan's hand. Bryan pleaded for help, but no one heard. The tide finally came in and Bryan screamed, but still no one heard. He cried, but no one was there to comfort him. The water rose over Bryan's exhausted body, and the boy drowned. The crab let go, but it was no help to Bryan. His body was slumped in the watery marshes.

Bryan's mother became concerned when the boy didn't come home after an hour. By evening she was hysterical as she ran up and down the beach calling his name. The marshes were dark, but the mother felt her way through them, searching for her son. The water was waist-deep in some places, but the distraught mother plodded on. It was almost dawn when she made her way home to her other children, hoping against hope that Bryan had returned in her absence. But Bryan's brothers and sisters hadn't seen him, and when the sun came up the entire family dispatched to the beach to look for their son and brother.

Perhaps Bryan never would have been found but for a pair of fisherman who were walking through the marshes in their hip boots a few days later. "What's this?" one of the men said to the other.

"Dunno, looks like a child to me!" the second fisherman exclaimed. And a child it was. The two men were sick at the sight of Bryan's poor water-bloated body. They carefully carried it back to shore.

"Wasn't there a boy reported missing a few days ago?" one of the men asked the other.

"By golly, I think you're right," came the reply.

It didn't take long to find Bryan's mother. All of the neighbors and most of the other townspeople knew about Bryan's disappearance. The funeral was small and very, very sad. Bryan was buried in a plain pine box.

His mother never forgot him, and she spent many hours a day for the rest of her life walking the beach, feeling her way through the marshes, trying to get close to the son she'd loved dearly. People began to think she was, as they said, "teched in the head," because she told her neighbors that often when she was down there near the spot where Bryan was found she'd hear his plaintive cry of "Help me! Help me!"

But there's a good chance that Bryan's mother wasn't "teched" at all. Since she's died many other people claim to have heard the cries of the little Crab Boy who died during the Depression, pleading, "Help me! Help me!"

DIRECTIONS: *From Murrells Inlet, take U.S. Route 17 South for three miles to Huntington Beach State Park.*

—JB

THE VENGEFUL SLAVE
Belle Grove Plantation
Middletown, Virginia

Belle Grove, an imposing mansion of sandstone that took six years to build, is steeped in history. Thomas Jefferson was one of the architects, and President and Mrs. Madison whiled away part of their honeymoon at Belle Grove. The place is haunted by Hetty Cooley, who some say was murdered there, some say committed suicide there, some say died by accident there, but who everyone concurs did succumb in a horrible fashion at Belle Grove.

The mansion and environs are worth seeing for themselves. A tour gives one a good feel of life in the Shenandoah Valley during the 1800s. Originally the land was in the possession of

Jost Hite, who moved to Shenandoah Valley in 1732, and was granted 100,000 acres. In 1782 Isaac Hite, Jr., Jost Hite's grandson, received from his grandfather a grant of 483 acres. Isaac began construction of Belle Grove in 1788, and the home was completed in 1794. It passed down from generation to generation of the Hite family until 1860, when Benjamin B. Cooley and John W. Cooley purchased the mansion with its original 483 acres plus another 136 acres. The pair, whose kinship I was unable to ascertain, paid $24,787 to the heirs of Cornelius Hite for this piece of real estate.

Benjamin Cooley, a bachelor, moved in with his small band of servants. Among the folk helping to keep the mansion running smoothly for Cooley was a slave girl named Harriette Robinson, who cooked and ran the house. She was strong-minded and willful, but she did a good job for her master. Harriette liked her position and, not being one to cotton to change, had made it known to the other members of the household staff that should the master choose to marry, she had no intention of welcoming the new mistress of the house with open arms. She intended, in fact, to make matters as difficult for the interloper as possible. It wasn't very long after the move to Belle Grove that Benjamin decided that the time had come for him to bring a bride to his new home. His quest for the right person ended when he met Hetty, a widow with children. After a festive wedding and a brief honeymoon, he brought his wife to Belle Grove.

True to her word, Harriette set about to be as ornery as any servant I've ever heard of! She not only told her friends and the others slaves how she felt about the new Mrs. Cooley, she told her new mistress right to her face. Every order that Hetty Cooley gave to Harriette was met with petulance at best and downright hostility at worst. One day Hetty, who was reputed to have an even temper, told Mary Moore, a spinster girl living at Belle Grove, that she was not going to take Harriette's slurs much longer. Hetty shouted in a burst of frustration that she'd taken more from this black servant than she'd ever take from a white person. She would not, and could not, live in the same house with Harriette Robinson any longer. Hetty vowed Mr. Cooley would have to do something with the slave girl.

For some reason I find hard to understand, Mr. Cooley didn't do anything with or to the slave girl, and matters went along pretty much as they had since Hetty had come to live at Belle

Grove. Harriette was so brazen that she often confronted her mistress, overtly threatening her. One of these occasions, just about a week before Hetty Cooley died, was witnessed by John Cooley, who later recounted the incident. Hetty was sitting in a room when Harriette entered and asked if Mrs. Cooley had found a stocking. "Mrs. Cooley said 'no I did not find it,' and Harriette accused her of hiding the stocking on purpose. When Hetty denied this, the slave girl accused her mistress of being a liar. Mrs. Cooley said 'if you tell me that I will take this stick and hit you!' She picked up a broomstick, hitting Harriette with it. The pair continued to struggle out into the passage. As I followed them out, I saw Harriette had Mrs. Cooley by the shoulders and was kicking her. They were right by the kitchen stairs, and I told Harriette if she did not go down, I would knock her down."

It was about a week after this that Hetty Cooley was sitting in the parlor with Mary Moore when Hetty excused herself and left. The time was about 2:30 in the afternoon. When Hetty didn't return, Mary Moore began to wonder what had happened to her. By five o'clock, Mary was becoming quite concerned, as Hetty had been known to have seizures. Benjamin Cooley wasn't at home; he'd gone to Alexandria, and Mary Moore was upset and confused, wondering what she should do about the strange disappearance of her hostess. Another thing troubling Mary was that she remembered Hetty saying she wouldn't be alive to see Lincoln become presdient. Mary Moore became increasingly agitated. The events that took place later that terrible evening and the days following proved that Mary Moore's worries were justified. Those events were chronicled at the trial of Harriette Robinson, who was charged with the murder of her mistress, Hetty Cooley.

I have a transcript of that trial, which took place in May 1861, at the Circuit Court, Frederick County, Virginia. While under oath, James Gordon, a tenant farmer on the Cooley place, said, "As I came over to the house that evening, I smelt something burning like wool. I told the old black man to go into the Negro quarter to see if anything was afire. I went on to the house, and Miss Mary Moore asked me if Mrs. Cooley was at my house. I told her no! I thought maybe she had gone to the stable looking for eggs and had fallen and hurt herself. I could not find her there. . . . The old man Louis Robinson told me . . . he had heard something groaning in the Smoke House, as if it was most gone. He called for the key and it could not be found till I got there and then somebody handed me the key. I don't know who it was. . . . I unlocked the door and pushed it open and saw Mrs. Cooley sitting between two hogsheads with her feet most in the fire. . . . She look to me as if she was nearly burnt up. . . . Her hair and face looked as if all burnt into crisps. . . . I picked Mrs. Cooley up and dragged her to the door and laid her down. Two of her skirts were taken off of her and nearly burnt up. . . . I called my wife to bring a quilt to carry her in the house on. Me and Louis Robinson carried her into her room . . . and then I started after the two doctors, Dr. Shipley and Dr. Guyer."

In Dr. Shipley's testimony at the trial of Harriette Robinson for the murder of Hetty Cooley, he said, "I was called upon by Mr. Gordon to visit Mrs. Hetty A. Cooley, who was reported to have been very badly bruised. . . . When I got to Mr. Cooley's, upon entering the house, I found Mrs. Gordon, Miss Mary Moore, and the prisoner standing in the entry. Mrs. Gordon and Miss Mary Moore were weeping very bitterly. . . . I repaired to Mrs. Cooley's room immediately. I found Mrs. Cooley lying upon the floor wrapped in a bed quilt. . . . I removed the coverlet from her face and when I did so she shrank back and said, 'Don't! Let me be.' . . . I never should have known her had I not been called to see Mrs. Cooley—and I am her brother! . . . When Mrs. Gordon and Miss Mary Moore asked what I thought of her, I gave the answer . . . I could do nothing for her, she must die. I returned to Mrs. Cooley and got one half of her face washed—the left side. At this time Dr. Guyer came in and entered into an examination. . . .

"It was suggested by Dr. Guyer that we had better get her garments changed and get her to bed. I assisted in taking off her outer garments and noticed that she had something tied around her neck in two knots—the knots were tight. When Dr. Guyer, in company with myself, made an examination of the extent of her injuries, first we noticed her bleeding freely, arterial blood from the nose. Upon the right cheek there was a severe wound, we subsequently discovered that the right cheekbone was broken at the corner of the eye. The right eye was sunken, whilst the left eye was protruded. . . . There were two flesh wounds upon the right side of the forehead, running back to . . . the temple. . . . There was also a flesh wound close and behind the right ear to the bone and about an inch and a half in length. . . . The nasal bones were broken as I discovered in subsequent examinations. . . . There were three bruises upon the lower portion of the left cheek and chin that resembled the imprints of knuckles. . . . There were also three distinct marks upon her throat, it appeared as though she had been grasped by the fingernails between the throat and the collar. Upon the front portion of each arm between the shoulder and the elbow there was the imprint of fingers as though her arms had been grasped by both hands of another person." Hetty Cooley's brother, still distraught from the experience, went on to describe in minute detail the other injuries he and Dr. Guyer had found that terrible night.

In further testimony Dr. Shipley recounted what followed: "This occurred on Tuesday night, and she died Saturday afternoon following. I was with her all night Tuesday night and nearly all the time afterwards till she died. I don't suppose I was absent six or eight hours all the time. I considered her insensible that night [Tuesday], unconscious of anything going on around her. About five o'clock next morning she seemed to have consciousness enough to recognize my voice. I asked her what hurt her? She replied that there was nothing the matter with her. I then asked if she had climbed up in the Smoke House to get a piece of meat and if she had fallen? She said after some hesitation 'Yes.' I did not consider her rational even when she answered these questions at that time."

During the time the ladies were getting the poor injured Hetty Cooley undressed so that the doctors could examine her more closely, Shipley and Guyer took it upon themselves to do a little detective work. Toward that end, the gentlemen went to the Smoke House where Mrs. Cooley had been found. Dr. Shipley told of their experience there in his testimony during the trial. "Upon close examination of that Smoke House, the first thing that attracted my attention was a pool of blood just inside the door and to the right as you enter. The next things were the steel hoops of her [Hetty's] skeleton skirt. They were lying upon the fire in a snug little pile—just as if they had been placed there. We then saw the spot where she was found in a sitting position between two hogsheads. . . . Both of these hogsheads had blood upon them. . . . We next noticed a large splotch of blood against one of the studdings. . . . We also found blood upon some boards lying upon a salting trough. . . . There was also a small pool of blood in the bottom of the salting trough. In one corner of the Smoke House there is a vacant space of about four feet square. In this vacant space, the ground floor of which is dirt, there was also a pool of blood."

It does sound to me as if the blood was too spread around for Hetty Cooley to have suffered her injuries in a fall from the rafters straight down to the hogsheads. The doctor was sure she'd been attacked. Shipley further stated, "My opinion was that she had been foully dealt with, after I had collected my thoughts, for it was some time after I saw her before I could form an opinion. I did not think she could have received the wounds from a fall." To enhance his case he told the court, "The hair that I showed in the presence of the court to Mr. Sperry and other witnesses and recognized by them as similar in color and texture to that found under the door of the Pig Room, is from the head of the deceased Mrs. Cooley." The Pig Room is a room that was used for slaughtering animals for food, and it is connected to the Smoke House by a flagstone walk. Dr. Shipley took dirt from the floor of the Pig Room, the walk, and the Smoke House. Those dirt samples were entered as evidence. The undergarments Mrs. Cooley wore when she was found were also shown to the court. The dirt on these garments was the type found on the walk, but it was dissimilar to what was on the Smoke House floor. The creases on Mrs. Cooley's underclothes appeared to have been made by dragging her by her heels.

As if this wasn't enough to convict Harriette, Mrs. Shipley testified that the dress which she'd seen the slave wearing the morning of the crime was hanging out to dry at the time Hetty Cooley was discovered lying mortally wounded in the locked Smoke House. According to the ladies who knew Harriette and were used to seeing her every day, she changed her dress only about once every two weeks, and the dress in question had just been laundered a scant two, or at the most three, days before the crime.

The question of Mrs. Cooley having a spasm, during which she thrashed around in the Smoke House, was put to rest by her brother, Dr. Shipley, who said, "Mrs. Cooley died with apoplexy caused by the injuries inflicted upon her brain. I have known Mrs. Cooley since her infancy. Her spasms grew out of disease. But she has had none since she became a mother. The family physician always told my father that would cure her." As for Hetty alluding to her own death by saying she wouldn't be around to see Lincoln become president, everyone who saw or came in contact with the lady that fateful February day agreed that she was in the happiest of moods and seemed in the best of health.

Another witness, Sally, a free black woman, didn't help Harriette's case when she told the court about a conversation she'd had with the prisoner after Hetty and Harriette had engaged in one of their frequent fights. Sally said, "We were outside the door, and she [Harriette] said, 'if I can't do anything else I will poison her.' She laughed and asked me, 'Have you got any poison?' I said, 'No indeed, I never had any poison in my hand in my life, and I never want any. If you would undertake such a thing as that they would hang you.' She said, 'I don't care what they do with me afterwards, I will have my revenge.' "

The consensus was that Hetty had been severely beaten in the Pig Room by an irate Harriette, who had pledged, even before she'd set eyes on her mistress, that she would not put up with Mr. Cooley marrying and bringing his bride to rule at Belle Grove. It didn't take long for the court to find Harriette Robinson guilty of inflicting the wounds on Hetty Cooley that had resulted in her death and then dragging the senseless woman from the Pig Room, where she had done the ugly deed, through the passage and into the Smoke House, then pushing her body into the fire and locking the door, leaving Hetty to burn painfully to death. A remorseless Harriette was packed off to prison. It's unclear what her sentence was but, considering the magnitude of the crime and the fact that she, a black slave, had murdered her white mistress, it's a pretty safe assumption that she was sentenced to hang.

For some reason, probably because at that time everyone was more concerned about the Civil War than about carrying out executions, Harriette languished in jail, along with many other black prisoners, for quite a spell. When federal troops marched through Shenandoah Valley, freeing black prisoners on the assumption they all were being held unjustly, Harriette, who no doubt had not thought she'd see the light of day again, quickly disappeared. No one ever heard of her again. But Hetty Cooley is still at Belle Grove. She walks down the flagstone path that leads from the Pig Room to the Smoke House.

In a 1930 book entitled *Virginia Ghosts*, Marguerite Dupont said, "More than fifty years ago an Englishman named Rose occupied this estate (Belle Grove). Miss Lucy Jones of Winchester visited the Rose family frequently. She was Miss Rose's intimate friend. Miss Jones states that the different members of the Rose family saw the ghost frequently—a white figure standing by the stone fireplace in the basement; gliding along the flagstone path to the Smoke House; again in the hallway of her former home, or looking from the windows at the big walnut tree."

After the Civil War, Belle Grove's ownership passed to several families. In 1907 Andrew Jackson Brumback bought the plantation, passing it on to his son J. Herbert Brumback in 1918. The younger Brumback operated an inn there until 1928. Francis Welles Hunnewell, a botanist from the north, purchased it from Brumback, hiring the noted Washington architect Horace Peaslee to restore it to its former glory. Hunnewell saw Belle Grove as a historically significant place, and so he stipulated in his will that upon his death the house and one hundred acres of the surrounding farmland would go to the National Trust for Historic Preservation. This organization has run the estate since Hunnewell's death in 1964. Belle Grove is used for historical and cultural programs and still functions as a fully operational farm. It is open to the public from April through October between the hours of 10:00 A.M. and 4:00 P.M. daily and on Sundays from 1:00 to 5:00 P.M. Special events are offered through the winter months.

DIRECTIONS: *Belle Grove is approximately one mile south of Middletown, Virginia. To reach it from I-81 take Exit 77, then State 627 to U.S. 11, go south on U.S. 11 through Middletown to the memorial column one mile south of town, take an immediate right on State 727, to Belle Grove. Or take I-81 Exit 75, north on U.S. 11 to State 727. To reach I-81 from Washington D.C., take I-66 through Front Royal.*

—JB

CHESSIE, THE SEA MONSTER
Chesapeake Bay
Maryland

It's true that Chessie isn't as well known around the world as her sister creature Nessie, the Loch Ness Monster, but she's a frequent topic of conversation and a subject for much research in the Chesapeake Bay area. Psychic Lynda Andrus of Andrus Phenomena Research Center in Lexington Park, Maryland, told me she's interested in Chessie on two levels. Lynda is intrigued by Chessie because her identity and origins are unknown. She could be an alien life form from another planet. She could be a heretofore unknown type of marine life. But Lynda is also interested in Chessie because the creature has been adopted as the mascot of the U.S. Fish and Wildlife Service in Annapolis, Maryland, in their campaign to clean up the Chesapeake Bay—a cause in which Lynda is passionately interested.

The sea monster has been the subject of much serious research since she first appeared in the 1970s. In spite of this and the many, many sightings (over fifty of which have been documented and are considered legitimate) by investigators, there are those who chose to think of Chessie as a joke, people who smile when Chessie's mentioned. They consider her a figment of a lot of overactive minds. I guess that's not surprising when you think of all the people who find it easy to reject anything that smacks of the paranormal.

The people at the Enigma Project in Reistertown, Maryland, have some pretty convincing evidence for those who care to read about Chessie. They have found that she is an enormous snakelike creature estimated by those who've seen her to be from five to fifty feet long. All of the folks agree that the creature they've encountered has a head shaped like a football. But that's about all they agree on. It's been reported that this elusive sea animal is black, brown, green, or reddish-brown; that she's a solid color and that she's multicolored. Some people estimate her girth at six inches, while others swear she's as thick as a telephone pole. Chessie has been spotted moving from side to side (which is the standard type of locomotion for

185

most water creatures) and moving up and down in an undulating motion (where humps appear above the surface of the water as she swims).

Michael A. Frizzell, of the Enigma Project, says his group has investigated Chessie from a neutral point of view. Their goal is to find the truth. According to Frizzell, there are several theories as to what, or who, Chessie may be—among them that she's an anaconda, an eel, an oarfish, some type of foreign matter (such as a log), or a species of animal unknown to marine biologists. The Enigma Project has addressed, and pretty much discarded, all of these theories.

Those people who think Chessie could be an anaconda speculate that many years ago, when ships from South America were frequent visitors to the North American ports, a few anacondas may have jumped the ship in the Chesapeake. To this Frizzell responds that anacondas are large constricting snakes which can live only in warm water. In addition, they're also most at home in fresh water, and the Chesapeake Bay has such a high salt content it's considered brackish. And the anaconda is light tan—one of the few colors no one has reported seeing.

It's just as unlikely that Chessie's an eel. Fizzell notes that eels breathe while under the water, and Chessie appears to be an air breather, surfacing frequently for oxygen. Eels found around Chesapeake Bay are not large (ranging from one to five feet in length) and are quite thin.

That brings us to the oarfish theory. This is considered highly unlikely, too, for while oarfish are long—some up to twenty feet—they're a silver color, again a color not among the many reported by Chessie watchers. And the body of an oarfish is thin. That doesn't sound like Chessie, with a girth up to that of a telephone pole.

To put to rest the guess that Chessie is only a log or some other inanimate object, the Enigma team has interviewed many people who've seen her move. These observers have been close to her, and they all swear this is a living, moving being of some type. It's remotely possible, however, that Chessie's a form of sea life that's yet to be discovered by marine biologists. These experts are dramatically divided in their opinions on this issue. There are a few who say it's the only possible logical explanation. (But then, they're looking for a logical explanation.) Most of the marine biologists questioned by Enigma thought it unlikely.

Bill Burton of the *Baltimore Evening Sun* wrote an article in 1982 suggesting that there was a correlation between the Chessie sightings and the times when the bluefish were running. From the data he collected, it appeared that when the bluefish were running, one was liable to encounter Chessie, but that there had been no sightings of Chessie when the bluefish weren't around. Strange! Could she offer the bluefish some sort of protection?

There have been many valid and confirmed sightings of the sea monster in Chesapeake Bay, as well as some reports given by people who just wanted to stir things up to be part of the excitement. In 1980, UPI carried a story entitled "Chessie Is Back." According to the article, G. F. Buddy Green, his family, and a friend of theirs were out for a Sunday boat ride when a snakelike creature appeared swimming in the water. According to Green, it was about twenty-five feet long and approximately six inches in diameter. On closer inspection, Green found that there were two snakelike animals and that they swam in an undulating motion. One of these serpentlike creatures was considerably larger than the other one. The larger of the two had humps on its back, and as it swam along, it kept putting its head under the water and then resurfacing—as if to get air. As the creature moved, Green reported, it created waves about a foot high or higher. He commented, "I've spent a lot of time on boats down in the Chesapeake, and I'm used to seeing a lot of strange sights, but never anything like this."

What Green didn't know at the time was that ten days before he and his family saw Chessie in the Potomac, there had been another sighting about fifteen miles downriver. The man, whose name doesn't seem to be on record, reported almost exactly what Green and his party described, with two major differences. While Green said the monster had humps, the first man didn't describe any. And when Green saw his monster she was underwater and coming up for air from time to time. The other man said he never saw her put her head under the water at all. Did these men see the same creature? It's entirely possible. Think about the differences in eyewitness reports to a crime. Everyone thinks they saw what happened, and yet often the descriptions of the event and of the criminal vary widely.

In 1983 Frederick C. N. Littleton, a reasonable and sane man who had practiced law for about thirty years and was a part-time boat builder, was sailing a twenty-footer in the upper

Chesapeake Bay when he had what he said was a weird experience. Littleton wrote to Bill Burton of *Bay Magazine* about what happened. "Saturday evening I anchored in Cabin John Creek, about two-thirds of the way in from the day market to the little dock on the south side. Sunday morning at about seven o'clock, I noticed what appeared to be the head of an animal held up on a stick and moving to the north about thirty yards from me."

Littleton grabbed his binoculars and through them saw a creature with a head about the size and shape of a football. The head was brownish in color and seemed to be covered with some growths resembling warts. Fred Littleton said there were protrusions where the eyes should have been, and the strange monster had a tapered snout, which it kept dipping in and out of the water. The sea serpent was black-green and smooth skinned. Littleton watched it swim around, slowly raising its head and back section and then disappearing below water before it dove out of sight. He said he thought there was probably another five or six feet in length to the creature which had remained below the water. Although this would still make it quite a bit shorter than other people have claimed Chessie to be, what Littleton saw could have been another creature of the same family or perhaps the smaller sea serpent that accompanied Chessie when Green and his family saw her.

In 1984 Chessie was spotted in Eastern Bay, a part of Chesapeake Bay that lies across from Annapolis, Maryland. The man who observed her was a credible businessman, who seemed to prefer to remain anonymous. He was interviewed by *The Queen Anne's Record Observer*, a Maryland weekly. The man described a creature with "an enormous head, more like a serpent's head" that he claimed broke the surface of the water only a few feet from his boat. He said the creature had big black eyes and looked him right in the eyes before it slithered under the water. That same summer there were numerous sightings of what people thought to be Chessie. One couple described Chessie as longer than their twenty-four-foot boat. Another person estimated her length was at least thirty-five feet.

In 1984 Charles Kirby, a twenty-four-year-old who had never believed in the legend of Chessie, was swimming in the bay with his nephew Michael Miller and Michael's friend Dwayne Bailuff. The trio had been horsing around in the water when they spied the monster swimming not far from them. The boys headed for shore, but Kirby stayed in the water observing Chessie. He later said in an interview, "If I hadn't seen it with my own eyes, I wouldn't have believed it. I don't care if no one believes me. . . . I know what I saw, I didn't imagine it." Chessie didn't seem upset by the trio, and she swam around contentedly about two hundred yards away from the shore for fifteen or twenty minutes. Kirby described the creature, saying, "It was huge, about as round as a telephone pole. It had two humps that kept coming in and out of the water. I would say it was about fifty feet from one end of a hump to the other. It's probably a lot bigger because we never did see its head or tail." Kirby reported that the way the creature moved reminded him of an inchworm crawling. After swimming in a leisurely manner, Chessie appeared to be frightened off by the shadow of a dark cloud that had formed overhead.

Early in 1986 an elderly man who'd once worked for the government swore he saw Chessie in the water near his home on Kent Island. But the most persuasive story that year came from Kenneth Boudrie, a resident of Waverly. Boudrie was passing the time on his dock with his friend Dr. Jack Bishop. It was about 6:00 P.M. on a Sunday, as Bishop told the story to the local newspaper, when Boudrie pointed in the water and said with amazement, "Hey, Jack, look!"

Bishop turned around to see the creature swimming along about one hundred yards offshore down the center of a channel. "He was going toward Watermelon Point from Easton Point," Bishop said. According to Bishop's description, Chessie was "coming out of the water in humps, one after another."

Both Bishop and Boudrie thought the creature they'd seen was from twenty to twenty-five feet long, and about twelve inches in diameter. The color, they concurred, was brown. It was moving swiftly and soon was out of sight. Bishop and Boudrie were both pragmatists and a little skeptical about what they'd seen until they heard that several people out on a sailboat had spotted the same thing at just about the same time. After that, Bishop said, "I believe in what I saw. I don't know if it's Chessie. But it's a large animal out there."

The most conclusive evidence that Chessie does exist, and is out there swimming around and maybe procreating in Chesapeake Bay, was obtained by Robert Frew. On May 31, 1982, Frew, his wife, and two children were swimming off the bulkhead of their Kent Island home when they spotted a large creature about one hundred feet from shore. Robert Frew quickly went inside his home, grabbed his video camera, and commenced to take a movie of the animal as it swam about. This videotape was brought to the attention of Dr. George Zug, chairman of Vertebrate Zoology at Smithsonian's Museum of Natural History. Dr. Zug previewed the tape with twenty-five other marine and fishing authorities at the museum. The zoologists found it fascinating but could reach no conclusion as to what it was. They seemed to agree, however, that it probably wasn't any known type of marine life.

Shortly after the Smithsonian viewed it, the tape was sent by the Enigma Project to Johns Hopkins Applied Physics Laboratory, where the staff tried to enhance the tape and the image on it, using a computer. The laboratory at Johns Hopkins was sufficiently interested in what they saw that they didn't charge the Enigma Project for their time or materials. The purpose of the computer enhancement was to get a clearer picture of Chessie and see if the marine experts could tell from that image Chessie's length, width, the speed at which she was traveling, and other data. Unfortunately, this project was abandoned just as it was looking very promising, because the Johns Hopkins Laboratory ran out of funding it could channel toward the Chessie tape.

Of course, Chessie brought out the crazies, and Chesapeake Bay became a hunting ground with many so-called sports hoping to catch and kill Chessie. A senator from Baltimore contacted the Enigma Project, offering his help in getting legislation to protect the sea monster. On January 29, 1984, the senator presented what was called the Chessie legislation to the Maryland Senate Subcommittee on Economic and Environmental Affairs. Many people who wanted Chessie protected gave testimony that day, and the tape Robert Frew took in 1982 was shown. The committee seemed interested, but when it was put to a vote they decided against Chessie and for the lunatics who consider her fair game.

Does Chessie really exist? There is no doubt in my mind she does. But whether she's an other-world creature or a form of marine life that's heretofore escaped the eagle eyes of marine biologists remains a question. If you visit the Chesapeake Bay area, perhaps you'll catch a sight of her undulating through the water, and you can form your own opinion.

DIRECTIONS: *Chessie has been seen in many spots all along Chesa-*
peake Bay and in its tributaries. To reach the Potomac River,
where she's often found, take Route 895 South out of Baltimore
to Route 97 South, to Route 3 South, to Route 301 South, to Route
234 East, to Leonardtown. Take Route 5 out of Leonardtown to
Point Lookout, at the mouth of the Potomac.

—JB

THE LEGEND OF MOLL DYER
Moll Dyer's Rock
Leonardtown, Maryland

This story was sent to me by my friend Lynda Andrus, a
psychic and the founder of Andrus Phenomena Research
Center in Lexington Park, Maryland.

Lynda says that during the late 1700s, a time when witchcraft
was widely thought to be evil and was universally feared, an old
lady named Moll Dyer lived in a hut on a stream that is now
known as Moll Dyer's Run. She was considered to be a witch
by the local people.

A hundred years ago Moll Dyer's story was recorded for the
St. Mary's Beacon by Joseph F. Morgan, Esq. In his account he
said, "Her history no one knew, but there were stories told of
her in another country where her lot was different and where
she had all that was refined and beautiful waiting on her every
step.

"Her tattered dress would at times reveal patches of an
embroidered kerchief or a bit of faded lace, which might recall
far off summers when the banquet hall rang with the music of
her laughter and courtly men worshiped at the shrine of her
loveliness. Great sorrow which crushed home and love out of
her young life, came upon her, and with hate for her kind in her

heart, she sought a distant shore to live out, alone and unloved, the remnants of her miserable existence."

Whether this was true or not, Moll was loath to discuss her past. On the few occasions when neighbors or townspeople questioned her about it she immediately turned and left the offender to seek refuge in her hut, where she would remain in seclusion for many days. During these times, those who had been an annoyance to her always seemed to suffer a run of bad luck. This gave rise to the rumor that Moll Dyer was a witch. In time Moll was blamed for all the troubles and mishaps of practically everyone living in Leonardtown. Finally some calamity of such magnitude that it affected the entire community took place. History doesn't record just what this pestilence was, but it does note that the entire population of St. Mary's County decided that they would get rid of Moll Dyer and her evil deeds once and for all.

Since Moll had been asked politely (and not so politely) to go elsewhere to live, her detractors knew this request would fall on deaf ears. So a meeting was held to determine just how the community could rid themselves of this evil forever. After much debate, a committee was selected to go to Moll's hut and set it on fire. It was the middle of winter and the temperatures were bitter. The theory was that Moll would have to flee and, having no place to come back to, seek shelter in another shack in another community.

It was an especially wintry night when the committee carried out the planned torching of Moll's shack. The old lady almost didn't get out alive. But Moll did manage to escape, and fled into the woods. The people who had gathered for the event cheered and returned to their homes, much relieved that they were rid of Moll Dyer.

The revelry continued for several days. Then about a week after the fire a young boy, hunting for his cattle who had strayed from the farmyard, came upon a gruesome sight. There was Moll Dyer kneeling on a stone. The old woman had one hand resting on the stone while the other was raised to the heavens. She had frozen to death because she had no shelter from the icy winter.

The story that circulated through the community was that Moll Dyer had died while beseeching her God to punish her persecutors by putting a curse on them and on their land. As if to support this theory, the townspeople were alarmed to find that the rock on which Moll Dyer's lifeless body had been found bore the clear impression of both her knee and her hand.

Morgan's article comments on the aftermath of Moll Dyer's death. "Many times belated travelers on this road have seen the ghost of Moll Dyer making her midnight visitation to her accustomed haunts. It is told, by those who have had the courage and endurance to watch, that once in each year, on the coldest night of winter, she may be seen wending her ghostly way from a point south of the run, where the remains of the hut still can be seen, to where the stone is, and kneeling in the same attitude as on that fatal night, as if praying that her curse may be continued.

"There are those who think that her prayer was heard when she asked that the lands be made barren and the flocks be decimated, as the country for several miles around the location of the hut is, to this day, with few exceptions, desolate and unproductive."

In the October 20, 1974, issue of *The Sunday Sun*, Philip Love reported the story of Moll Dyer. He found the usual facts about the community's feelings toward Moll—about the fire, about the rock. Philip Love, who had a beach house in the area, had tried in vain to find Moll Dyer's Rock. Finally he gave up and went home. A syndicated column he did on Moll and his failure to find her rock resulted in a barrage of letters. One came from James Norman Simms of Silver Spring, Maryland. In his article Love says, "Simms wrote that his schoolteacher mother, May Magdelene Simms, had been a Dyer, and he'd learned the family history from her. She told him that two Dyers landed at St. Mary's City in 1690 after being chased out of England and Ireland because they were Roman Catholics. Their most noteworthy descendants were a Dr. Dyer, who practiced medicine in Washington and Prince George's County, and his son, Father Edward Dyer, the first American provincial of the Sulpician Order in the United States. Simms seemed to think that Moll was a descendant of these Dyers."

Another answer Love had was a phone call from Woodrow Bennet, a resident of St. Mary's County who ran a grocery store near Moll Dyer's Run. He told Love that he knew exactly where Moll Dyer's Rock was and would be glad to take him to it. Love eagerly returned to his cottage at St. Mary's County Beach. When Love met Bennet for the trek to see Moll's Rock, he had a number of other people with him, among them a Christian brother.

Love says, "As we followed Bennet up a steep grade, I spotted the charred remnants of a small building and asked facetiously if it had been Moll's hut." Bennet replied that it wasn't, and explained it was the house of a man named Dan Wills. The Wills house had burned a few years earlier. Then Bennet added that many folks—those who believed in and feared Moll Dyer's curse—thought she had been responsible for this fire because the house had been on land Moll had condemned.

Bennet, Love, and their party climbed over a fence, walked through woods and meadows, and finally Bennet pointed to a dark ravine, explaining, "There it is, Moll Dyer's Rock! There isn't another one like it anywhere. . . ."

One of the children in the party jumped on the rock and put his fingers in the indentations made by Moll Dyer's fingers so many years before. Love's wife wanted to freeze the moment on film, but as she snapped her camera, the flash refused to operate. Since it was too dark to take a picture successfully without light, Love snapped his camera in an attempt to capture the scene. The results were the same. No flash! Bennet smiled and commented, "Moll's hexed your cameras."

From that time on the little band of explorers met with nothing but irritations. First Anne Greene, a friend of the Loves, dropped her sunglasses and stepped on them, breaking them beyond use. Then, while the group was making its way back to the cars, Brother Joseph bumped his head on a fence. One of the girls tore her jeans, and another member of the party received a terrible gash on her finger while tangling with a berry bush. Love himself was stricken with a painful kink in his knee.

Charles Fenwick, a St. Mary's County historian, was de-lighted to hear that Love had uncovered the elusive Moll Dyer's Rock and promised to have it moved to the local historical society for everyone to see. But apparently Moll wasn't pleased that her rock was going to be disturbed. Although the owner of the ravine in which the rock rested was more than willing to let the community have the stone, the committee from the histori-cal society who were going to move it seemed jinxed. One or more of these people was always ill when the appointed hour to move the rock arrived. Finally a time was set to remove the rock and everyone was enjoying good health. Then the storms came and flooded the area, making it impossible to get near Moll Dyer's Rock.

Eventually the weather broke, and the committee, down to a man, was feeling wonderful. But the large truck they needed to move the rock wouldn't run. By the time it had been repaired and a new date had been set there was illness again. And so it went.

Fenwick retired and Thurston Baxter took his place as president of the historical society. The new president was afraid the location of Moll Dyer's Rock was fast becoming common knowledge. He feared souvenir hunters might descend on it and chip away pieces to add to their treasures. With this in mind Baxter convinced the Maryland National Guard to make removing the rock a weekend field project. Eight guardsmen from St. Mary's and Calvert counties had their work cut out for them. It took a lot of digging and grunting and groaning to unearth the rock. When it had been fully exposed, it was thirty-eight inches long, twenty-three inches wide, and seventeen inches high. This giant weighed 875 pounds. They succeeded in dragging the rock out of the ravine, loading it on a truck, and driving it off to its new home in front of the St. Mary's County Historical Society Building, where it still resides, attracting tourists, the curious, and those who wish to communicate with the spirit of Moll Dyer.

Many questions still go unanswered. Who was Moll Dyer—really? Was she a descendant of the Catholic Dyers who escaped to this country in an effort to practice their beliefs in peace? Maybe. But there are other stories about her beginnings. In *Intimate Glimpses of Old Saint Mary's*, George Morgan Knight, Jr., claims, "Mouldy Dyer was an Indian maid who gave her love to a handsome young 'paleface' who seduced her and promised to marry her. Instead of doing so, he disappeared."

When a baby was born to her, the Indian maid took it in her arms, as the legend relates, and, kneeling on a stone by the run, held it out over the water and vowed vengeance on the paleface for his unfaithfulness. So solemnly did Mouldy Dyer make her oath that she left the impression of her knee in the stone. "The Indian's knee print is readily visible today in the stone. Despite the passing of the years, it has been preserved.

"Some claim that the weeping of Mouldy Dyer can be heard on dark stormy nights when the run floods the highway, holding up traffic. According to the legend, it is flooded by the tears of the Indian maid who still weeps for her lover to return."

Through the years, other people have found their cameras balky when they've attempted to snap a picture of Moll Dyer's Rock. Others have reported having sharp pains or lingering aches from being near the rock. But some people have snapped photos with no opposition. Lynda Andrus told me, "In the five years I have visited Moll Dyer's Rock, I have never experienced any camera malfunctions. I haven't suffered any aches or pains like those that other people have reported either. Instead, I feel sensations of loneliness and abandonment."

Perhaps that's because Lynda's psychic powers are finely honed and she senses that Moll Dyer may not have done any of the evil deeds attributed to her. She may have been just a friendless old woman.

Although Moll Dyer's Rock is easy to find, her grave is elusive. No one seems to have been successful in finding it, although many have tried. Lynda Andrus is among those who would like to find Moll Dyer's grave. "I have tried many times in vain to find the resting spot of Moll Dyer," Lynda told me. "So instead I sit by her rock and try to comfort the spirit that some say is as cold as ice."

Someday, if you're driving through Maryland, maybe you'll stop by St. Mary's County Historical Society, kneel on the rock where Moll Dyer knelt, and put your fingers where her fingers fit on that terrible night when Moll froze to death because of the hatred of a hysterical town.

DIRECTIONS: *Leonardtown is right on Route 5 in southern Maryland.*

—JB

TWO TRAGIC STORIES
The Bridge on St. Andrew's Church Road
Hollywood, Maryland

While I was working on *Haunted Houses, USA,* I contacted many people who were helpful with the book. Some of them are psychics and several of them are now friends. Lynda Andrus, founder of Andrus Phenomena Research Center in Lexington Park, Maryland, qualifies as both. She very graciously consented to help me with some haunts for this book as well. This story of the ghosts of St. Andrew's Church Road came from her.

There's a bridge on St. Andrew's Church Road that crosses over a dark, swampy area. This spot is home to at least two restless spirits, and a sad story is attached to each. One of them is about a young man who marched off to defend his country during World War II, leaving behind a pregnant bride. The usual V-Mail crossed the ocean with vows of eternal love written on those crowded little pages. The young wife gave birth to a baby boy. They were both ecstatic, as they had been hoping to have a son, and now their dreams had come true. The father wanted so much to return home to Maryland to see his baby and the wonderful girl who was his wife.

As luck would have it the war was winding down, and with victory in sight the young soldier was sent home. His orders didn't leave him time to notify his wife. Imagine her surprise when she answered the telephone in the middle of the night to hear the voice of her beloved husband. He was, he said, in Hollywood and would be home just as soon as he could drive the car he'd borrowed from a buddy out to St. Andrew's Church Road and home.

The young wife was overcome with excitement, so instead of waiting for her husband, she walked down the road to meet him. It would mean seeing him sooner, she reasoned, even if only a few minutes sooner. The girl quickly, but carefully, dressed her son for his first meeting with his father. Then she set out, down the road toward town, running as fast as she could while carrying the baby.

There's a bad curve in the road just by the bridge. As she

started around it, her husband was approaching it from the other side. He was, he later admitted, driving far faster than caution would dictate. But he was, after all, going to see his only son for the first time. As he sped around the curve the woman clutching the infant in her arms suddenly appeared in the road, but it was too late. There was no way he could stop the car fast enough. As he careened into his astonished wife, he glimpsed the look of fear on her face just before he saw the baby fly out of her arms and into the cold water of the stream that ran under the bridge.

His wife was dead, and the baby was never found—not a trace, although bands of people combed the area, supposedly covering every inch of it. Since that time, especially on cold winter nights, people crossing the bridge often hear the sound of a baby crying. The noise comes from the dark waters of the creek that so completely swallowed up an infant many years ago. The creek has been dubbed Cry Baby Creek.

Another ghost who hangs around the bridge on St. Andrew's Church Road is manifest in the form of a black woman who jumps out of nowhere right in front of automobiles crossing the bridge. She's caused more than one accident.

Who is this female with little regard for the motorists she scares? The story goes that there's an old slave cabin right near the bridge. This is the last remaining cabin of a group that belonged to an old plantation. Other signs of the plantation that once operated on the site have long since vanished. The plantation was magnificent for the owners but not a grand place to be a slave. Back before the Civil War the man who owned the place abused his slaves. The women were used to satisfy his insatiable sexual desires.

The cabin that's still standing was inhabited by a group of slaves, among them an extremely beautiful young black girl. She deeply resented the fact that the master visited her so often—a fact he thought should make her proud. After months of ill treatment, the young girl devised a plan. One night when the master arrived expecting a warm bed as usual, he was greeted instead by an iron skillet over the head.

The poor slave girl hadn't meant to kill him, just to stun him and then run off as other slaves had done. But her arm was strong and her aim was true, and when she looked down she realized what she'd done. Quickly the girl packed what few things she had and ran as fast and as far as she could. But it wasn't far enough.

The next morning the master was found dead on the floor of her cabin. A posse formed to catch the young murderess. They took along a number of fierce dogs. The girl had reached the swamp on St. Andrew's Church Road when the dogs overtook her. The men in the posse, who considered themselves heroes, quickly killed her.

Most people from Hollywood, Maryland, believe the woman on the bridge is the ghost of the young girl who was so unfairly killed without a trial those many years ago. Perhaps she's trying to tell her side of the story.

DIRECTIONS: *From Baltimore take U.S. highway route 301 South 48 miles to the town of T.B., where 301 merges with Route 5. Stay on Route 5 for 38 miles to Highway 4 (St. Andrew's Church Road). Travel east about three miles to bridge. From Washington, D.C., take Route 5 to Highway 4 and the bridge.*

—JB

THE UNHAPPY FIDDLER
Scott Run Bridge
South of St. Georges, Delaware

In the mid-1800s the bridge over Scott Run was a simple affair made of wood. It was crudely constructed and probably none too safe, but it served as a means for local people to cross the stream. Somewhere near the bridge there was a small wooden house. It wasn't much of a dwelling, but it was home to Ebenezer, an old man who had lived there all his life. When he'd been a boy things had been quite different. Though Ebenezer's family hadn't been well off, the small house had been comfortable and the boy's father had worked steadily. There was always food on the table and love in the house.

Ebenezer was an only child. From the time he was an infant,

he'd loved music. He sang little ditties and would listen endlessly to anyone who played a musical instrument. Even as a young child he'd been drawn to the violin, and so his parents were especially grateful when a farmer who lived nearby offered to teach their son how to play the instrument. Ebenezer was a smart boy and an apt pupil. The farmer was amazed at how fast the youngster picked up the intricacies of playing the violin. Of course, it was hard for young Ebenezer to practice, as he had no violin of his own. His parents started to save whatever money they could toward buying their son a fiddle. It took them two years, but finally they had enough to purchase a secondhand violin from the widow of a local man who had left behind him a fiddle he'd rarely played.

They saved the surprise for Christmas. It was the happiest day Ebenezer had ever had. He was just fourteen, and never before had he received such a wonderful gift. He vowed to make his family proud. He'd learn to play that violin so well that he'd make a fine living with it. He'd buy his mother and father all the things they'd never had, he mused, as he cradled the new violin lovingly in his arms. And learn to play he did. In a short time there was nothing more the local farmer could teach him. Ebenezer started composing his own violin solos. He was a popular entertainer at local weddings.

The next winter, when Ebenezer was only fifteen, a serious strain of influenza hit the area. Everyone in the family was very sick, and to Ebenezer's horror, his mother and father died within a few days of each other. Being an only child he had no one to console him. Oh, the neighbors were nice enough, but in a short time they were back to their own concerns, tending their own families. The orphaned boy was all but forgotten. Occasionally one of them would invite Ebenezer for a home-cooked dinner. Other than that the boy was left pretty much on his own.

Ebenezer did odd jobs around the town and kept the cabin neat and clean. He cooked his own meals mostly from the vegetables he grew and the small amount of meat he could afford on his meager earnings. And he played his violin—he played it every spare minute that he had. The cabin seemed so empty without his parents that the boy took to sitting on the railing of the bridge over the stream, playing his fiddle and serenading the animals in the woods, the neighbors, and anyone else who cared to listen. He had few friends.

As the years went by Ebenezer withdrew more and more. Pretty soon it was just him and his fiddle. The young man still missed his family and remembered the wonderfully warm times they'd had before that awful winter. By the time Ebenezer was thirty he was considered strange and was pretty much avoided by the local people. This only added to his loneliness and for solace he played the violin even more. When Ebenezer was about forty-five the local children began taunting him. They'd stand on the bridge, shouting names at him as he played his fiddle and tried to shut out what he now considered the cruel world. Ebenezer lived to be well into his seventies—alone, friendless, and a legend. Some people considered him dangerous (which he wasn't). Others just considered him different, which, by the time he was an old man, he might have been. He longed to talk with the children who made him the butt of their cruelty—to know the solace of some little companionship, but all he had was his fiddle—the violin his parents had sacrificed so much to get for him those many years before.

One day as Ebenezer was balanced on the rail of the bridge playing his violin, a particularly aggressive band of older boys approached him. They screamed the usual insults, and then one nasty teenage boy gave Ebenezer a small shove. To the children's surprise (and probably Ebenezer's dismay) the old man lost his seating on the bridge railing and fell headfirst into the water below, still clutching his violin. The stream was swollen from the spring rains and Ebenezer disappeared. The kids ran off, all vowing not to tell. But the story surfaced about the time Ebenezer's body was discovered facedown on the banks of the stream.

One day a few years later, as a group of young children were crossing the bridge, one of them dropped a penny and it rolled across the bridge and into the water. The children were delighted to hear the strains of a violin coming from the water below the bridge. The music continued for a few minutes, then stopped. The kids went on their way, but like most kids they carried the story home and told of the penny and the violin music to anyone who'd listen. One of the children's parents decided to go to the bridge and throw in a penny to show his son nothing would happen. To the father's surprise, he heard violin music. News of this happening spread like butter on hot bread, and soon many people were visiting the bridge to throw in a coin and listen for the sound of Ebenezer's violin. Visits to the bridge became a popular pastime. Many people felt that the best time to hear the violin music was in the dead of the night. But maybe that just sounded more spooky.

There's one story about a Delaware city couple who were entertaining guests. In order to supply something different for their amusement, the couple held the party at the Scott Run Bridge. They gave each of the guests a supply of pennies to throw into the stream. The people were delighted when lovely violin music came from the stream each time a penny splashed in. Every one of the partygoers heard it (which wasn't always the case with the people who'd been to the bridge before). When the party broke up, the guests agreed it was one of the best times they'd ever had. A few people who knew of the legend and thought the music was just a bit too clear finally questioned the host and hostess. The couple laughingly admitted they'd planted a violinist right under the bridge.

But Scott Run isn't just a hoax for bored socialites; many serious ghost hunters have heard Ebenezer's music as he plays his violin under the Scott Run Bridge. Most people who've been there say all you need is a few coins and a strong belief to hear Ebenezer's fiddle.

DIRECTIONS: *From Wilmington, take Route 13 South past St. Georges, two miles to bridge.*

—JB

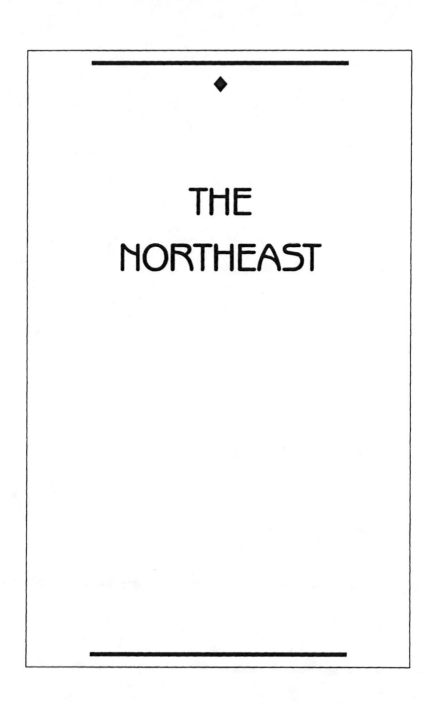

THE
NORTHEAST

WINDOW TO UNKNOWN WORLDS
Chestnut Ridge, Pennsylvania, and West Virginia

The one-hundred-mile-long, two-mile-wide region of the Allegheny Mountain system known as Chestnut Ridge, stretching from West Virginia to southwestern Pennsylvania, is a veritable "twilight zone" of other-worldly phenomena. Some say there are magnetic forces along the ridge that attract unearthly events and beings, that it is a "window" to unknown worlds. Not only is this mountainous expanse a center of Unidentified Flying Object (UFO) sightings, but also the occasional appearance of that shaggy, unsavory creature of lore and legend known as Bigfoot, apparently no stranger to dense woodlands of the area.

As if these phenomena weren't enough, other weird events on the ridge have been reported over the years: unexplained earthshakes and underground sounds, fireballs crashing, strange falls of ice and metallic residues, unusual animal killings, and the appearance of black panthers.

Some UFO experts theorize that conditions on Chestnut Ridge allow a glimpse into alternate worlds or other dimensions. This notion is similar to my theory that haunted landscapes are places that may permit us to step into other dimensions of time. Other UFO authorities believe that something about the ridge itself attracts real, live beings from outer space.

The Pennsylvania Association for the Study of the Unexplained (PASU) was founded in 1981 by Stan Gordon, an electronics technician. PASU is an all-volunteer, nonprofit research unit that investigates strange and unusual occurrences, a clearinghouse for reports of UFO sightings and other phenomena, widely recognized by law-enforcement officials and news agencies. Gordon, who has been studying unexplained phenomena since 1959, is an internationally recognized authority on the subject of UFOs and Bigfoot.

A recent surge of UFO sightings along the ridge began in

August 1987. On numerous occasions, law enforcement officers, reporters, pilots, or other trained observers were among
the witnesses. During 1988, for the first time, there were UFO
cases reported each month "that could not be explained away,"
says Stan Gordon.

This wave of sightings continued into early 1989 and then
decreased. Nevertheless, dedicated people go out to watch for
UFOs on many a clear evening in townships along the ridge.

Not necessarily "flying saucers," some of the ships that have
been seen by multiple witnesses are quite spectacular. For
instance, one of the UFOs reported to PASU in February 1988,
seen by many independent observers over Cambria County (not
on Chestnut Ridge), was likened in size to the Goodyear blimp
and compared to a small cruise ship in the sky, with several
rows of lights along each side.

At this writing, most of the UFO activity on the ridge is
centered around Westmoreland County, in the towns of Ligonier, Latrobe, and Derry. The three other Chestnut Ridge
counties—Fayette and Indiana counties in Pennsylvania, Preston County in West Virginia—have been inundated with sightings at various other times.

Of the 350 UFO reports PASU received in 1988 (and this
figure is constantly increased as previously unreported cases
come to light), the greater percentage can be explained by
naturally occurring events. Some of these might be legitimate
aircraft, planetary activity (such as when Venus and Jupiter
appear side by side, giving a "headlight" effect), meteors, space
debris, weather balloons, kites, unusual atmospheric conditions, and pranks. One creative group of youngsters found a
way to get white plastic rubbish bags to fly by inserting a strip
of lighted birthday candles.

That leaves a troublesome forty percent of the Chestnut
Ridge sightings for which no apparent explanation can be found.

Professor J. Allen Hynek, the elder statesman of UFO studies in this country, says the wave of sightings that began in the
forties is developing a new trend. The appearance of humanoids
is being reported in a growing number of cases. (In some recent
incident near Saltsburg, Pennsylvania, the humanoid was described as four feet tall, with large eyes, a large, long head,
pointed ears, and pincherlike hands.) "The strangeness index
has gone up," Hyneck said in an article by L. Stuart Ditzen that
appeared in *The Columbus Dispatch* (April 7, 1985). It was

Hyneck who coined the phrase "close encounters of the third kind" to describe these visits by alien beings.

The reported ability of UFOs to hover silently and/or accelerate silently at tremendous speeds defies natural explanation, Hyneck said. "In our physical world, we don't have objects that can do those things."

One of the most intriguing reports of a UFO landing in Pennsylvania happened on December 9, 1965. The object's descent was witnessed by literally thousands of observers from Canada through Pennsylvania. It appeared to be an orange fireball leaving a long smoke trail visible for twenty minutes over Michigan and Ohio. Near Detroit, private pilots felt shock waves as it passed and reported that an aircraft must have exploded and was probably going down in Lake Erie. Spewing out flaming debris that started a series of blazes in the states over which it passed, the UFO made a thirty-degree turn between Cleveland and Akron, Ohio, crashing finally in a densely wooded area near Kecksburg, Pennsylvania, at 4:45 P.M.

What followed then was some kind of cover-up by the U.S. Air Force, reminiscent of those we've seen graphically dramatized in science-fiction films. (After living through the eighties, it's no longer paranoia to believe that government officials would withhold the truth of an event from the public.) By 7:30 that evening, air force personnel, with the help of the state police, had cordoned off the area, ejecting volunteer searchers as well as the merely curious who had converged on the crash site to find out exactly what had landed somewhere in those woods. Then the military clamped on a news blackout and imposed martial law.

Late that same night, according to the eyewitness reports, the 662nd Radar Squadron from the Oakdale Army Facility retrieved a large object, which they loaded onto a flatbed truck, concealed under a tarpaulin, and hauled out of the woods.

A nineteen-year-old volunteer fireman, member of the civilian search team that first located the object, described it in a taped interview with Stan Gordon of PASU.

"It plowed a path as it came in at probably a twenty-five- or thirty-degree angle, taking off the tops of trees fifteen or twenty feet high. It didn't make a crater but a trench about seven feet deep at the end, and the unique thing is there was no fire. I was amazed because it was a fireball when it went over. It wasn't hot. There was no steam or vapor, the trees were snapped off but not burned.

"In the ditch was the 'airplane,' or object of the search, but it was totally foreign. There were no wings, glass, fuselage, or rotors; no shrapnel like an explosion. It was round and metal, seven to nine feet wide—at least, the part we could see. I don't know how much was buried. I could easily have stood up in it.

"The metal was an unfamiliar color like tarnished silver or off-color gold. I'm a machinist, and I've never seen metal like it again, either solid or liquid.

"It looked like a deflated beach ball pushed down and crumpled up, and toward the bottom, it had a ring or a bumper eight to ten inches wide, raised up from the surface. This bumper had writing, like ancient Egyptian hieroglyphics—straight lines, dots, different figures—nothing I could understand.

"Nobody wanted to go down into the hole, even though the ground wasn't burned, and we were talking about what to do. I guess it was fifteen to twenty minutes until the first person [went] in . . . a state policeman. Right behind him was a man with no uniform but who reeked of authority. They ordered us out, evacuated the search teams. Military people were coming up the road carrying firearms. Military trucks and state police cars were coming up. They roped off the area. I saw an air force van.

"When we got back to the firehall, the military throwed us out of there. It was wall-to-wall military. They took a house, too [a nearby farmhouse]. A little later a flatbed truck with something big covered in a tarpaulin—it had an escort in front and back with lights flashing—left the area, and it wasn't slowing down for no one."

The family whose farmhouse was commandeered by the U.S. Air Force that night confirmed for Stan Gordon part of the fireman's story. They said that a military truck was driven into the field with something large loaded on the flatbed. Air force officers were observed to be armed and wearing rubber gloves; some men wore decontamination suits. The family was told to say it was a meteorite.

No details were forthcoming the next day for the local paper, *The Greensburg Tribune-Review,* to report. Sometime later, a state police source said the object was a meteorite that broke up in the atmosphere and left no trace. The air force would not confirm that it found anything.

PASU's attempt to follow the paper trail of this event, using the Freedom of Information Act, hasn't turned up much additional information. The *Blue Book* file sums up its report as follows: "The search was called off about 2:00 A.M. and nothing was found." In a document that describes the December 1965 activities for the radar squadron involved, December 9 is blank.

When not being buzzed by UFOs, Chestnut Ridge is enlivened by the emergence of Bigfoot, described as a longhaired, foul-smelling two-legged creature six to eight feet tall with a torso that shows no distinct neck or waist and arms that hang down below its knees. It eyes glow red in the dark, and it likes to hang around trailer parks. The sounds Bigfoot makes have been likened to a bird chirping, a baby crying, or asthmatic wheezing. Pets are liable to be skittish when Bigfoot is lurking about, but then, the shapeless creature makes human beings pretty nervous, too.

The earliest recorded Bigfoot report, a sighting near Indianhead in Fayette County near the ridge, goes back to 1931. This ugly fellow, who bears a familial resemblance to the Abominable Snowman, was glimpsed again in 1972, on a hill that can be seen from the window of the coffee shop in Greensburg's Sheraton hotel. Since then there have been yearly sightings of the creature(s). In 1988, an important year for UFOs over the ridge, there were also twenty-eight reports of Bigfoot encounters.

More than thirty caves have been discovered in the low, wooded mountains of the region, and there are countless stone ledges, hollows, and dells. It's a perfect place for an introverted "missing link" to hide from humankind.

PASU has made many casts of Bigfoot footprints, some showing great detail. Most of these have been three-toed, thirteen to twenty-one inches long. A podiatrist estimated that whatever made some of these tracks would weigh between 450 and 600 pounds. But no one has been able to take a clear photograph of this elusive creature haunting Chestnut Ridge, especially Westmoreland County and areas near Pittsburgh.

Bigfoot is most likely to be seen by hunters and other woodsmen; these witnesses often prefer to remain anonymous for fear of the ridicule of their peers. They feel free to file these sightings with PASU, however, because Stan Gordon guarantees confidentiality to all reporters of Bigfoot and UFO incidents if the witnesses request it.

Fortunately, Sam Sherry, a veteran hunter and fisherman, was not shy about revealing his encounter with Bigfoot. One night, as he was unloading his pickup to go night fishing in Loyalhanna Creek alongside Chestnut Ridge, this weird, hairy, red-eyed fellow approached him and beat its fists on its chest. Bigfoot smelled like a wet dog and looked like a walking overcoat, Sherry said, as it followed him to his vehicle and put its hands on the hood so heavily that the truck sank in the mud. Sherry yelled at the creature, scaring it off into the woods. Now Sherry hopes to encounter Bigfoot again, trap him, and make his point to the scoffers, not to mention a profit.

Bob France would also like to see Bigfoot again. After sighting the shaggy fellow up on the ridge, France now goes looking for him on weekends with a camera in hand and fruit for a lure. Bigfoot is thought to be a vegetarian, except for occasional forays into flocks of domestic geese. France would like to be the first to provide a bona fide photo of the man-beast.

Another witness encountered Bigfoot along a railroad track on the first day of doe-hunting season. An awesome sight, the creature who blocked the man from entering the trailer park where he lives was bigger than a bear and walked upright.

In January 1990 Stan Gordon wrote me that the new year had started off with "a great set of fresh Bigfoot tracks near Ligonier, in the hot Westmoreland County side of the ridge. The tracks were found early on New Year's Day in the snow. They are about fourteen inches long, nine inches wide, and three-toed." Stan sent photos of the tracks, which showed up quite clearly. Since the snow was not deep, the footprints went through to the grass beneath.

Underfoot or overhead, there is still plenty of excitement on Chestnut Ridge. Something about the area seems to make it a hotbed of unexplained phenomena.

Michael J. Klein, who heads a NASA-based project called the Search for Extraterrestrial Intelligence (SETI), has stated that the circumstantial evidence is growing that humankind is not alone in the universe. Most encouraging are the studies showing that comets and cosmic dust particles contain the complex organic compounds that are the chemical precursors of life. Presumably, life could have begun anywhere in the universe where there's a hospitable planet like Earth in a life-sustaining relationship to its sun. Advanced civilizations could be sending out radio signals, and that's just what SETI's engineers are listening for . . . that needle of intelligent sound in the haystack of the heavens. Since this not-inexpensive project is government funded, apparently some officials do give credence to the possibility of alien beings of other worlds.

The question is, are these alien beings so far advanced beyond our own knowledge and capabilities that they have crossed incredible distances into our solar system, in journeys that would take generations to achieve (according to our laws of physics), in order to scout out our planet? Or are these sightings and abductions that sincere people have experienced the result of a window in time, perhaps into our own planetary future, as hauntings may be stepping into the past?

Whatever the explanation, if you want to scan the sky for UFOs, travel along Pennsylvania's Chestnut Ridge and keep your eyes open as well as your camera ready. If you're a hiker or spelunker, there's always the exciting thought that you could meet Bigfoot on the trail. Checking in with Stan Gordon at PASU (see Contacts, page 276) will put you in touch with the county where it's all happening. If the past few years are any indication, the action is sure to be someplace on Chestnut Ridge right now.

DIRECTIONS: *Chestnut Ridge runs between Preston County, West Virginia, through Fayette, Westmoreland, and Indiana counties in southwestern Pennsylvania. The Pennsylvania Turnpike crosses the ridge, going west toward Pittsburgh, at about the midway point. Route 711 runs parallel to the ridge.*

—DR

THE JERSEY DEVIL
Pine Barrens, New Jersey

M any natives of this section of New Jersey are convinced that a creature not of this world resides among them. They call it the Jersey Devil. There are many versions as to how this strange and frightening character came to haunt the area. One of the most-told stories, sent to me by Shawn

Garrett through COUD-I (an organization that collects unusual data), goes this way: Back in 1735 a local couple, Abigaile and Arthur Leeds (the first names change with different renditions), were expecting their first child. They were in their thirties and had about given up hope of ever having a baby when they found out that Abigaile was pregnant. Of course, they were ecstatic. Abigaile took very good care of herself during her pregnancy. The couple had great plans for their child.

One cold evening in October Abigaile went into labor. Her husband rode quickly to summon the doctor. The eagerly awaited moment was approaching. It was a long and painful labor, during which Arthur paced the floor of the living room in the tiny house on the edge of the woods. After what seemed to him like an eternity, Arthur heard a small cry from the couple's bedroom. Relief and excitement filled his being. At last, he was a father.

The exhilaration was short-lived. In a few minutes, the doctor appeared at the bedroom door and gave Arthur the sad news that while his wife would in time recover, the long-awaited baby had lived but minutes.

It was a stormy night. The sky was streaked with lightning and thunder roared, but Arthur Leeds fled from his home out into the deluge, seeking solace he knew not where. As he ran through the night Arthur kept hearing that pitiful cry of his son. It resounded in his head until Arthur thought he was going mad. Suddenly his eyes came to rest on a bush, and he realized the crying wasn't in his mind but came from someone hiding under the foliage. As Arthur looked further, he was greeted by two huge eyes staring out at him. On closer inspection, he found a small creature the likes of which he'd not seen before. It seemed completely helpless.

Arthur was not a cruel man and, realizing that the baby creature would die if left on its own, he scooped it up and carried it back home. Exhausted from her ordeal, Abigaile had fallen asleep. Arthur quietly wrapped the small thing in a dry blanket and put it in the basket that had been intended for their baby.

In the morning, as Arthur tried to comfort Abigaile, there was a cry from the basket. Arthur had forgotten about the strange being he'd left there the night before and started to explain to his wife. But the explanation fell on deaf ears. Abigaile staggered out of bed and walked as fast as her aching body would allow across the room to the basket. She picked up the small, babylike creature and cradled it in her arms. After a day of feeding and caring for it, the Leedses made an unusual decision. They'd keep this tiny bit of life that was sent to them in their darkest hour, and they'd raise it as their own child—the child they knew now that they'd never have.

The creature proved to be a joy to them. It had a sunny disposition and always tried to please. But there was no disguising its unusual looks. This adopted creature they loved had batlike wings, huge, protruding eyes, a wraithlike body with stubby legs, and hands and feet that terminated in claws instead of toes and fingers. The couple vowed they would shelter their charge from other people, keeping it at home, protected from prying eyes at all times. One day, Abigaile and Arthur were outside their house a short way off, picking berries, when two of the town's ladies came calling. Had the Leedses been in the house, they'd have put the creature in another room. But as luck would have it, when the ladies got no answer to their knocking, they pushed open the unlocked door and entered the Leedses' house.

Hearing a cooing sound coming from the basket in the corner of the living room, they tiptoed over to see what the Leedses had there. "It's probably a kitten," one of the women said to the other. They were shocked when they peeked in and saw two huge eyes staring and claws reaching up to them. Piercing screams were followed by cries of "It's the devil's baby," as the ladies ran, tripping over each other, to get out of the house.

Realizing there was a commotion in the house, Abigaile and Arthur hurried inside to see what was happening. To their dismay, their new family member had disappeared, probably frightened off by the hysterical yelps of the nosy neighbors. Though the Leedses searched and searched, they couldn't find the creature who had won their hearts. The years passed, but the couple never recovered from their grief.

In time Arthur died, and a saddened Abigaile made a daily pilgrimage to the cemetery, placing flowers on the graves of her husband and the tiny son she had known for only a brief minute. Abigaile was disturbed by the rumor of a large monster who was said to be roaming around the area; but, although she was apprehensive, she still made the trip to visit her loved ones every day. One stormy afternoon just at dusk, she braved the rains and went to the graves. As Abigaile knelt praying she felt someone's eyes on her. Turning, too numb with terror to scream, she saw the creature she and her husband had taken into their home and hearts. Although it was grown now, she recognized it instantly. And the creature recognized her, too, for it put its wings around her in a comforting gesture.

The story goes that the winged creature visited Abigaile in her home every day from then until her death, and that it still roams the cemetery and the Pinelands in an effort to console the family that had loved it.

Several other versions of the Jersey Devil persist. In one, an American girl was cursed for falling in love with a British soldier and having his baby, which had wings and claws. Then there's the tale of a woman who had twelve children and said that if she had another one she hoped it would be the devil. She was pregnant again within a few months and had twins, neither of which looked human. The mother smothered one, but the other got away. That creature is said to roam the cemetery in New Jersey still.

According to an account of the Jersey Devil carried by the *Asbury Park Press* in October of 1988, a man who lived in Howell Township encountered the Jersey Devil in 1981. He described the creature as having a furry body, huge feet with three toes on each one, large teeth, and standing about six feet tall. He was quoted as saying, "We had ten dogs there, and the dogs would put their tails between their legs and run away. . . . It made some kind of noise like a growl. But it never seemed to hurt anything."

Another gentleman claimed that the Jersey Devil had "killed hogs, sheep, chickens—and once in a while a woman or child."

In addition to roaming the cemetery, this creature has been reported in the Pine Barrens and South Jersey marshes—just about where the coastal area meets the pines. Whether or not there is any validity to this old tale, it does seem certain that some strange being has been seen by a number of people over the years lurking in the Pinelands near Howell Township.

DIRECTIONS: *Howell Township is due west of Asbury Park. Get on Route 33 south of Asbury Park, at Ocean Grove. Follow to Howell Township.*

—JB

LET THERE BE LIGHT

Robert Erskine's Grave
Ringwood Manor Cemetery
Ringwood, New Jersey

Dan and Pauline Campanelli live in a wonderful house, a miniature fairyland in New Jersey. And they share their house, at least their land, with a ghost. These two extraordinary people are artists, writers, and psychics. They are a truly lovely couple, and their house was one of those I wrote about in *Haunted Houses, USA*. When they heard Dolores and I were writing this sequel, Dan and Pauline were quick, to share this haunt and their experience with me.

Robert Erskine was a very important member of the Continental Army. As surveyor-general he was invaluable to George Washington, providing him with accurate maps which made it possible for Washington's troops to be in the right place at the right time—an essential element to winning any war. Erskine served the colonies loyally, meeting with Washington and adding his expertise to that of the other men who helped win our independence. When the war was over, Erskine settled in what is now New Jersey, and he became one of the area's leading industrialists.

Erskine was as successful at business as he'd been at surveying for the country, and soon he had amassed a considerable fortune—enough to make him comfortable for the rest of his days. Robert Erskine was still a young man when he decided to build Ringwood Manor. It was a showplace coveted by many of the local folk. He lived there with his family for the remainder of his life, and then, as he had requested, he was laid to rest in a small cemetery on the grounds of his palatial home. One would think that would be the end of it. But it seems Robert Erskine's sleep is an uneasy one.

Robert didn't seem to be content to stay put. His ghost must have been pushing and pulling on the walls of the vault in which his body was interred, for one night, to everyone's surprise (maybe even Robert's), one of the bricks from which the walls of the vault were constructed gave way. It popped out of its place, falling to the ground with a plop. The ghost of Robert

Erskine followed, and it's been cavorting around the area ever since.

Many of the curious who've visited the cemetery when the moon is full have been disappointed, but many of those brave enough to venture there when the moon is dark and the night inky black have encountered the ghost of Robert Erskine sitting on top of the vault, swinging a lantern in one hand. Some of these visitors have even reported that Robert Erskine, ever the gentleman, has escorted them down the dark road to the old bridge that led them out of the cemetery.

About twenty years ago ghosts and other folklore were high on Dan and Pauline's list of collectibles. They had been gathering these bits of interest for years and had quite a group of them. Eager to share and educate others about the spirit world, the Campanellis started giving talks on the paranormal and the many haunted places that they'd found over the years, sharing their knowledge with their audience. Ringwood Manor was among these places.

One night in the early 1970s Pauline and Dan gave a rousing good lecture to a church youth group in New Jersey. Ringwood Manor and Robert Erskine were major topics. The audience was an interested one, and as Dan and Pauline warmed up to their subjects, they could feel that they had the undivided attention of everyone in the hall. Not that there weren't skeptics. The questions that came after the talk included several from a trio of young men who had serious doubts about the authenticity of what they'd heard. The Campanellis did their best to answer all the queries, but they knew that when they left that night there were still at least three people unconvinced of the existence of ghosts.

Unknown to Pauline and Dan, the three young men made plans to visit Ringwood and see for themselves what, if anything, went on there. It was nearby, and they'd been intrigued by the story. A few nights after the lecture, when the moon was at its darkest, the trio set off for the cemetery. They fully expected to be able to call the Campanellis in the morning, tell them about the experience, and report they'd seen absolutely nothing. However, the phone call they made was quite different from the one they'd planned, and they placed it long before the sun rose.

Pauline said she and Dan had just settled in for the night when the phone rang. Pauline picked it up and heard a frantic voice on the other end babbling almost incoherently. "What's wrong?" Pauline asked the agitated fellow. "Just calm down and tell me slowly."

The young men had piled into a car belonging to one of them, the caller related, and proceeded to the cemetery gate, where they parked the car and walked to the grave. The trio sat around for quite some time, exchanging jokes and confidences as young people do, and waiting for the ghost. Just about the time they were ready to give up and leave the cemetery, one of the boys saw a hazy bluish light hovering just above Robert Erskine's vault. "Look at that!" he commanded his companions in a whisper.

"Look at what?" one of his comrades replied.

"Oh, my . . ." cut in the third young man.

All of them stared at the unmistakable blue light. "There's got to be a logical explanation!" exclaimed the one who'd originally seen the light.

After a few minutes the three screwed up their collective courage and walked around the vault. They looked very carefully on each side of it for a wire that would indicate someone was pulling a prank with a blue electric light. The young men were very thorough, but no wire was to be found. They thought maybe the light was some kind of flashlight operated by batteries, but close inspection showed that the light had no case of any kind—it was just a blob of light.

"Let's get outta here," cried the three almost in unison. They could feel the hair standing up on the napes of their necks by now, and they were all more than a little frightened.

As they ran back toward the car, one of the trio looked back. "Oh, my God, it's following us," he bellowed to his mates. Now they were really petrified. The driver fumbled for his keys as the blue light hovered behind the car, waiting for no one knew what. It seemed like a lifetime before he found the keys, opened the doors, and they all piled in, locking the doors behind them.

As they took off in a cloud of dust, one of the men looked behind and gasped. "It's coming right up to the car." The next thing they knew the blue light was in front of the car. The driver went faster, but no matter how fast he drove the light stayed the same distance from the car. When they slowed down, it slowed down. When they sped up, it sped up. It stayed about ten feet above the ground. Just when it appeared they'd never be rid of the blue light, they came to the main road, and the light vanished just as completely and quickly as it had appeared on the vault.

The fellow on the phone that night wanted Pauline and Dan to tell them what to do. They were sure the blue light was going to appear again and follow them home.

It took Pauline about an hour to calm his fears and convince him to tell his companions that the light was not the manifestation of a malevolent spirit but only that of Robert Erskine, politely escorting his guests through the dark night.

DIRECTIONS: *From I-80, take Route 17 North to Sloatsburg Road. Follow Sloatsburg Road to Ringwood Road. Go west on Ringwood Road to the park entrance.*

—JB

THE STUBBORN GHOST
The Bowery
Manhattan, New York

They say such things and they do such things on the Bowery, the Bowery
I'll never go there any more.

Those who do go to the Bowery may encounter the ghost of Peter Stuyvesant, colonial governor of the New Netherlands, a Dutch colony founded in what is now New York. He was a stubborn old coot. At least by the time he arrived in New Amsterdam he was middle-aged, which was old by the standards of the day. And he had always been stubborn—so stubborn, in fact, his associates had dubbed him Stubborn Pete. He was stubborn when the British, who far outnumbered his men, came to take over the New Netherlands. Perhaps it's his stubbornness that keeps coming back to haunt the Bowery, a section of New York that once teemed with mortal suffering. For the Bowery was named after the house in which Peter

Stuyvesant lived during his years in America—the house in which he died in February 1672. This is his story.

Peter was born in Holland in 1592 to parents of modest means. His father was a minister who preached the gospel, baptized babies, and did anything and everything the oppressive government might ask of him. Little Peter grew up uneventfully then joined the military. He was stationed in the West Indies. Like cream, Peter rose to the top, and soon he was director of the West India Company's colony of Curaçao—a post he held for ten years, from 1634 until 1644. His resignation came quite unexpectedly in 1644 when he led his troops in attacking the island of Saint Martin. Peter took a shot to the calf that was so severe his leg had to be amputated. He wore a wooden leg for the rest of his life. But no ordinary leg was good enough for Peter; his artificial leg was adorned with bands of silver.

In 1645, the West India Company assigned Stuyvesant to be director of the New Netherlands. He was to replace William Kieft, who would remain in a lesser position. Transportation and the wheels of progress moved slowly in those days, and it wasn't until two years later that Peter finally arrived in New Amsterdam, the capital city of the New Netherlands, to take on his new responsibilities. The rumors of his bravery in battle had preceded him, and he was greeted by the settlers with great enthusiasm. In due time they let it be known that they wanted a representative government and were delighted when Stuyvesant agreed. A board of nine people was selected out of eighteen whom the citizens proposed. This board was supposed to confer with Peter and his council. They were to be consulted whenever the council chose to do so about matters in the colony. Of course, the board wasn't summoned very often and when they were, Peter stubbornly refused to act on any of their suggestions.

Peter Stuyvesant was fiercely loyal to the West India Company—this loyalty was not felt by most of the colonists. After Oliver Cromwell died in 1658, Charles II mounted the throne of England. No man hated the Dutch more than this king, who held them responsible for the murder of his father and making Charles beg for money that was rightfully his through the will of his sister. He also detested the new colonies to which many of his tyrannical father's people had fled.

Charles was loose-lipped when in the arms of any of his many mistresses, and no sooner had he decided to punish the colonists in America than he revealed this secret during one of his amorous tête-à-têtes. Alas, his paramour was no more closed-mouthed than the king and quickly passed on his plans, news of which reached the colonies by the time Charles had barely gotten out of the lady's bed. By 1659, it was general knowledge in America that the British were coming.

Peter, who felt he'd done the best he could to give the people of the New Netherlands their way, was surprised and displeased when he found that most of them were pretty apathetic about whether they were ruled by Holland or England. The colonists concluded that they were never going to return to Holland and that the West India Company hadn't exactly been sympathetic to their needs over the years. Maybe, just maybe, the English would have a more ready ear with which to hear their griev-ances. It had been the experience of the good citizens of the New Netherlands that the company was greatly concerned with little things (it insisted on setting the fares on the ferry that ran to Long Island, and it enforced its rule about saloons closing at an early hour). But when it came to big matters (like defense), the colonists were on their own. The West India Company was usually too busy with its own troubles to bother helping the settlers. This disenchantment wasn't shared by Peter Stuyve-sant, who stubbornly supported the company and its wishes.

This was the social and political climate in New Amsterdam in 1664 when four British ships entered the harbor and dropped anchor. Stubborn Pete was unable to accept the fact that his people had lost their loyalty to the company. First he sent messengers running hither and yon, telling the people of the New Netherlands that the British ships were in the harbor and summoning the men to bring their guns and rally in New Amsterdam. He relayed through his messengers that it was vital that they unite to save their homes.

Poor Peter; he waited and waited but only a handful of men appeared. But Peter hadn't gained his nickname for nothing. He planned to defend the New Netherlands with a few willing men. A count of the available men, the available cannons, and the available ammunition was sobering even to our hero. There was enough power to defend their spot in paradise for just about three hours if they were lucky. Richard Nicolle, commander of the British ships, was well armed and had men to spare. Daunted but not defeated, Stuyvesant decided to act as if he had the advantage. The best defense being a good offense,

Peter sent a very strong letter to Nicolle, demanding to know what his intentions were when he anchored four ships in the harbor of a friendly colony.

Nicolle's answer was swift—he had come by order of His Majesty the King of England and his brother the Duke of York. His mission was to reclaim the property that rightfully belonged to the British crown. Of course, Peter had known all along that was what they intended, but he was stalling for time in the hope of getting support.

Stuyvesant then sent a committee of New Amsterdam's leading citizens to go in person and, ever so carefully, question the English about their intentions. They were polite and so were the English, but Nicolle held to his position. The ships, he gently said, were in the harbor to reclaim the property that rightfully belonged to the British throne. He declared firmly but very nicely that he wanted an immediate surrender of the town. When one brave colonist questioned Nicolle as to what right he had to disturb a peaceful nation, he answered that he wasn't about to debate that point and anyone who cared to question his presence had best argue that case before His Majesty the King and that that would be difficult because the king was residing in London. The little band of colonists returned to relay their failure to Peter. Later that day Nicolle dispatched a messenger to Stuyvesant, saying exactly what he had told the committee but adding Nicolle's promise that the colonists' rights would be respected. In his note Nicolle also vowed that anyone who failed to comply with the order to surrender would be dealt with harshly and considered a prisoner of war.

Peter knew his people would give in immediately if they knew they'd be treated well. So he pocketed the letter, determining to have one last try at discouraging the British. Since the enemy didn't seem to be making any great effort to come ashore, Stuyvesant told his people that the British occupation was a temporary one and that with just a little effort on the part of the colonists they could be persuaded to leave. He set his small band of men to looking like they were a large band of men. Right in sight of the ships they started moving guns back and forth and shoring up bulwarks with rocks and earth hauled in wheelbarrows. Although the British were supposed to be terrified, they hardly blinked at all this effort. Then another group of colonists approached Nicolle, this time with a very firm letter from Peter Stuyvesant threatening dire action against the British ships if they didn't leave the harbor. Nicolle probably had a good laugh over that one. But, ever the gentleman, he politely told the weary colonists that they should inform their leader that he had been sent on a mission and he would accomplish the mission. In addition he said that unless the colonists surrendered by Thursday (this was Saturday) he would be forced to open fire on their fort. But, he added, if he saw the white flag of surrender on the walls of the fort, the colonists would find him to be a fair and compassionate man.

If it had been left to Peter, they'd have dug in their heels and fought to the last man, but he knew he'd be fighting alone. The colonists had lost what little spark they'd had. He sent a dispatch to the West India Company that read, "Long Island is lost and Neiuw Amsterdam itself has been called upon to surrender. We have no soldiers, we have no gunpowder, we are short of food. Furthermore, the citizens are completely disheartened. They cannot see that there is the slightest chance of relief in the case of a siege, and if the island falls into the hands of the invaders, they fear for the lives of themselves and their wives and children. It is clearly apparent that this town can't possibly hope to hold out for more than a few days." His letter continued to say that the colonists had come to hate the company and that he really couldn't blame them since "every suggestion for improvement made either by myself or others has been disregarded and goes unanswered." For reasons unknown, this letter never reached Holland.

It was on the eighth of September, 1664—a Monday—when Peter Stuyvesant signed a proclamation that conceded the surrender of the colony he had come to love. This act took place at Fort Amsterdam. It was the last official document signed there. When Peter Stuyvesant was through he held his head high as he marched at the front of a handful of soldiers away from the fort, away from the land that had become home, onto the ship *Gideon*—the ship that would eventually carry him back to Holland.

Stuyvesant's return to his native land wasn't out of choice but out of what he perceived as duty. The British seemed perfectly willing to have him stay in their colony and in fact treated him rather well until he left. But the West India Company needed a scapegoat to save face over the loss of its possession, and Peter Stuyvesant was it. Just before he set sail, the officials who had been thwarted by Peter in their attempt to establish self-rule summoned him to what had been the town hall of New Amsterdam and wished him godspeed.

On this occasion of fond good-byes, the well-wishers presented Stuyvesant with a letter addressed to the West India Company. It explained that Stuyvesant was not responsible for the loss of the colony, that he had, in fact, done all he could to prevent it and in the end had acted in the only way he could. At first the board of directors of the company wasn't disposed to treat Peter with kindness; its members were angry that they'd been made fools of in the eyes of the world. But gradually, as the embarrassment of the loss lessened, the company went on to other problems and left Peter Stuyvesant alone.

He remained in Holland about a year, but all this time he felt a restlessness, a desire to go back to the New World. In 1666 Peter returned to America and came to live at his farm on Manhattan, which he named Bouwerie. He was in his seventies by this time and lived out the remainder of his life enjoying his garden. His active interest in politics seemed to have dissipated, and he was content to listen to what was taking place—not adding his own two cents' worth. In 1672, shortly after his eightieth birthday, Peter Stuyvesant died.

Perhaps he regrets not getting involved in the politics of the area; perhaps he's just too stubborn to give up on life; perhaps he's warning the people who walk the Bowery to get off his land. No one seems to know why Peter still haunts the streets, but there's no doubt that the apparition that appears on the Bowery is Peter Stuyvesant. Who else had a wooden leg adorned with silver bands?

This ghost has been seen by many people—among them sightseers, the poor unfortunates of the area, and the artists, writers, and yuppies who seem to have discovered the Bowery.

DIRECTIONS: *Stuyvesant is buried at St. Mark's-in-the-Bowery at Second Avenue and Tenth Street. You may encounter his ghost there or strolling down Stuyvesant Street to Cooper Square and the head of the Bowery. (The Bowery was originally the road to Governor Stuyvesant's farm.) Look for a fellow with a wooden leg and a broad-brimmed hat.*

—JB

THE GHOST WITH REGARDS FOR BROADWAY
New York, New York

The name of Mathew (with one *t*) B. Brady conjures up images of the pictures he and his associates took during the Civil War. His expertise with a camera and his ability to select and train people to work along with him resulted in photographs that helped the public understand, better than any words ever could have done, the horror and misery of the war that tore our country apart.

But there's more to Mathew Brady's tale than this. Some of the facets of his life may help explain why his ghost is seen on the street that runs in front of the site once occupied by Brady's first studio at Broadway and Fulton Street. The ghost of Mathew Brady reportedly approaches people, usually prosperous-looking young mothers out for a stroll with their babies, and asks if they would like a picture taken—for a fee, of course. As the women start to answer him, usually surprised by his period clothing (as surprised as anyone can be by anything they see on New York streets these days), he vanishes, evaporating into the New York afternoon. There are those people who say the ghost simply can't be that of Brady because it doesn't make sense that this famous photographer from the Civil War would be soliciting business on a New York street. Perhaps they don't know his life story.

Mathew B. Brady was born in Lake George, Warren County, New York, in 1823. He had a love of nature, a feeling for shapes and forms, and even as a child he was drawing pictures to amuse himself. By the time he was sixteen, Brady was quite adept at sketching and painting—so much so that William Page, a well-known artist of the era, took an interest in the boy and chose Brady to study with him. Page was astounded with the progress his pupils made in the first year, and the instructor suggested that Brady study art at the local university. Brady was flattered and had every intention of doing what his mentor suggested. But, when he went to sign up for painting classes, he became involved in a conversation with Samuel F. B. Morse.

The topic of that discourse was the fairly new process of putting images on various materials. The process was called daguerreotype, and it was to become very popular. Morse's enthusiasm for his subject was boundless.

Morse's impact on Brady altered his life. Instead of studying art as he had intended, the boy signed up for courses in the new medium. Mathew Brady was a young man with an imagination. Not content just to snap pictures, he experimented with materials on which to print them. He became a master of composition and very adept at obtaining just the right expressions on the faces of his subjects. Brady was scarcely twenty-one years old when he opened his first studio at Broadway and Fulton Street. In the beginning he took family pictures—shots of parents and children. That may partially explain his return to the area and the fact that he approaches young mothers strolling with their babies.

Shortly after Brady opened his first studio, he entered one of his daguerreotypes in the annual contest sponsored by the American Art Institute in New York. He won a prize in this most prestigious exhibit. The next year, when he was twenty-two, Brady entered another of his daguerreotypes in the contest. This time he walked away with a gold medal in his category. Mathew was pleased, but he wasn't entirely satisfied for, although the gold certainly proclaimed his excellence in his field, it wasn't the top prize in the show—only the top prize in the category in which he had entered. He vowed that the next year he'd be best—and he was. At age twenty-three, he beat out all the other, older, more experienced photographers, and his work took the most coveted award in the American Art Institute show. Mathew Brady was most pleased, but not one to rest on his laurels, he started to investigate ways in which to make his craft more important. One of his first endeavors toward that end was to produce art books with many pictures and a small amount of text explaining them. The idea caught on, and Mathew Brady's books were in demand by society's most sophisticated people.

Over the next fifty years Brady collected pictures of statesmen, politicians, and anyone else of importance. When people made headlines, Mathew Brady made pictures of them. He sold these pictures to people who made lithographs or woodcuts of them to run in the periodicals of the day. In no time at all, the byline "from a daguerreotype by Mathew Brady" became a familiar sight. Things were going so well for the photographer that in 1847 the young man opened a branch of his gallery in Washington. It was an instant success, and from then on presidents and members of their cabinets went to Brady's gallery to have their official portraits done. Staff members who ran the gallery for Brady were well schooled in his ways with a camera and strove, just as the master himself would have, for the perfect expression and the perfect pose.

Brady now offered tinted pictures and daguerreotypes on ivory as well as the conventional black-and-white images, and the public loved them. It was in this climate of acceptance that Mathew Brady opened a school of photography, training young men in the art of using a camera. Many of the most talented of these students ended up working for their instructor. Mathew Brady stood at five feet six inches. He was lean and healthy, a dynamo of energy, and considered quite nice-looking—if not handsome. He was married to Julia, a girl he loved dearly, and his business was flourishing. It would seem he had the world by the tail, but for one thing—Brady's eyesight was failing rapidly. Every few months he went to his doctor and got thicker and stronger glasses. They'd help for a while, but always his vision would dim and he'd return to the doctor for another pair of glasses with stronger lenses. By 1853, when he moved his New York studio to a gallery over a saloon on Broadway, his eyes were so bad he relied on his associates to do most of the camera work.

His new studio was decorated in a style befitting someone who'd attained Brady's degree of success. The walls were adorned with gold wallpaper set off by luxurious, intricately embroidered drapes. The carpets were soft and velvety, and the furnishings were of the finest rosewood. Not only politicians and statesmen frequented this posh picture palace, but the cream of New York society found their way there to be pampered and immortalized on film as only Mathew Brady, or one of his staff, could do. By the time the gallery moved to these posh new quarters, the daguerreotype had been pretty much replaced by the ambrotype. Although Brady's eyesight had failed to the point where he relied heavily on his staff, he had trained them well, and a picture bearing his credit line was still in great demand and commanded a high price.

Brady stayed in his lovely studio over the saloon for about seven years. In 1860 he made his next and last move—still on

Broadway but this time at Tenth. Abraham Lincoln, a fast-rising politician at the time, went to Mathew Brady's new (and even more elegant) gallery to have his portrait done soon after the move to Broadway and Tenth. Brady was a great admirer of Lincoln's, and this was one picture he took himself. He sought with care to get the expression that would portray Lincoln as the kind, intelligent man he thought him to be. The picture was a huge success and was always one of Lincoln's favorites. It was circulated widely during the election. In fact, after he was elected president in 1862 Lincoln made the statement, "Brady and the Cooper Union speech made me president of the United States."

The Civil War caused Brady to rethink his work and what he must have considered his mission in life. Leaving his galleries in New York and Washington in the able hands of his associates, Brady went to see Lincoln in an attempt to persuade the president to allow Brady and a hand-picked few of his associates to go into the war area and onto the battlefields to take pictures that would show people on both sides of the Mason-Dixon Line what hell this war really was. Lincoln listened patiently to what the photographer had to say, then he thought for a few minutes before he gave his answer. "I can let you go to the front," he said. "But I can't in good conscience give you any of the Union's funds to cover your operation." Although Brady had hoped for more, he took the note Lincoln gave him that would give him and his staff entry to the dangerous war areas.

Mathew Brady had amassed over $100,000 from his work as a photographer, and he was willing to spend every cent of it if it would help the people understand what was happening to their country. Brady, poor eyesight and all, was present at many of the Civil War's most bloody battles, dodging bullets and taking the pictures that have become so famous and are synonymous with his name. Although Brady's photographers consisted of twenty separate units that spread out and covered just about every major battle and event in the Civil War, Brady took many of the pictures himself. He was at Bull Run, and the pictures he took at Antietam caused Oliver Wendell Holmes to write in the *Atlantic,* "These terrible mementos of one of the most sanguinary conflicts of the war, we owe to the enterprise of Mr. Brady of New York. Anyone who wishes to know what war is, need only look at the series of illustrations."

Ever aware of what he could and couldn't do with his craft,

Brady taught his associates to bypass the real action shots because the events happened too fast for the film of the day to record. Instead they filmed the fear that was part of the anticipation of a battle and the aftermath of the bloody confrontations, the mangled, mutilated bodies—bodies of sons and husbands, bodies of men whose lives had been ended, who would never grow old with the people they loved because of this terrible war that had turned our countrymen against each other. Brady's photographs depicted the suffering on both sides. He hoped to show people that whether a man wore a gray uniform or a blue uniform his dead body was a terrible and regrettable sight.

After the South surrendered and during the time when the Union troops were disbanding, wearily making their ways home to pick up the pieces of the lives they'd abandoned to protect their ideals, Mathew Brady went to see the defeated Robert E. Lee. One would think, after all the blood that had been shed and after his defeat, Lee wouldn't be eager to talk with the photographer from the North. But Lee found Brady to be a compassionate man. So much so that he allowed the photographer to take a picture of him. It was one of Brady's personal favorites, that portrait of Robert E. Lee, his son, and his aide, standing on the porch of the Lee home in Richmond, Virginia. It showed in it all the courage of the man, all the anguish of his defeat, and his sorrow for the many men he'd seen die.

Brady had to pay the men who worked with him during the war. He'd needed the supplies with which to take the pictures, and it all added up to a great deal of money. By war's end, Mathew Brady had spent all of his $100,000 on his Civil War project and had charged over $25,000 in supplies. Although he'd sold hundreds of his pictures to the press and had literally thousands more negatives, the costs far surpassed the profits, and Mathew Brady found himself wiped out financially. After the war Mathew Brady returned to New York and to his financial problems. The people who'd run the gallery for him during his absence had done an admirable job, but the business still hadn't shown nearly the profit to which Brady had become accustomed. And he still owed that $25,000 for supplies. Understandably, his suppliers became reluctant to extend him any more credit.

Brady, not one to lie down and accept defeat, looked around for ways to pay off his debts and get his business back on solid footing. But bad luck in the 1800s, like bad luck in the 1900s, arrived in bunches. Mathew Brady's wife, Julia, became extremely ill about this time, requiring his almost undivided attention and piling up a sizable amount in doctor and hospital bills. Brady had little choice; he was forced to sell the studio in New York and several other pieces of real estate he'd acquired during his golden days.

There were thousands of negatives from Brady's Civil War pictures stored in a warehouse in Washington that he leased from the government. Because of his severe financial and personal problems, Brady got behind in his rent. The War Department, with complete disregard for the contribution that Mathew Brady had made during the Civil War, confiscated the negatives. It was a good swap for the government, and the War Department knew it. They'd acquired over six thousand negatives valued at around $150,000. Fortunately, there were people who remembered Brady and how hard he'd worked to help the people of the country understand the war. General Benjamin Butler and General James Garfield knew that an injustice was being done, and they bucked the powers who ran the War Department on Mathew Brady's behalf. At first their pleas went unheeded, but finally, in an effort to get the pair of determined generals off their backs, the thieving government officials agreed to pay Mathew Brady $25,000. Though it was far less than he should have received, the money came at a most welcome time. (James Garfield, of course, went on to become president of the United States.) By the time Brady got his hands on the $25,000, his wife was suffering terribly. The money barely covered Brady's bills for supplies, his wife's hospital bills, and the cost of the funeral—for Julia died soon after Brady received the cash.

Mathew Brady, once the photographer of statesmen and the elite of New York; Mathew Brady, the man who gave to his country in the best way he possibly could during the Civil War; Mathew Brady, who had had it all, was financially ruined, almost totally blind, and all alone by 1874. A nephew finally took him into his home and cared for him for about two years.

Brady loved to walk the streets of New York, to smell the city odors—different with each season—to feel the cold winds on his cheeks in the winter and the warmth of the sun on his face in the summer. He spent these hours reminiscing about the good times, about his successful business, about his wife.

He knew the city well, and his nephew thought it best to let him wander as he wished. One day, as Mathew Brady walked up the street toward his nephew's house after enjoying a turn in the nearby park, he lost his sense of direction. As he stumbled off the curb, a car drove around the corner of the street and ran into him. Brady was rushed to the hospital, and it looked for a while as if he wouldn't recover. But Brady was a fighter, and little by little he regained his health until he was strong enough to return to his nephew's home.

Not one to lie around feeling sorry for himself, Brady began to plan an exhibit of his war photos. He was pleased with the way things were going, and then one morning just two weeks before the exhibition was scheduled to open, Brady's nephew went to wake his uncle and found that the famous photographer had died in his sleep. The exhibit opened on schedule and enjoyed great critical acclaim.

Mathew Brady was given the burial he deserved. His body rests in Arlington National Cemetery among those other heroes of the Civil War. His body rests there, but his spirit is often seen on Broadway at Fulton, asking a young mother if she'd like to have a picture taken. Perhaps he's returning to a place in which he knew happiness, trying to recreate that wonderful time when he and his craft both were young. The spirit of Mathew Brady doesn't appear to be in pain, as so many spirits do; he just walks along Broadway, holding his camera, trying to ply the trade he loved so much and at which he was so very good.

DIRECTIONS: *Follow Broadway through Greenwich Village, just past the Civil Center (on left)), to Fulton Street. St. Paul's Chapel, which was built between 1764 and 1766, stands on one corner of Broadway and Fulton Street.*

—JB

THE GHOST AT FORT TICONDEROGA

Ticonderoga, New York

Inverawe! Inverawe!
Where art thou, Inverawe?
I wait at Ticonderoga.

Being of Scottish descent, I was intrigued to hear that we have a clansman's ghost right here in the United States. The spirit has lingered for over two centuries at Fort Ticonderoga, waiting for revenge on a man who is long dead. In a way it's a sad tale because it involves two good men who should have been friends but became mortal enemies as a result of circumstances they couldn't control.

"Here lies the body of Duncan Campbell of Inverawe, Esqre., Major to the Highland Regiment, aged 55 years, who died of wounds he received in the Attack of the Retrenchment of Ticonderoga or Carrillon, on the 17th of July, 1758." That's how the tombstone on a grave at Union Cemetery, Fort Edwards, New York, reads. There's quite a story behind those words. The man whose mortal remains lie beneath the stone was caught up in a moral dilemma that resulted in his death and the haunting of Fort Ticonderoga by a spirit who still roams the fort on stormy nights, clad in a tartan stained with blood. The ghost is looking for Duncan Campbell, the man he vowed to kill at Fort Ticonderoga. As he stumbles along the walls of the fort, this revenant can be heard to scream in a voice filled with pain and in such a roar that it can be made out over the wailing of the storm, "Inverawe! Inverawe! Where art thou, Inverawe? I wait at Ticonderoga."

The beginning of this saga of betrayal involves two decent men, both named Campbell. In the year 1742 one Donald Campbell of Lorn was involved in the overthrow of Prince Charles Edward of Scotland. The other, Duncan Campbell of Inverawe, commanded a regiment of the Black Watch that had been ordered to prevent the Prince's involuntary surrender of the crown. It's unclear whether Donald and Duncan were cousins, brother's, stepbrothers, or what the blood relationship was, but it seems certain that one did exist. The unhappy story began on the west coast of Scotland in a town called Argyle-

231

shire. One night, after Duncan Campbell and his regiment had spent the day burning the homes and properties of those people in the district of Lorn who were suspected of being part of the insurgence, he became separated from his men. Unfamiliar with the area, he managed to get himself hopelessly lost.

The terrain was rocky and Duncan was hungry and exhausted, when he was met on a narrow path by a band of men. One of them stepped to the front, saying, "What are you doing here, Inverawe?" (It was the custom in Scotland to call a man who was a leader in his town by the name of that town.) "Have you lost your way?"

Duncan Campbell was surprised to be known by this stranger, and he was more than a little apprehensive as he asked, "How do you know who I am?"

"No matter how I know," came the reply. "I do know and I also know that you're a brave man, the type of man I can respect. I will do you no harm. Is there a way I can be of service to you?"

"I am hungry and I would like to rest and then get back to the road where I left my men and on my way to Inverawe."

"Follow me then," said the stranger. It was a long, steep climb over the rocky hills and through prickly bushes, but at last they came to a cave. The stranger provided Duncan with a meal and let him rest. Then, as the man was about to lead Duncan to the road to Inverawe, he said, "You were the leader of the regiment that burned my home today, but you are also a Campbell. I know that these things happen in war, and I hold no personal hatred of you. We are Campbells, and I have no wish to kill or injure a Campbell. What I would hope to get in return for sparing your life is a commitment that should you ever have the chance to help me if the fates conspire against me, you will do so—that you will be as good a friend to me as I have been to you this night."

Duncan Campbell swore he would always be ready to help his rescuer and that should their paths cross again, he would greet him as a friend. Donald Campbell led Duncan back through the thickets, down the rocky path to a road that Duncan knew and from where he could find his regiment and make his way back to Inverawe. The two parted with a firm handshake.

In time the Black Watch disbanded and the members returned to their respective homes. Years passed. Duncan's castle at Inverawe became a place for parties and other social gatherings.

Many of the men and women who attended these functions were virtual strangers to Duncan Campbell, but he and his lovely wife were known as great hosts. One night, after much revelry at home, Duncan of Inverawe retired to his bedchamber. His wife had her own rooms in the castle, as was often the case in those days, and he was alone.

Duncan had scarcely settled into bed when he heard a creaking on the stairs. In a moment he realized that he was hearing the unmistakable sound of someone trying to climb the stairs without being detected. Before Duncan could reach the door of his bedroom it was flung open, and a wild-eyed man in tattered clothes entered the room. Duncan was alarmed, not only by the man's appearance but by the bloody dagger he had clutched in his right hand. "Don't be frightened," implored the man. "Don't you recognize me? I was one of the guests at your party tonight. On the way home I encountered a man, a robber I thought, and I killed him. His friends are after me. Please, I beg of you, hide me. They will be here in a short time. Please swear you'll help me."

He no sooner had the words out of his mouth than there was again a noise on the stairs. As Duncan Campbell pushed the man into a secret compartment in the floor, he said, "I'll help you. I swear by the oath of Cruachan."

"Where is the murderer?" came a roar as a trio of men burst into Duncan Campbell's room.

"I have murdered no one, sir," replied Duncan of Inverawe. "Quite the contrary, what are you assassins doing in my bedchamber in the middle of the night? I will fight you to my death."

One of the men stepped forward and answered in a lower tone of voice, "We have no quarrel with you, sir, but we have a reason to believe that one Stewart of Appin is hiding in your castle. He was seen lurking around here not an hour ago. This Stewart jumped brave Donald Campbell of Lorn and plunged a dagger into him until the Lorn was dead."

Duncan Campbell was stunned. What had he done? He'd given his most sacred oath, the oath of Ben Cruachan, to the murderer of Donald Campbell, the man to whom he owed so much. He'd sworn to help Donald Campbell if ever the opportunity arose, but he'd not given the oath of Cruachan as he'd done in haste to the other man. For the oath of Cruachan was the oath of Inverawe, and it meant that no matter what a person did or had done—though you might disagree with him entirely—if you had given him that oath you must welcome him into your home, make him comfortable by your hearth, and make his enemies your enemies. Duncan Campbell was a moral man. He knew that he must keep faith with the oath of Cruachan and the terrible man to whom he had given it. Telling lies he regretted as they came from his mouth, Duncan assured the trio that no Stewart had entered his castle that night—they were mistaken.

Duncan was in a bad spot. In no way did he want the murderer of his savior, friend, and relative Donald Campbell in his home. But he'd taken the most sacred Campbell oath. So he feigned concern and offered to help Donald Campbell's compatriots find the killer. In a pretense of doing so, Duncan let the three men away from his castle, away from the murderer.

When he returned home he found a cowering, sniveling man begging him for assistance. Although Duncan was acutely aware of the oath he had taken, he simply didn't feel he could allow this assassin to remain in the castle at Inverawe. He told Appin he'd lead him to a nearby cave, where the man could hide out until the searchers gave up and went about their business. The path to the cave was steep and hazardous, and the two men carried lanterns to light the way. Duncan left Appin with food and one of the lanterns, which he cautioned him to light only if it was absolutely necessary. Although he was finding his new companion increasingly distasteful, Duncan promised to return the next night with more food.

It was extremely late indeed when Duncan Campbell finally lay on his bed to sleep. But sleep was to elude our hero that night, for no sooner did his eyes close than he sensed something was wrong. Peering out from his bed, Duncan saw that the room was filled with a dull blue light. He was chilled to the bone when he detected a human form stealthily approaching the bed. On closer inspection, he was more than a little startled to see that the form belonged to none other than Donald Campbell of Lorn. Donald's face was pale and he was clutching a gray tartan around his shoulders. As the apparition approached the side of the bed, he flung back the tartan, revealing a dagger wound penetrating his heart. The blood was still flowing from the gash made by his assailant.

The ghost had few words for Duncan, but those few words were meant to remind him of his vow of friendship those many years ago. "Inverawe! Blood must flow for blood! Shield not the murderer!" cried the ghost of Donald Campbell before it faded and disappeared, taking the blue light with it.

There was no sleep for the weary Duncan Campbell after that. He arose and walked around the dark room, trying to convince himself that what he'd seen was just a figment of his imagination or a bad dream. In the morning, Inverawe attempted to go about his usual tasks, but thoughts of the apparition of the night before kept getting in the way. "Am I losing my mind?" he asked himself.

Good to his word and his oath of Cruachan, a few hours after nightfall Duncan Campbell packed a basket of food and made his way to the cave where the murderer hid. To his surprise, as he approached the cave he could see the lantern burning brightly. "You will be found if you do not put out your lantern!" scolded the man's rescuer.

"Aye, it matters not. I cannot stay without the light. Every time I turned it down, I was visited from the beyond by strange creatures, threatening my very life."

Duncan was even more disgusted with the man than he had been the previous night, and again he sorely regretted his vow of Cruachan. "If you burn the lamp, you do so at your own risk," he said, leaving the man and returning to his castle for what he hoped would be a much-needed sleep.

For a few hours it seemed he would get his wish; the Inverawe slept soundly. Then suddenly he was startled into wakefulness by the same apparition who had visited the night before. It was obvious that this time Donald Campbell was much angrier than he'd been on his previous visit. This time he expressed his ire at having been defied by Duncan and implored him to think before he helped the murderer again. He cautioned Inverawe that though he had tried to overlook this hostile action, if it happened again it would not be forgiven. As Duncan Campbell sat up searching for the right words to say to the ghost, it disappeared again. There was no further sleep for Duncan that night. He regretted deeply having given the oath of Cruachan to the cowardly man he found so offensive. But give it he had and he could see no way out without sullying the reputation of the Campbells of Inverawe.

The next day was more difficult than the day before had been. Night finally came, and again he filled a basket with food and climbed to the cave. Again he noticed that the lantern was burning brightly, again he warned the fugitive that he was making it easier for a search party to find him. The man was looking much the worse for wear. He muttered about the demons that plagued him every time he turned off the lantern. Inverawe tried to convince the haggard man to give him the lantern, but the murderer clung to it as if his life depended on keeping it lit. Duncan left after asserting he'd take no responsibility for what happened to the man because of the lamp.

That night Duncan Campbell bolted the door to his bedroom and locked his windows. But his head lay uneasy as he anticipated the visit from his savior turned tormentor. Just as Duncan thought he might have foiled the intruder, the bluish light appeared and a disturbed apparition materialized. This time Donald Campbell's ghost roared with great fervor. "Inverawe! My warnings have been in vain. The time is now passed. Yet blood must flow for blood! The blood of the murderer might have been offered up. Now your blood must flow for his! We meet once more at Ticonderoga!" Then the apparition disappeared, never to return again.

The next night, when Duncan Campbell visited the cave, he found the blanket and the lantern he'd given the assassin, but there was no sign of the man. Obviously he'd been found and dealt with.

As time went on, Duncan Campbell almost forgot the prophecy of the ghost of Donald Campbell of Lorn. He once again knew restful nights. He rarely thought about Ticonderoga—a place of which he'd never heard.

In the mid-1700s the Black Watch was again called to service. War was raging between France and England over land in the New World. Inverawe was made a major of the 42nd regiment and sent with his men to Albany, New York. The men often sat around talking to fill the hours until they were called to battle. One night the subject of ghosts came up. Duncan Campbell paled. Colonel Francis Grant, Duncan's superior officer, was quick to notice the change and asked Inverawe if indeed he had seen a ghost. The man answered that he couldn't see one then, but that he had seen an apparition and was fated to see him again. At that point Duncan related the story to Grant and, according to legend, Grant wrote it in his diary.

A few days later the brigade left, advancing to St. George. They were going to march on Fort Carillon. The troops hid out around the area waiting for the order to attack. During this time, while Inverawe was walking along the banks of a river, he came upon a figure clad in gray tartan. The man flung back the plaid that he had clutched to his chest, revealing a stab wound streaming blood. Duncan knew that the hour for his death was approaching.

On questioning Grant, Inverawe found that the town known as Carillon had another name—it was also called "Ticonderoga."

A total of 1,100 English attacked the fort. They fought bravely for hours, but the French far outnumbered them, and when the battle ended 306 English were dead and 316 injured. Inverawe was among the wounded. When Grant came upon him he tried to assure his friend that all would be well and he would recover from his wounds. But Duncan Campbell knew better. It was plain to him that, though his wounds seemed superficial, this was the end. He told Grant that this Ticonderoga was the Ticonderoga about which he'd been warned.

The wounded, including Duncan Campbell, were moved to nearby Fort Edward, where Campbell quickly developed an infection. After lingering in torment for a few days, he died. Duncan Campbell was interred in the State Street Cemetery in Fort Edward. After a few years his body was moved to the Union Cemetery and buried there beside Alexander Gilchrist, who had claimed kinship with the Campbells of Inverawe. The body was moved one more time but still kept in the Union Cemetery atop a hill in Fort Edward.

But the ghost of poor old Donald Campbell, knowing that Inverawe hadn't been killed at Ticonderoga as was to be his fate, evidently didn't learn of his later demise from the wounds. Donald Campbell of Lorn still roams the halls of Fort Ticonderoga, seeking the vengeance he feels is his due and crying out into the stormy nights to anyone who'll listen, "Inverawe! Inverawe! Where art thou, Inverawe? I wait at Ticonderoga."

DIRECTIONS: *From I 87 take Route 74 East about 25 miles to the fort.*

—JB

LEPKES AT EASTON CEMETERY
Easton, Connecticut

I t was in an article on the front page of the *The Wall Street Journal* (a newspaper that is not given to supernatural flights of fancy) that I first learned about the Warrens, founders of the New England Society for Psychic Research. Ed Warren, whose business card identifies him as a demonologist, uses the medium of art to paint his impressions of haunted scenes; his wife, Lorraine, is a clairvoyant. This Connecticut couple is high on the list of America's best-known ghostbusters. The Warrens have been lecturing for over twenty years on the college circuit and have taught classes in demonology and paranormalology at Southern Connecticut State University. (I can't help but reflect that university curricula have loosened up a bit since I was of college age.)

As seekers of the supernatural, the Warrens have investigated literally thousands of hauntings and other paranormal phenomena. Ed has been present at more than two hundred exorcisms, a term that the public hardly knew until the advent of *The Exorcist* and *The Amityville Horror,* and he was one of the few people authorized to examine the original files on which *The Exorcist* was based. The Warrens also were chief investigators of the celebrated Amityville case, which they say was not a hoax but a terrible reality. Their experiences have convinced them "beyond a shadow of a doubt" of the reality of ghosts and demons.

It was Ed who first introduced me to the word *lepke*, which he tells me is the correct term for a ghost that manifests outdoors. Although I was unable to find *lepke* in any dictionary or encyclopedia, I'm inclined to take this new term on faith, because Ed really knows his ghosts. And Ed says that a number of people have reported to him that there are lepkes at Easton Cemetery.

These particular ghosts at Easton Cemetery are not your run-of-the-mill wispy apparitions that trail through moonlit paths at midnight but spirits that show up in broad daylight and who look and talk for all the world like flesh-and-blood, living people. Their clothes may look a bit old-fashioned, but they can hold a sensible conversation with anyone who happens to be visiting the cemetery. The only giveaway is their penchant for mysterious disappearance.

Ed Warren had been hearing these reports about Easton Cemetery for some time but had never encountered the apparitions himself. Then a curious thing happened, which he related to me.

The Warrens had a friend named Ethel Whittaker, who was a psychic photographer. Ethel passed away after a long illness, the last part of which she spent in a coma.

About ten months ago, Edward went out to Easton Cemetery to photograph some ghost impressions. These phenomena, he explained to me, are the faces that occasionally appear on gravestones, usually formed by the growth of lichen. He was there taking pictures around noontime when a well-dressed older woman wearing sunglasses joined him in the deserted cemetery. Ed was immediately struck with her resemblance to his deceased friend Ethel Whittaker.

"Taking pictures of ghosts?" she asked him with friendly interest.

Ed said that he was, and apologized for the rough clothes he was wearing. "I look like a bum," he said jokingly. Meanwhile, he was glancing around to see how the woman, who was wearing high heels, not hiking shoes, had arrived at the cemetery, but there was no car other than his own in sight.

"That's what you always look like," said the woman, which was exactly the kind of remark that Ethel used to make. After conversing with the Ethel look-alike for fifteen to twenty minutes, Ed asked her where she lived, but she was rather vague in her reply. Then he asked her how she had come there, and she pointed down across the fields to where there was a stand of trees, saying that her car was parked on a dirt road in back of the trees.

"I have to go home now and make dinner for my husband," the woman said finally. By now Ed had an inkling that there was something unusual about this encounter, and he asked if he could take the woman's picture. She agreed, and he persuaded her to remove her sunglasses for the photo. There was no doubt that she could have been Ethel Whittaker's twin. All the time this uncanny resemblance was going through Ed's mind, he was also wondering how a woman in high heels was going to walk over those fields, with stone walls and some barbed-wire fences, to get to her car.

After he had taken the woman's picture, Ed busied himself taking others and became absorbed in his work. When he looked up, the woman was far across the field near the trees. Ed even ran around by the paved road to see if there really was a car parked out of sight there, but he didn't see any kind of vehicle.

When he got home, Ed told Lorraine about this strange meeting in the cemetery, and she said he ought to have that roll of film developed without delay. Neither one of them was quite sure that the woman's likeness would appear, but it did. They took the photo to Ethel Whittaker's husband, and he broke down and cried when he saw the picture, convinced it was Ethel whom Ed had met at the Easton Cemetery.

Most apparitions are transparent and prefer to lurk in the shadows. Often, they are only glimpsed from the corner of one's eye, giving a jolt to the heart, before they disappear. If they speak at all, they seem to be doing so in another time frame, not addressing those living in the present. So it's a rare thing indeed for there to be a place where ghosts, or lepkes, appear to be as lifelike as you and I, not to mention articulate. But the ghosts encountered at Easton Cemetery seem to have stepped solidly into our own reality.

If you enjoy visiting haunted cemeteries, as we do, you may want to check out the one in Easton. And don't take the presence of other visitors there for granted—they just may be lepkes.

DIRECTIONS: *Easton is on Route 136 in southwest Connecticut. Easton Cemetery is located near the Easton Baptist Chruch on Route 59 in Easton.*

—DR

THE FIERY SPECTER OF THE PALATINE
Block Island, Rhode Island

Down swooped the wreckers, like birds of prey
Tearing the heart of the ship away,
And the dead had never a word to say. . . .

In their cruel hearts, as they homeward sped,
"The sea and the rocks are dumb," they said:
"There'll be no reckoning with the dead."
  —*The Palatine,*
  JOHN GREENLEAF WHITTIER

It was two days after Christmas in 1738 when the *Princess Augusta,* out of Rotterdam and bound for Philadelphia, went aground at Sandy Point on Block Island and fell into the hands of waiting salvagers. On the map, the island looks like an inverted pork chop. It's only six miles long, with the high cliffs being a meaty expanse to the south and the low land jutting like a sharp bone at Sandy Point to the north.

Details of the nightmarish voyage of the *Princess Augusta,* popularly known as the *Palatine,* are still in dispute. The appalling events following the shipwreck, as told in Whittier's poem, are hotly denied by Block Island natives, some of whom are descendants of the original settlers.

"In regard to the poem 'Palatine,' Whittier wrote later, "I can only say that I did not intend to misrepresent the facts of history. I wrote it after receiving a letter from Mr. Hazard of Block Island, from which I certainly inferred that the ship was pillaged by the islanders. He mentioned that one of the crew, to save himself, clung to the boat of the wreckers, who cut his hand off with a sword. . . . Mr. Hazard is a gentleman of character and veracity, and I have no doubt he gave the version of the story as he had heard it."

Whatever the truth behind this hearsay report, ever since that freezing night in December when the *Princess Augusta* went aground, a phenomenon known as the Palatine Light has been seen off the coast of picturesque, wind-sculptured Block Island, a burgeoning art colony in recent years. The specter begins as a point of light dancing on the waves, grows into a blaze, increasing in size until it assumes the proportions of a

241

three-masted ship—a ship made of fire—sailing back and forth
along Sandy Point Beach, scene of the tragedy. Sailors have
sworn that this specter came so close to their own ship they
could make outmasts, rigging, and even passengers.

> *Now low and dim, now clear and higher,*
> *Leaps up the terrible Ghost of Fire,*
> *Then, slowly sinking, the flames expire,*
>
> *And wise Sound skippers, though skies be fine,*
> *Reef their sails when they see the sign*
> *Of the blazing wreck of the Palatine!*
> —*The Palatine,*
> JOHN GREENLEAF WHITTIER

The three streams of fire forming the masts and the details
that appear to be passengers make this apparition look like a
sailing ship rather than like the phenomenon known as St.
Elmo's fire. The latter is the popular name of an electrical
discharge that sometimes occurs on the ocean during thunder-
storms, named after sailors' patron saint, Elmo.

I first learned of the intriguing Palatine legend in an article by
Tom Drury called "Clandestine Actions," which appeared in the
Providence Journal Sunday Magazine, August 6, 1989. After
further research, I discovered that no two accounts agreed on
the nature and cause of this strange apparition. This then, is
the story of the last voyage of the *Princess Augusta,* with its
conflicting suppositions and my own conclusions.

In addition to captain and crew, the ship set out in August
1738 with 340 German emigrants from the Palatinate district
west of the Rhine. These hardworking, hopeful families had
packed up all their worldly possessions and ventured forth to
settle in the New World. But the Atlantic Ocean threw every
dirty trick in its book at the *Princess Augusta,* and the voyage
was plagued by stormy misadventure. Time after time the ship
veered off course and as winter approached, still had not
reached Philadelphia. Sometime during the intervening months,
the captain died (some say he was murdered), and the crew
began to prey upon the passengers. Many cruel tales are told
of the passengers' plight, of which we can never be sure, but
one fact emerges. When the *Princess Augusta* went aground in
December, there was in its hold "15,000 weight of bread"—yet
a number of the passengers had already died of starvation and
others were seriously weakened. One imagines that the emigrants had run out of whatever provisions they brought with

them and been forced to pay inflated prices for food from the ship's store. Those without a hoard of valuables to barter for bread had starved.

In those years, Block Island natives earned their living from farming, fishing, and salvage. The latter was no small part of their income. Tides and currents are treacherous around what some mariners call Stumbling-block Island—and it's been estimated that the southern coast of Rhode Island from Westerly out to Block Island may be one of the largest marine graveyards on the Atlantic coast.

Some accounts, including Whittier's, have suggested that the floundering *Princess Augusta* was led astray with false lights. But the wreck-strewn history of the island—not to mention the raging weather of the night in question—suggests that no nefarious assistance was needed to cause the grounding. It was snowing so heavily that the crew couldn't see the water in front of them. Suddenly the acting captain saw some great mass like a dark gray cloud loom up in front of him. The order he shouted to veer hard to port was already too late.

After the grounding the ship was still in one piece on Sandy Point. More than a hundred of the German emigrants, called Palatines, made it to shore. In their pitiful condition, two women froze right there on the beach. Twenty more shipwreck victims died later and are buried on the island.

The survivors must have been cared for by islanders. "Most of them" one early account reads, "were carried to the house[s] of Edward Sands . . . and Simon Ray. . . . Many of these passengers, weakened by starvation and disease, soon died and were buried on a little spot west of the house of Wm. P. Lewis, Esq., and their graves, without a fence, or a name, though of late too closely approached by the plowshare, still remind us of the ship *Palatine.*" The graves still exist in the southwest corner of the island.

The evidence indicates, however, that the overwhelming concern of the islanders, from the moment the *Princess Augusta* crashed onto their shore, was more for the cargo than the victims. The townspeople who rushed to Sandy Beach kept urging the acting captain to let them take the cargo off, but he refused for three days. Since he'd also ordered his crew to uncable the anchor, on the fourth day the ship drifted free and was smashed on the rocks of the island's west side. Now the cargo—including the possessions, gold, and jewelry of the

Palatines—was in imminent danger of being lost. The islanders went immediately into action, apparently looting as much of the cargo as they could get their hands on. Only when the governor of Rhode Island, alerted by two of the island's officers, sent his men to seize all goods and preserve them for the owners was part of this cargo recovered. But the salvagers were still allowed to claim a one-third share. As if that weren't enough, some of the goods were used to defray the Palatines' expenses, meaning whatever the islanders were charging to house and feed them. The pitiful remainder was divided up among the survivors.

The historical accounts don't say what became of these impoverished people after that. We do know that only one of the Palatines chose to make her home on Block Island. Distinguished by her unusual height and known as Long Kate, she married a slave belonging to Nathaniel Littlefield and bore him three children, named Cradle, Mary, and Jenny. In her later years she gained a reputation among the islanders of being a witch, since she told fortunes and sometimes went into trances, during which she claimed she traveled back to her home west of the Rhine.

Some of the *Princess Augusta's* fittings were made of a hard wood called lignum vitae, which the islanders found useful for fashioning into mortars and pestles, although the task was not an easy one. The tough wood had to be bored full of holes, over which a heated cannon ball was placed to burn out the desired cavity. It is said that the heirs who inherited these pieces found that they shared a peculiar charcteristic—at midnight, they would dance around the room of their own volition.

Apparitions have been reported in the southwest end of the island, one of which is a woman in a white dress who holds a clock in her arms. Perhaps she is a Palatine woman still trying to save a family treasure.

The legend that the islanders set the *Princess Augusta* on fire—or that a woman and child were trapped on board and perished screaming in the flames—probably is not true, since the motivation was clearly to salvage, not destroy, the valuables on board. One report does state that a woman passenger refused to leave the ship, but most accounts deny that the ship was burned. The legend persists largely because the north coast of Block Island is indeed haunted by a ship of fire.

One eyewitness to the phenomenon, Dr. Aaron C. Willey, described it vividly in a letter dated 1811. "This curious irradiative rises from the ocean near the northern point of the Island. Its appearance is nothing different from a blaze of fire. . . . Sometimes it is small, resembling the light through a distant window, at others expanding to the highness of a ship with all her canvas spread. When large it displays a pyramidical form, or three constant streams . . . somewhat blended together at the bottom but separate and distant at the top, while the middle one rises higher than the other two. . . . The duration . . . is not commonly more than two or three minutes. . . . It is seen at all seasons of the year, and for the most part in the calm weather which precedes an easterly or southerly storm. . . .

"This blaze actually emits luminous rays. A gentleman whose house is situated near the sea, informs me that he has known it to illuminate considerably the wall of his room through the windows. This happens only when the light is within a half mile of the shore, for it is often seen blazing at six or seven miles distant, and strangers suppose it to be a vessel on fire."

I can't close this story, with the questions it raises about the eighteenth-century Block Island salvagers, without noting that 8,719 gold medals for extreme heroism were awarded by the Carnegie Foundation to Block Islanders between 1904 and 1947, for the many occasions on which they distinguished themselves in rescue work when ships were in danger off their shores.

DIRECTIONS: *Block Island is reached by ferry from Galilee, Rhode Island, or New London, Connecticut. A schedule may be obtained from Interstate Navigation Co., Nelseco Navigation Co., Box 482, New London, Connecticut 06320, or by calling—in Connecticut—(203) 442-7891 or 442-9553, or—in Rhode Island— (401) 789-3502 or 783-4613. If you plan to visit the island, I suggest you phone or write the nice people at the Chamber of Commerce, Drawer D, Block Island, Rhode Island 02807, (401) 466-2982, who will send you, on request, all you will need to know about restaurants and accommodations. During the summer, with advance reservations, you can take your car aboard the ferry. Otherwise, a very pleasant way to see the island is to take a taxi tour. Or you may prefer to rent a moped.*

—DR

THE VAMPIRE GHOST OF CHESTNUT HILL CEMETERY
Exeter, Rhode Island

Rhode Island Historical Cemetery 22, behind Exeter's Chestnut Hill Baptist Church, is a family cemetery. The few new monuments show the same family names that are repeated in faded, moss-hidden lettering on the older gravestones that lean at tipsy angles. In some places, what must have been tiny evergreen plantings have grown so high and wide with the passage of time as to completely hide the memorial markers they were set out to decorate.

One afternoon in October, with the late sun bringing out magical highlights in the autumn foliage, my husband, Rick, and I walked the uneven rows looking for three particular graves. We were searching for the final resting places of Mary E. Brown and her two daughters, Mary Olive and Mercy Lena Brown. Mercy's spirit is said to haunt this cemetery. There are many Browns buried in the Chestnut Hill Cemetery, and it took us some time to find the family grouping of four headstones, which also included George T. Brown. This husband and father had believed so fervently in vampires that he'd caused the bodies of his wife and daughters to be exhumed and examined for the telltale evidence: fresh blood in the veins.

The headstones face west. It may have been a trick of the lowering light, but the sun that illuminated three of the headstones and their inscriptions cast the top half of the fourth headstone into shadow, making the old engraving nearly indecipherable unless you got really close. Close enough to hear a whisper, or was that just the October breeze stirring in the evergreens?

The fourth headstone bore this legend: *Mercy L., died January 18, 1892, aged 19 years.* "Please help me. Let me out," are the words that some visitors hear her whisper.

I noticed that a single delicate pink blossom on a foot-high green stalk leaned its head against Mercy's stone, perfectly centered, as if intentionally planted there. Not so, of course. It was only an errant sprig of wild clover.

Two noted vampirologists have stated that Rhode Island is a kind of Transylvania of the western hemisphere. More incidents of vampirism have been reported in the southern part of this state than in any other area outside of Eastern Europe, according to Raymond McNally, an expert on Dracula, speaking at the University of Rhode Island in 1975. Stephen Kaplan, who calls himself America's foremost vampirologist, ranked Rhode Island fourth among the fifty states in 1988, judging by reports received at the Vampire Research Center he operates in Elmhurst, New York. Either way, it's a disturbing statistic.

Unless you've grown up in a remote corner of the world where films and television have never penetrated, you know that a vampire is the legendary manifestation of the "undead," a deceased person who, instead of resting in peace, preys on the living. The food of their immortality is human blood; their victims are usually asleep and helpless. In the morning, two little marks on the neck indicate what has happened, and the victim will become progressively weaker as the attacks continue. The inevitable result is death. Sometimes the victim also joins the ranks of the "undead," and the infestation spreads throughout a community.

Vampires have a "half-life" that allows them to go about only during the night hours, sometimes in human form, sometimes in the form of a bat. A mirror will detect this demon, because a vampire shows no reflection. A shaft of sunlight, a silver cross, or a necklace of garlic will ward the demon off. So will a little black dog on whose brow you have painted an extra set of eyes with white paint. A wooden stake through the heart is the standard method of killing a vampire. Naturally, this desperate act must be accomplished by day, when the demon is powerless. At least, using a stake was the way it was done in Romania. But in Rhode Island, the method employed was slightly different. In this New England state, the vampire's heart was cut out of its body and burned.

As the story is told, vampirism in Rhode Island started in the pre-Revolutionary era, with a prosperous farmer called "Snuffy" Stukeley, the nickname referring to his butternut-brown homespun jacket. He rejoiced in his fourteen children, some already grown to adulthood. But in the midst of peace and plenty, Stukeley began to have a recurring nightmare. In this distressing dream, he witnessed half of his orchard withering before his eyes. Soon after that, his oldest, Sarah, sickened and died, probably of tuberculosis. One by one, other children became ill, and Stukeley, like Joseph in the Bible, came to a frightening interpretation of his dream—it was a prophecy. Not his orchard but his children were fated to succumb.

Five more of them did, and were buried beside Sarah. During their last illness, all of these children had complained of nightly visits from Sarah. Finally, Mrs. Stukeley, worn out with nursing, began to experience the same unearthly visitations. A frantic Stukeley consulted with learned men of his day, and the diagnosis was that vampirism was the probable cause of the family's misfortune. Much less was known in those days about how a contagion is passed from one person to another.

With the help of a group of neighbors, Stukeley dug up the six children who had perished and examined their bodies. Five of them were decomposing, but Sarah's, although she had been the first to die, was in surprisingly good condition. Her eyes were open, her hair and fingernails had grown, and there was fresh blood in her heart and arteries. Clearly, she had been possessed by a vampire and had become one herself. Stukeley removed Sarah's heart to a nearby rock and burned it. A seventh child, who was already ailing, died soon after, but the rest continued in good health.

The story of the Stukeley vampire, becoming a Rhode Island legend over generations, must have preyed upon the mind of the Brown patriarch, Mercy's father, when ill health began to plague his family. He applied the same remedy as Stukeley, and the Brown incident, which happened over a hundred years ago, has resulted in a haunting.

Consumption, as tuberculosis was called then, was a frequent visitor to New England homes, but no one ever got used to the way it attacked people who appeared robust and hardy, even pink-cheeked in the presence of the initial low-grade fever. But soon the victim became tired, thin, and pallid, except for those feverish spots on each cheek. It looked as if something were draining the very life out of the coughing consumptive, who struggled for every breath.

That's the way it took George Brown's wife, Mary, and six months later Mary Olive, the oldest daughter. Four daughters and one son remained, all in apparently good health. About four years later, the son, Edwin, took ill. He and his bride, Hortense, went out to Colorado Springs so that Edwin could benefit from the healthful air and the mineral springs. While he was gone, his sister Mercy sickened and died in a very short time. When Edwin returned a month later, he, too, began to fail and was cared for at the home of his father-in-law.

Apparently, the thought of losing his only son was the final blow to George Brown. Like Stukeley, he consulted with others more learned than he, and the ugly specter of vampirism was raised again. Nothing would do but to exhume the three bodies in Chestnut Hill Cemetery.

Dr. Harold Metcalf, the district medical examiner, was called in, and one chilly morning in March, George Brown, Dr. Metcalf, and a group of Brown's friends carried shovels into the cemetery and began their grisly work.

Autopsies were performed on the spot by Dr. Metcalf. As might be expected, the bodies of the mother and sister, buried years before, were decomposed, but the body of Mercy, who had died more recently, was not. To the relatives present at the exhumation who had also attended Mercy's wake, it appeared that the body was not in the same position as it had been when the casket was nailed shut.

As requested by the family, Dr. Metcalf removed Mercy's heart and liver, and when he did, blood seeped from those organs and dripped onto the ground. The doctor tried in vain to explain that this was not unnatural. The vampire had been discovered! George Brown carried his daughter's heart and liver to a large flat rock in the cemetery, and his attendants burned them to ashes. Then the ashes were carefully scooped up and saved. According to legend, ashes of a vampire's heart have the power to cure its victims. Dr. Metcalf was instructed to stir a pinch of these ashes into the medicine that was prescribed for Edwin, and so he did.

Two days later, March 19, 1892, the whole story was front-page news in the *Journal-Bulletin,* under the following headline:

EXHUMED THE BODIES
Testing a Horrible Superstition in the Town of Exeter
BODIES OF DEAD RELATIVES TAKEN FROM THEIR GRAVES.
They Had All Died of Consumption,
and the Belief Was That Live Flesh and Blood Would Be Found
That Fed Upon the Bodies of the Living.

Another newspaper account designed to titillate "inquiring minds" of the day carried this banner:

THE VAMPIRE THEORY
That Search for the Spectral Ghoul in Exeter Graves
NOT A RHODE ISLAND TRADITION BUT SETTLED HERE
It Originated in Europe—Cremation of the Heart
of the Sister for the Consumptive Brother
to Eat the Ashes.

The article closed with this sentiment: "Mr. Brown has the sympathy of the community."

But alas, the macabre antidote didn't work, and Edwin died a short time later.

Many articles have been written through the years, in the same *Journal-Bulletin,* about the Browns of Exeter. In recent times Karen Lee Ziner, staff writer for the newspaper, interviewed two present-day relatives of the Browns, Reuben Brown and Louis Peck, both of Exeter.

Reuben Brown was quoted as saying that six or seven young girls on that side of the family had died before Mercy was exhumed. "My father believed she was a vampire. He said all those girls had the mark on their throat when they died. . . . I used to know a man who unearthed [Mercy]. He said he saw them cut her heart out and burn it on the rock. . . . It appeared Mercy had moved in the grave. She wasn't the way she was put in there. But he said there were no more deaths after that. That's what he said."

Louis Peck said, "It's true, my people did this. . . . I remember as a kid my mother wouldn't allow us to touch those rocks." Peck went on to relate a story that happened when he was a much younger man. One windy night he and some friends went up to the cemetery where Mercy was reburied, and there was a bright blue light hovering over the four graves. "God, she was bright, that's the part that stuck in you. I have no idea what it was." When Peck told others about the blue light, it turned out that a neighbor, also a member of the family, had seen the same light, and people on the other side of the family had had the same strange experience.

This is not a unique phenomenon. Blue lights bouncing and darting about gravestones manifest so frequently in haunted burial grounds that they are known as cemetery lights.

Ed and Sally Cloutier, who had followed the Brown saga with great interest, tried three times to record Mercy's voice, and the third time, around nine at night, they left the machine recording and came back later. When they replayed the cassette they heard a dry rasping whisper saying, "Please help me." This was reported by C. Eugene Emery, Jr., in the *Providence Journal Magazine*, the Halloween issue, 1979. A psychic investigator named Marc Seifer was called in by the Cloutiers, and he went up to Chestnut Hill Cemetery with a tape recorder, special photographic film, a Geiger counter, and a silver crucifix—but he found nothing. He and other experts have listened to the Cloutier tape and believe the rhythmic breathing to be the scraping of the tape reel; they cannot detect a voice.

Our visit wasn't at night. In fact, it couldn't have been a more ghost-dispelling day, full of bright sunlight, when we investigated the Chestnut Hill Cemetery ourselves. I felt there is an unmistakable energy hovering over those graves, something that makes you turn back sharply to look again. If it is Mercy's spirit, I believe she does want to tell us something. Her side of the story, perhaps.

Over the years other cases of vampirism were whispered about in Rhode Island—in Wickford, Greenwich, Kingston, Coventry, Hopkinton, Richmond, and other communities. The story is told that a man named William Rose of Peace Dale, a village in South Kingstown, similarly cut out the heart of his deceased daughter and burned it in 1874.

There is talk of a vampire named Bob in Pawtucket in recent times. (Personally, I think names like Vladimir, Hugo, or Ramon would be much more appropriate.) This contemporary incident was reported by Gerry Goldstine from an interview with Stanley Kaplan that appeared in the *Providence Journal-Bulletin* in 1988. Bob is five feet three inches tall and weighs about 115 pounds.

DIRECTIONS: *Heading north from Connecticut on I-95, take Exit 5 onto Route 102 toward Exeter. Follow signs to the Chestnut Hill Baptist Church, which will be on your left. Heading south from Providence, Rhode Island, take Exit 9, Route 4 and proceed south to Route 102. Turn right onto the Route 102, following Exeter and Baptist Church signs. The cemetery is right behind the church. Mercy Brown's grave is near the center, to the left of the road that runs through the small cemetery.*

—DR

A Witch Hunt and Its Haunting Heritage
Salem, Massachusetts

If a whole city can be haunted, that city is Salem. I grew up in Massachusetts, and when we were teenagers, the spookiest thing we could do on Halloween was to make a pilgrimage to Salem. It was common knowledge that ghosts lurked around every ancient oak tree and behind each mossy gravestone in this historic North Shore city. At the center of most hauntings, the researcher finds a strong personality, a dramatic event, and/or some pressing unfinished business. All three were present in abundance in the Salem witch hunt of the 1690s.

The perception generally held during my youth was correct. Salem has its ghosts, and if you visit the place and are at all sensitive, you will feel their presence. You should be prepared to encounter the restless ghosts of Salem in any quiet, shadowy corner of the city, but certain places are particularly well-known haunts. Some of the historic mansions on Essex Street have had manifestations. I can personally testify to an unusual experience in the House of Seven Gables. Although Seven Gables belongs to the later period of Nathaniel Hawthorne, there is a connection between the famous American author and the Salem witch trials, as this story will relate. The ghost of the accused wizard Giles Cory is said to appear from time to time in Salem near the old jail whenever some calamity is impending in the community. Gallows Hill, where the executions took place, once a desolate, windswept summit, enjoys a similarly eerie reputation. In modern times, it has become a pleasant residential neighborhood called Gallows Hill Circle, located on Witchcraft Heights.

Twentieth-century Salem does nothing to live down the clouded reputation of seventeenth-century Salem Village—quite the contrary! Its motif is the silhouette of a witch, and many of its tourist attractions commemorate the decade or so when hunting and hanging so-called witches were God's work and Salem's holy mission.

The Salem witchcraft hysteria began in 1692, ironically in the

252

home of its God-fearing, straight-laced minister, Reverend Samuel Parris. Tituba, the minister's West Indian slave, secretly told fortunes and supernatural stories to his daughter and niece. Later, her circle of eager listeners was enlarged to include a number of teenage friends. There wasn't much fun for young girls in Salem in those days. Life was a hard and serious business, punctuated only by marathon services in an unheated church. These pubescent females craved something—they knew not what—at least, a glimpse into the future to see the face of a husband-to-be.

Tituba's rituals and mutterings could be downright scary, not to mention sinful. If caught, the girls, as well as Tituba, could look forward to severe punishment. It wasn't long before fear and guilt affected the youngest of the girls. The minister's impressionable nine-year-old daughter Betsy, Tituba's favorite, began barking like a dog and scurrying about on all fours. This surprising affliction received a great deal of attention, especially on Sundays when Betsy's father was embarked upon one of his tediously long sermons. The hysterical reaction quickly spread to the minister's niece, who was two years older, and soon, every one of Tituba's "girls' club" was convulsing, barking, choking, and screaming. This strange malady could have had a physiological cause originally, depending upon what Tituba used in her dinner concoctions. Jimsonweed, for instance, which grew abundantly in the area, causes convulsive seizures, spasms of pain, and burning and twitching of the extremities. However the symptoms began, they continued for years after any exposure to poisonous plants the girls may have had.

Before long, a fatal question was asked of the girls by consulting ministers and doctors: "Who afflicts thee?" When the afflicted girls began to answer this question, timidly at first and then with growing boldness, Salem Village achieved its unique chapter in New England's history. Before the hysteria was over, nineteen people had been hanged and one crushed to death under heavy stones. Many more were imprisoned and had their lands and goods seized, since the property of a witch was forfeited to the city. Honest, hardworking families were ruined financially and torn apart by betrayal. Old feuds were dusted off and given new weapons of accusation. Salem Village was out to destroy the devil and all his cohorts, but unhappily, the town fathers were unable to recognize the real culprits, the pale, suffering daughters with downcast eyes who threw fits at the drop of a Bible.

The victims in this village drama were mostly women in their forties and fifties, many of them matrons supervising large households, strong-minded ladies at the height of their power in the community; bossy spoilsports, no doubt, to the circle of young accusers.

The recorded words of Mercy Short, addressing the spectral tormentors who were giving her fits, are especially revealing: "What's that? Must the younger women, do ye say, hearken to the elder? They must be another sort of elder women than you, then! They must not be elder witches, I am sure. Pray, do you for once hearken to me!"

Mercy had her wish. The magistrates hearkened only to the girls and their "spectral evidence." No one who handled the subsequent investigations and trials had legal training. Harvard was still only a divinity school. No American-educated person had received a founding in English common law. In fact, the presiding dignitaries didn't even allow the accused persons to be represented by legal counsel—if they could have found any.

The chief evidence against the accused was spectral. That is, one or more of the tranced girls would claimed to have seen a vision of the accused person either consorting with the devil or persecuting the girls themselves with pins and pinches. In rather a neat twist, the mediumistic girls even witnessed the devil holding one of his unholy meetings right on the church grounds. This close brush with the contagion really frightened the elders. The devil and his witches were responsible for mysterious wasting illnesses, inexplicable fatal accidents or sudden deaths, runaway cattle, spoiled butter, and lascivious night visits to lonely farmers.

Since it was believed that the devil could never take the spectral form of an innocent person, anyone the visionaries saw meeting with the devil must be guilty. The accused was then submitted to two tests.

The first was an intimate body search, looking for a wen or a wart, which, if found, would be the witch's extra teat for suckling the devil. Today's strip searches are no more thorough and embarrassing than the inch-by-inch inspections visited upon the modest puritans of Salem.

If the accused had managed to get to midlife without such a

blemish, he or she was brought into court to confront the celebrated circle of girls. Without exception, each accused person was greeted with screams and convulsions, clear evidence of spectral torture. Touching the witch was thought to bring relief from her power, rather like grounding, so one of the afflicted girls would be dragged over to touch the accused. That touch would bring her instant relief and wrap up the case for the prosecution.

After the investigations came the trials. Any witch who confessed could escape a sentence of hanging and be kept alive to name other witches and wizards, which some of them did. Others stood firm, refusing to belie themselves or implicate others even when their foot was on the gallows ladder.

One of the implacable inquisitors through all these preliminary examinations was Magistrate John Hathorne. His descendants later added a *w* to the family name, making it Hawthorne. Magistrate Saltonstall from Haverhill took a dim view of the proceedings and resigned. A third magistrate, Jonathan Corwin, let Hathorne take the more active part and confined himself to listening and recording his impressions. If he had misgivings, he kept quiet about them. Despite his passive role, the house on Essex Street where he lived in 1692 and where some of these preliminary examinations took place, now called The Witch House, is one of those that is haunted.

A few learned ministers in Boston, hearing of the troubles in Salem, got together and wrote a document that questioned the validity of spectral evidence, but the magistrates in Salem were not persuaded. Nor were they influenced by a half-century of blameless living, a spotless reputation, and petitions avowing good character signed by neighbors.

Particularly touching is the story of Rebecca Nurse, an aged and sickly matron whose eight grown children were fiercely devoted to her. Not only that, but her seven sons- and daughters-in-law also spoke highly of her, which means she must have been practically a saint. All but one neighbor (whose pigs she had chased out of her precious flax field) signed their names to a petition on Rebecca's behalf. This action took real courage. Anyone who came to the defense of an accused friend was often "called out" by the girls shortly thereafter.

Although she was quite deaf and ill, Rebecca presented her innocence so strongly in court that the jury returned a not-guilty verdict. Not having any knowledge of legal proceeding, the judges thought it perfectly proper to send the jury back to reconsider. The jury got the message, and came back with the desired "guilty."

Rebecca Nurse was hanged on the gallows tree and her body thrown into a ditch with the other witches who had been executed that day. The whole town attended, with the visionary girls taking places of honor; executions were considered to be morally edifying. Rebecca's family came quietly at night to rescue her remains and give them a proper burial at a site they kept secret from everyone in the community.

Rebecca's two sisters were subsequently accused. One of them, Sarah Cloyce, managed to escape hanging until the witch-hunt hysteria had passed, but the other, Mary Esty, also was executed on Gallows Hill.

Although the majority of those prosecuted were women, a number of men were victims also. Of these, Giles Cory, whose ghost still walks in Salem, is perhaps the most famous. His wife, Martha, known for her sharp tongue, had been particularly scathing to the afflicted girls. In fact, when she witnessed her first exhibition of demonic possession, Martha had simply thrown her head back and laughed heartily at the girls. She had paid for her disbelief by being the next they called out as a witch. Giles had been bemused at the time, almost believing he could have been mistaken about the good character of his wife. Sometimes he'd felt she prayed too long at night instead of coming to bed.

After Martha died on the gallows tree and Giles himself was called out as a wizard, the eighty-year-old man realized his naïveté. He refused to utter one word in court, knowing he could not lawfully be sentenced unless he made a statement. The magistrates ordered that he be taken to an open field near the jail and laid in a shallow pit with a stout beam across his chest. Heavy stones were placed on the beam to force a statement out of him. As the last verse of an anonymous ballad about Cory goes.

> *"More weight!" now said this wretched man;*
> *"More weight!" again he cried;*
> *And he did no confesson make,*
> *But wickedly he dyed.*

As the hysteria grew, a few accused persons wisely fled, among them John Alden of Boston, the firstborn son of John and

Priscilla Alden, the Puritan lovers made famous by the poet Longfellow.

A valorous sea captain and soldier, Alden boldly strode into court on a fine May day to face the rumors that he was "the tall man from Boston" named by Tituba. Scoffing at the girls, he called their fits "juggling tricks." They responded by tumbling into a heap when he looked their way, screaming that his spectral self was nicking their tender flesh with his sword. Fortunately for Alden, his position was such that he was put under house arrest in Boston instead of jail in Salem. Reluctant to cut and run, Alden held out until September before fleeing. "The devil is after me," he cried to friends who took him in.

The more status and money one had, the easier it was to escape, of course. New York, because it had a large component of the sensible Dutch, offered safe haven to Alden and others.

The witch-hunt horror was finally ended by the ghost of Mary Esty, Rebecca Nurse's sister—a fascinating example of a strong spirit coming back to this dimension to right a wrong. So amiable and compassionate a woman was Mary Esty that her very jailers pleaded for her to be spared. But under that gentle demeanor there as a woman of powerful spirit. Even when she knew there was no hope for herself, Mary continued to plead for justice, trying to influence the magistrates on behalf of others who had been accused and were awaiting trials. Although she failed in that attempt, she rose from the dead to continue her fight.

At the time of her hanging, the ghost of Mary Esty appeared to Mary Herrick, a seventeen-year-old girl living in Wenham. "I am going upon the ladder to be hanged for a witch," the apparition said, "but I am innocent and before a twelfth-month be past you shall believe it." Then Mary Esty vanished before the horrified girl's eyes.

Mary Herrick knew Mary Esty and believed she was a witch deserving of hanging, so she said nothing to anyone of this first visit. And yet it was a troubling visitation. The body of belief about witches contained some unwavering canons, like the one about the devil being forbidden by God to take the shape of the innocent, which made spectral evidence conclusive. Another significant canon held that once a witch had been executed, she would lose the power to return and torment the innocent. This was the most important reason why a witch must be hanged rather than simply imprisoned. If a witch like Mary Esty could return, the hangings had lost their therapeutic value. Or else Mary Esty had been innocent after all. Pondering these matters, young Mary Herrick, not surprisingly, began to have pains in her stomach.

Back came the ghost of Mary Esty, this time accompanied by the ghost of Mrs. Hale, the pious wife of the Reverend John Hale of Beverly, Massachusetts, who had also been hanged as a witch. Mary Esty told the girl she'd come back to vindicate her cause and convinced Mary Herrick that she must report these apparitions to Reverend Gerrish, the girl's pastor, and Reverend Hale. Mary Herrick did so, and the two learned gentlemen instantly perceived that the canons governing so-called witchcraft were not true, and the admission of spectral evidence was a travesty. The Reverend Hale marshalled his forces and his evidence, and courageously attacked the Salem court's proceedings. He found that the wounded families of Salem Village, and elsewhere, were ready to listen to reason at last.

Chief among other opponents of the witch hunt were the Massachusetts ministers (one of whom had already gone to the gallows for wizardry), with the exception of Reverend Parris of Salem, who still stood foursquare for the spectral evidence of his girls and the others.

Finally these tranced young ladies accused one innocent person too many. Rather drunk with their own power to topple the mighty, this time they called out Governor Phips's wife, Lady Phips. The governor was astounded. He'd been keeping himself aloof from the hysteria, letting Deputy Governor Stoughton handle the contagion. Knowing his wife to be innocent of such deviltry, he realized that all the other women probably had been innocent, too. Immediately, the governor ordered the release from jail of all accused witches.

Of course, innocent or not, these women had to pay the costs of their keep in jail and the irons used to restrain them before they would be let go. A few had sufficient savings, but most had to wait quite a while before relatives could scrape together the necessary capital or someone took them as an indentured servant in exchange for paying their way out of jail. Tituba, still alive because she'd had the good sense to confess, was sold this way.

January 15, 1697, was set aside as a day of fasting in Massachusetts, to repent the wrongs committed during the witch hunt. The people of Salem Village, with practically no family untouched by the madness, refused to pay the Reverend Parris's salary until finally he was forced to go elsewhere. Parris did not escape some retribution; perhaps the ghosts of Salem's victims had a hand in it. His beloved elder son, Noyes, died insane.

Nathaniel Hawthorne, one of early America's greatest authors, was born in Salem in 1804. The legacy of the witch trials haunted him especially because his ancestor, Judge Hathorne, had played a part in condemning the innocent. Nathaniel Hawthorne must have felt this all the more keenly because he was also descended from Philip English. English had lost his pious wife, who sickened in prison while they were both awaiting trial and died shortly after the couple managed to escape; he blamed the investigator Magistrate Hathorne for this personal tragedy. All of English's property had been confiscated when he and his wife had fled on the eve of their trial with its certain conviction; he held Sheriff Corwin (nephew of Magistrate Jonathan Corwin whose Essex Street house is haunted) accountable for those losses. These two men English hated with a Puritan's unforgiving fervor. After the general amnesty, English attempted unsuccessfully to get his property back from Sheriff Corwin. So when the latter died, English seized his corpse and held it for ransom. This didn't work either. The distraught English died deranged. On his deathbed, English forgave Hathorne for the grievous indignities inflicted upon him and his wife, but only to save his own soul. "If I get well," English said, "I'll be damned if I forgive him!"

English must have turned over in his grave when one of his daughters let bygones be bygones and married the son of Magistrate Hathorne. This was the lineage the pale, handsome Nathaniel Hawthorne brooded over and exorcised in his novels, particularly *The House of Seven Gables*.

One of Hawthorne's most famous books, this novel tells the story of the relentless working out of a curse on the Pyncheon family of Salem who has inhabited the House of Seven Gables for generations. The ancestral Colonel Pyncheon has built this home on the property of a man named Maule who, through Pyncheon's efforts, was executed for witchcraft. As Maule had stood with the halter around his neck, he'd cursed his enemy, saying, "God will give you blood to drink." (This very same curse was actually voiced by one of the first three women to be charged, Sarah Good, and directed to the magistrates, of which Hawthorne's ancestor was one.) In Hawthorne's story, many Pyncheons suffer disastrous losses of life and fortune before a pretty young girl, Phoebe, comes to live with her aunt Hepzibah, one of the last of the Pyncheons. Hepzibah has fallen on such hard times that she's had to open a cent-shop in the mansion. The curse is lifted when Holgrave, a descendant of Maule, falls in love with and marries Phoebe.

The real House of Seven Gables wasn't Hawthorne's home. One of his cousins, Susan Ingersoll, lived there, and he visited her often. "The venerable mansion," Hawthorne wrote, "has always affected me like a human countenance, bearing the traces not merely of outward storm and sunshine, but expressive, also, of the long lapse of mortal life, and accompanying vicissitudes that have passed within."

This historic home, open to the public, is generally so crowded now that it is difficult to feel its vibrations. Such was not always the case. Although I had been to Salem many times as a child, I first visited Seven Gables as a young woman. I went with a friend and our children at a time when the beautiful home was relatively empty. I fell in love with the upstairs bedroom with its window seats overlooking the sea, and I marveled at the hidden staircase behind the fireplace. But downstairs, my friend and I were both seized with a hysterical response to house's atmosphere, somewhere between laughter and terror.

As we learned when we compared notes later, for several minutes, when we were standing in the re-creation of Hepzibah's cent-shop, we both had the experience of being catapulted into another time. To tell the truth, we practically ran out of the place, and my friend kept gasping, "witches, witches." She was trying to describe the presences she'd encountered, but somewhat inaccurately. The victims of the witch hunt certainly were not in league with the devil, and, anyway, the old religion of witchcraft (called Wicca) predates the Christian notion of Satan. Perhaps it was Sarah Good whose apparition my friend saw while we were talking to the pleasant lady behind the counter of the cent-shop. I had felt pretty weird myself, as if I were looking at two people at once.

I've been back to Seven Gables since but never had the same alarming but memorable experience.

Salem enjoyed a glorious maritime history, sometimes forgotten in the interest over the witch trials, and the city boasts many homes of splendid architecture built during that period. One of these, the Ropes Mansion on Essex Street, a stately eighteenth-century home open to the public, is haunted by two people not connected, as far as we can tell, to the witch hunt. One of these ghosts is Judge Nathaniel Ropes, a Tory, who died a few days after the house was stoned by angry revolutionaries. The judge still walks around his former home, occasionally setting off the burglar alarm. The second ghost is that of Abigail Ropes. Years after the judge's death, Abigail was in the upstairs bedroom of the mansion one evening when her petticoat caught fire from the fireplace flames. Although she screamed for help, the servants didn't hear her and she was consumed. People passing the house at night still hear her agonized screams.

Nathaniel Hawthorne himself saw a ghost in the Salem Athenaeum Library. The young author used to spend an hour each afternoon reading at the library, where a strict silence was always observed among the patrons. Hawthorne used to nod quietly every day to one of the other regular patrons, the eighty-year-old Reverend Harris. One day, Hawthorne was saddened to learn that his friend had passed away. But the next day, when Hawthorne went to the library, there was Reverend Harris seated in his favorite chair as usual. Harris seemed about to speak to Hawthorne, but no words were forthcoming. Not wanting to disturb the other patrons, Hawthorne never could bring himself to inquire whether they, too, saw the apparition of Harris. After a week of these visitations, Harris's shape came no more to the Salem Athaeneum. If he had ever doubted, there was no question about Hawthorne's belief in ghosts after that experience.

Salem is a pleasantly spooky place to visit around Halloween time! The waterfront city sponsors a Haunted Happenings Festival October 21–31, including a haunted house (not the *real* ones), psychic fair, masquerade balls, magic shows, candlelight tours, ghost stories, and much more. Several psychic readers are available in Salem. One is located at the Lyceum, original homesite of Bridgit Bishop, the first witch to be dragged to the gallows.

DIRECTIONS: *Salem is located 16 miles north of Boston, Massachusetts, off Route 128, via Route 1A South. The helpful chamber of commerce can be contacted by writing Visitor Information Center,*

Old Town Hall, 32 Derby Square, Salem, Massachusetts 01970, or calling (508) 744-0004.

The House of Seven Gables at 54 Turner Street is open daily from 9:30 A.M. to 5:30 P.M. from July through Labor Day. From September to July, the hours are 10:00 A.M. to 4:30 P.M. An admission fee is charged. For information, telephone (508) 744-0991.

The haunted Ropes Mansion, which also offers an important collection of Nanking porcelain and Irish glass, is at 318 Essex Street. The hours June through October are 10:00 A.M. to 4:00 P.M. Tuesday through Saturday, 1:00 to 4:30 P.M. Sunday. A fee is charged. Call (508) 744-0718.

The Gabled Witch House, the home of Jonathan Corwin, one of the judges in the witch trials, and scene of some of the preliminary examinations, is located at 310½ Essex Street. From mid-March to June, it is open from 10:00 A.M. to 4:30 P.M.; July through August, 10:00 A.M. to 6:00 P.M., Labor Day to December 1, 10:00 A.M. to 4:30 P.M. An admission fee is charged. Call (508) 744-0180.

Salem Witch Museum, at 19½ Washington Square North, presents a multisensory re-creation of the events of the witch hunt. It is open year-round from 10:00 A.M. to 5:00 P.M.; in July and August, the Museum stays open until 7:00 P.M. Admission is $3 for adults; reduced rates for seniors and children. Call (508) 744-1692.

At the Witches Dungeon Museum, 15 Lynde Street, you can tour a re-creation of the Salem jail where witches were held and see a live presentation of the trials. The museum is open daily from May through November, 10:00 A.M. to 5:00 P.M. An admission fee is charged. Call (508) 744-9812.

Gallows Hill is off Essex Avenue at Almeda Street. Take a right at Almeda from Essex, opposite Salem Hospital. The site of Gallows Hill is on the northern side of Almeda.

—DR

AMERICA'S STONEHENGE
Mystery Hill, North Salem, New Hampshire

I f you're gifted with a sensitivity called "far memory," which is the intuitive or psychic knowledge of ages past, you'll want to visit this complex in New Hampshire and have a go at solving the enigma of its builders. So many theories have been proposed—and so many debunked—that some reputable archaeologists are afraid they will be thought cranks if they seriously investigate the site. Although new evidence is being discovered constantly as less timid scientists continue the archaeological exploration of Mystery Hill, there are as yet no commonly accepted conclusions about America's Stonehenge, as it is called by its present owner, and that's what makes it a perfect psychic trip.

Myth, mystery, and megalithic astronomy combine to make America's Stonehenge one of this country's most intriguing landscapes, and certainly a prehistoric site about which there has been the most heated speculation. Who would expect to find in New England what is clearly a sacrificial table with grooves cut in the four-and-a-half-ton stone slab for a runoff of blood? It looks like a giant gravy platter, big enough to accommodate a large animal or a man. Sure, we've heard about the Aztec sacrifices in South America, but this is homey New Hampshire, where we look for picture-book towns with white-steepled churches, not dark stone passages and chambers for the worship of forgotten deities. It is said that H. P. Lovecraft, the granddaddy of horror fiction, was inspired by a visit to Mystery Hill in 1937 to write "The Dunwich Horror," one of his premier tales of terror in New England.

Long before Columbus arrived, this thirty-acre complex was built by a people about whom we know very little. It wasn't until the 1960s that we even learned the true antiquity of this puzzling site. It was then that analysis by the carbon-14 dating method proved that charcoal found between stones at an excavation was at least three thousand years old. Then, with a later series of tests, the figure was revised to four thousand years (2025 B.C.). That's pretty far back, about the same time that England's Stonehenge on Salisbury Plain was being constructed, the Egyptians were just discovering the use of papyrus, and a court musician in China cut the first bamboo pipe.

So while Egyptians were planning libraries and the Chinese were piping their earliest five-note tunes, here in the New World, an ancient people were raising four- to eleven-ton standing stones on a desolate granite hill in present-day New Hampshire, aligning them to specific solar and lunar events.

Before the incontrovertible evidence of carbon dating showed its real age, some experts with a "flat earth" mentality were still maintaining that America's Stonehenge merely consisted of a bunch of Colonial root cellars, where settlers stored their potatoes and turnips against the winter frost—or possibly they were sheep enclosures.

The first "discoverers" of the strange structures must have been the American Indians of early New England, who left evidence that they had occupied several peripheral points but had probably avoided the main site. Some of their artifacts dated to about 1000 B.C.

The first private owners of the hill were the Pattee family, who lived there between 1823 and 1849. After the Pattee house burned down, the unexplained stone complex became a local curiosity, a pleasant place for an afternoon's excursion and picnic.

About this time many tons of slabs were carted off from the site and used to make curbstones for the streets of Lawrence, Massachusetts. Needless to say, much priceless evidence probably was lost or destroyed during those years.

No one attempted any research on Pattee's Caves, as they were called then, until William Goodwin bought the property in 1930. His pet theory was that Irish Culdee monks had built the structures around A.D. 1000 and lived there while attempting to christianize the natives. In his well-meaning but amateurish efforts to clean up and uncover the various features of the site, Goodwin also muddied up the evidence, but by no means as sweepingly as the stone robbers before him. Apparently unshaken by the presence of the sacrificial table, which would have been rather incongruous in a monastery, Goodwin wrote a book called *The Ruins of Greater Ireland in New England.* It's been reported that Goodwin's view so impressed the Archbishop of County Kerry in Ireland that he offered $100,000 for the site. Whether that story is true or not, Goodwin never did sell the property, but willed it to Malcolm Pearson.

In 1957 Robert E. Stone leased the site, then called Mystery Hill, becoming its owner in 1964. In 1982 its name was officially changed to America's Stonehenge.

It was Robert Stone who deduced that a number of the monoliths had astronomical significance. With his cousin, Osborn Stone, an engineer, they have found some fascinating correlations. Observed from the viewing platform, one stone aligns with the setting sun at the winter solstice, another at the summer solstice. One stone is positioned on the true north line, and others connect to celestial bodies on different important days, not only of the astronomical year but also of the Celtic calendar—the "May Day Monolith" aligns to the position of the sun on May 1, the Celtic festival of Beltane.

And there are many other exciting features. The cavelike structures of America's Stonehenge have been built by the drystone method, held together by their own weight and careful positioning, the oldest construction technique known to man. They are roofed by great horizontal slabs. Descending the eastern side of the hill, the various chambers, some dwarfish in size, only two or three feet high, form a complex that includes many low stone walls.

The sacrificial table, standing on four squat legs, is centered like an altar, and below that a covered passage leads to the largest chamber, twenty-two feet at its widest part with a six-and-a-half-foot ceiling. From this Y-shaped chamber, a shaft, thought to be a speaking tube, leads to an opening under the sacrificial table. If a priest stood in the chamber and spoke through this tube, its resonance would produce an eerie oracle, perhaps pronounced at the time of the sacrifice. Below the speaking tube is a niche just the right size for a person to hide and observe activity at the altar through a small opening near the floor.

Two long stone drains, one sixty feet and one forty, were built to carry water downhill and prevent the chambers from becoming flooded. Two wells have also been discovered. Quartz crystals found in one well were probably mined from a vertical fault in bedrock found beneath it. Crystals had a magical significance and were also used as tools by many ancient cultures. The other well may lead to a subterranean chamber as yet unexcavated.

A carving of a running deer, or possibly an ibex, has been found in the Oracle Chamber. Carved letters or signs on stones at the site have been variously interpreted. In 1975 Barry Fell, an epigrapher (specialist in ancient inscriptions) who knows about a half-dozen ancient alphabets, described a triangular-shaped inscribed stone that he studied at Mystery Hill as evidence of a Celtic-Carthaginian partnership in exploration and settlement of the site. Other archaeologists have, of course, disagreed, claiming that this particular Celtic alphabet, called Ogam or Orgam, was unknown at the time to which Fell refers. It appears that the story the marked stones have to tell has yet to be deciphered in a way that is generally acceptable to the scientific community.

One of the most fascinating hypotheses about this and other sites that show an advanced knowledge of astronomy has been propounded by Jean Hunt (*Mensa Bulletin,* October 1989, Number 330). Man is known to have existed on this planet for some thirty-five thousand years and the rise of civilization, from the first chipped stone ax to space travel, has happened only in the last five thousand years. Hunt theorizes that there may have been other civilizations in previous millennia that rose, flowered, and died so completely that all record of them has been lost. Well, almost all. Knowledge of these other civilizations may have come down to us in the form of myths, specifically those that tell stories of wizards, magicians, powerful fairies, canny elves, and other strange beings who were somehow wiser than those who told tales about them in subsequent dark ages.

You'll note that some of these myths speak of a people who were smaller, such as elves. Hunt reminds us that Dr. G. Elliot Smith, an anatomist, pointed out the existence of a small people, under five feet three inches in stature, with long rather than round heads (dolichocephalic), who were in Egypt around the time that the pyramids were built. These same long heads, different from those of modern men, were reported among the Minoans, the Phoenicians, in the British Isles as the *Preteni* (from which the name Britain is derived), in North and South America as the Red Paint People, and with the Hawaiians as the *Menehune.* The wise little people of legend who could do marvelous things beyond the ken of their mundane neighbors may have had a basis in reality, Hunt suggests. So rather than try to discredit the astronomical knowledge implied by mega-liths like the one in New Hampshire, the scientific community should be open-minded enough to study them objectively.

One piece of evidence to support the advanced civilization

theory that Hunt cites is Alexander Thom's conclusion, based on careful engineering studies, that megalith builders from Egypt to America all used a measurement called the megalithic yard (2.72 feet). That's pretty hard to explain unless there was some kind of central wisdom or set of uniform standards to which all of these people deferred. And these megalith builders of three thousand, four thousand, and five thousand years ago showed a remarkable skill in mathematics and construction as well as astronomy that just doesn't fit into the primitive picture of prehistoric peoples that has generally been accepted. If Hunt's theory is right, these remarkable feats may have marked the end of an older civilization, not the beginning of our newer one. If there's any truth in this conjecture, then America's Stonehenge may be part of a worldwide civilizaton, now lost in the darkness of prehistory, whose history has been preserved only in children's fairy stories.

Although it's not a traditionally haunted place, America's Stonehenge is an obviously sacred site that is well worth visiting. Meditate upon its mysteries, and perhaps the vibrations of the past will speak to you there.

America's Stonehenge is open to visitors daily from May to September, 10:00 A.M. to 4:00 P.M. In the peak tourist time of June through Labor Day, hours are extended to 9:00 A.M. through 5:00 P.M. The site is also open on weekends in April and November only, 10:00 A.M. to 3:30 P.M. Admission is $5 for adults, with discounts for seniors, students, and children (under age 6, free). Group rates are available, advance notice required. For further information or other arrangements, call (603) 893-8300 or 423-2530, or write America's Stonehenge, P.O. Box 84, North Salem, New Hampshire 03073.

DIRECTIONS: *From I-93, Exit 3, take Route 111 East (approximately 5 miles) to Island Pond and Haverhill Roads. Follow Haverhill Road south to the entrance.*

—DR

THE CHARMED LIFE (AND AFTERLIFE)
OF OCEAN-BORN MARY
Henniker, New Hampshire

I t's no surprise that the spirit of Mary Wilson Wallace lingers on in New Hampshire. Obviously, she was a survivor from the moment she took her first breath. And if it weren't for her charmed aura, a boatload of Scots-Irish families would never have made it to America. This group of hopeful emigrants would have been mysteriously lost at sea instead of joining friends and relatives in the town of Londonderry, New Hampshire.

In the summer of 1720, the ship *Wolf* sailed from Londonderry, Ireland, packed with families seeking a better life in the New World. The *Wolf*'s destination was Portsmouth, New Hampshire, and it enjoyed a calm crossing until the ship approached the Massachusetts coast. There the crew and passengers were horrified to see a much faster ship bearing down upon them. Flying from its mast in the ocean breeze was the Jolly Roger.

Spanish pirates, led by the notorious blackguard Don Pedro, soon swarmed over the *Wolf*'s decks. The emigrants' small hoards of money and jewelry were roughly ripped away from them, and the captain's cabin was looted for gold and valuables.

Satisfied that there was nothing more to be had from the harassed passengers and crew, Don Pedro ordered his men to dispatch the entire group by having them walk the plank, which was a popular spectator sport among pirates in those days. Sometimes these brutes saved a few of the prettier women for a while.

No sooner had the rollicking pirate crew got the plank in place than a strange sound was heard—the unmistakable cry of a lusty newborn infant. Hidden under sacks and blankets, Elizabeth Wilson had just given birth belowdecks.

Cutthroat through he was, Don Pedro evidently had a soft spot deep down in his villainous heart because he immediately ordered that the plank-walking party be halted while he viewed the baby. The tiny girl's father, James Wilson, wrapped her in a bit of blanket and brought her up on deck. She was a plump, pretty infant—not one of the red-faced, wrinkled types—and the sight of her moved Don Pedro to tears, which must have been as astonishing to his men as it was to the cowering emigrants.

All those aboard the *Wolf* would be spared, Don Pedro said, if the Wilsons would name the child Mary, which had been the name of the pirate captain's beloved mother. (Possibly he said Maria, and it got translated into Mary.) Naturally, the Wilsons were glad to agree, and everyone sighed with relief when the pirates got back onto their own ship to sail away.

But a few minutes later, Don Pedro returned and boarded the *Wolf* a second time, along with a few of his men. Had the pirates only been toying, then, with the passengers and crew of the *Wolf?* No, Don Pedro's men were loaded down with gifts that the pirate captain wished to present to the Wilsons—fancy clothes, coins, and jewelry taken from other not-so-fortunate victims. Don Pedro was eager that his mother's namesake be given a good start in life.

He himself carried a bolt of rare Chinese silk brocade in a beautiful sea-green shade, which he laid on the bed beside Mary. "Let this be made into a gown for her wedding day," said Don Pedro to the Wilsons, who swore that they would. (At that point, they would have sworn to anything.)

This time the pirate ship departed for good, and the *Wolf* sailed on to Portsmouth. As planned, the passengers continued their journey to Londonderry, which at that time was no more than two rows of cabins along West Running Brook. The residents there were celebrating a unique harvest—the first field of potatoes grown in North America. The newcomers had quite an adventurous tale to tell friends and relatives who awaited them!

These fortunate survivors may have thought they'd seen and heard the last of Don Pedro, but such was not the case. While they were clearing and planting their little farms in Londonderry, Don Pedro was counting his ill-gotten wealth and fondly remembering the tiny girl he thought of as his goddaughter.

James Wilson died soon after the Wilsons' arrival in Londonderry, but Elizabeth remarried. Her second husband, James Clark, was to be the great-great-grandfather of Horace Greeley. Mary was raised in the Clark home in Londonderry.

Every year on Mary's birthday, the whole community celebrated the *Wolf*'s miraculous deliverance from the pirates.

Birthday parties were not the norm in those days, but being a child, little Mary probably took it as a matter of course that her day should be the village's biggest event. To her fellow towns-people, she was always known as Ocean-born Mary from her first birthday fete to her last.

Although child mortality was high in the 1700s, Mary grew up to be strong and beautiful. She had thick, lustrous red hair and green eyes. Those who knew her described her as strong-minded, quick of comprehension, full of good humor, speaking always with a charming brogue, and elegant in her manners. But she was tall for a girl in the 1700s—six feet—and towered over the young men in the neighborhood.

Still, Mary managed to find a handsome young man who was taller than she, Thomas Wallace. In 1742, when she was twenty-two years old, they were married. Elizabeth Wallace Clark had kept her promise to Don Pedro and had made Mary a lovely wedding dress from the bolt of blue-green Chinese silk for the ceremony. How becoming it must have been to a girl with Mary's coloring!

Mary's granddaughter and great-granddaughter both wore that same dress on their wedding days. When the dress fell apart from age, a piece of it was framed and hung in the Henniker home where Mary spent the last part of her life.

The Wallaces had four sons before Tom died in 1740. The boys grew up—not a one of them under six feet eight inches tall—to fight in the American Revolution. Robert, their second son, became active in politics and helped to frame New Hamp-shire's constitution.

At this point Mary's story diverges into two versions.

According to some sources, Don Pedro determined that the time had come to retire from the strenuous life of crime on the high seas. He decided to buy a house in Henniker, New Hampshire, not only because it was pleasant country where, at that time, no one was gunning for him, but also because the goddaughter he remembered so fondly lived nearby. Perhaps the pirate had sired no children of his own.

When Don Pedro discovered that Mary was a widow raising four sons, he invited her to bring the boys and live with him in Henniker, where he would see to it that they lacked no comfort or luxury that his riches could provide.

Mary accepted this invitation and moved in with Don Pedro,

perhaps sharing with him the secret of where he buried his
fortune, thought to be somewhere on that property.

One day when Mary was out in their coach and four, Don
Pedro was murdered by someone trying to steal his cache of
gold and jewels. Apparently Mary had felt some foreboding
about this event, because she came rushing home earlier than
expected, only to find Don Pedro lying facedown in the orchard
with a sword in his back.

One of the apparitions that has been seen in our time is the
hurried arrival of a coach and four from which a tall woman is
seen running into this Henniker house. Some people have
witnessed Mary throw something into a well in the yard as she
passes it. Groans are heard coming from the orchard. Local
ghost watchers say this supernatural scene occurs every Halloween.

In the second version of Mary's story, other sources say that
the Henniker house was built for Mary by her son Robert, who
wanted her to have the grandest house in the surrounding
country.

There is one interesting fact, however, on which most
sources agree. In 1781 an elderly Spanish gentleman, assumed
to be Don Pedro, was living in that house. Whether he was the
owner and Mary the guest, or vice versa, is the question. In
any case, the Henniker house was his abode for some time,
maybe until he died.

So, everyone wonders, what became of his fortune? In some
versions of the story (even ones in which Robert built the
house), Don Pedro requested that Mary bury him under the
hearthstone in her kitchen, which is a slab of granite eight feet
long and thirty inches wide. Some say the old pirate buried his
treasure, not himself, under the hearth, but he placed a curse
on it: anyone who digs up the treasure chest will die. Despite
this curse, I believe this hearthstone has been thoroughly
investigated, perhaps more than once.

Mary lived on in the house after Don Pedro died (or departed), where in the course of the following years she entertained many celebrated guests. Daniel Webster visited often,
and President Franklin Pierce came by to meet the legendary
Ocean-born Mary. General Lafayette, who stayed with almost
every well-known family in America, also stayed at Mary's
house and planted a tree in the front yard.

This amazing woman died at the ripe old age of ninety-four,

but one can't say she gave up the ghost, because she didn't. She's buried at Henniker Cemetery, and even there her tall figure sometimes has been seen wandering about. Her head-stone is inscribed as follows: *In Memory of Widow Mary Wallace, Who died Feb. 13, A.D. 1814, in the 94th year of Her Age.* Beneath this legend, there are two more words: *Ocean Mary.*

The house in Londonderry where Mary grew up with her mother and stepfather was taken apart board by board and moved to Compton, Rhode Island, where it was reassembled. It's called the Sea-Born Mary House, and I've even heard rumors that Mary's ghost strides about in that location from time to time, but I was unable to pin down any more details.

Since 1830, subsequent owners of the Henniker property have dug in and around the house, looking for Don Pedro's treasure, but no one has said they found it. The kitchen has been taken apart at least once. A well in the cellar found filled with stones has been cleaned out and searched. Mediums, dowsers, and people wielding metal-finding equipment have combed the old property pretty thoroughly.

The story of Mary's apparition throwing something into the well (not the one in the cellar) interests me in regard to the treasure's location. Sometimes homes as old as Mary's have had several wells over the generations. Maybe there's still a closed, undiscovered well on the property.

One couple who owned the house in recent years said that Mary's ghost haunted the place, exerting a protective influence against storm or fire damage. The next owners said the place is not and never has been haunted, that the previous couple had made up the story in order to interest tourists. And local folklore still tells the tale of Mary's coach and four appearing every Halloween.

Whatever the true facts are, the Henniker house is still private property, but you can visit Mary's grave at Henniker Cemetery. Keep watch for a tall, red-haired woman, as full of life as a ghost can get!

DIRECTIONS: *Henniker is on Route 114 in southwest New Hamp-shire. There is more than one Henniker cemetery; the one where Ocean-born Mary (Mary Wallace) is buried is easy to find because it's right behind the Henniker Town Hall. Traveling south on Route 114, continue ¼ mile past a blinker at the center of town to a small park area. The town hall will be on your right, the cemetery to the rear. Mary's grave is twelve rows back on the right.*

Mary's Henniker house is privately owned, and its residents do not appreciate having people take up a vigil on Halloween (or any other time) to watch for Ocean-born Mary. Everyone I talked to in the process of researching this story stressed the owners' wish not to be disturbed by tourists.

—DR

CONTACTS

American Society for Psychical Research, Inc.
5 West 73rd Street
New York, NY 10023
Researches and educates on the subject of paranormal phenomena; publishes journal.

Andrus Phenomena Research Center
Lynda Andrus, Director
2016 Hermanville Road
Lexington Park, MD 20653
Organization aids people in freeing earthbound souls (ghosts).

Collectors of Unusual Data International (COUD-I)
Raymond Nelke, Director
2312 Shields Avenue
St. Louis, MO 63136
Members swap clippings about anomalies.

Ghost Research Society
Dale D. Kaczmarek, President
P.O. Box 205
Oaklawn, IL 60454-0205
(312) 425-5163
Publishes The Ghost Trackers Newsletter; *Kaczmarek also lectures and conducts tours of haunted locations.*

Haunt Hunters
Phil Goodwilling and Gordon Hoener, Directors
2188 Sycamore Hill Court
Chesterfield, MO 63017-7223
Psychic investigators.

Louisiana Mounds Society
Jean Hunt, President
3330 Eastwood Drive
Shreveport, LA 71105
Publishes a newsletter on archaeological sites and finds, with emphasis on the prehistoric; lists books on subject.

Parapsychology Institute of America
Stephen Kaplan, Director
P.O. Box 252
Elmhurst, NY 11373

Parapsychology Resource Center
Kelly Roberts, Psychometrist
P.O. Box 2715
Escondido, CA 92025
Seminars, investigations, consultations.

Parapsychology Sources of Information Center
Rhea White, Director
Plane Tree Lane
Dix Hills, NY 11746
Supplies reference material to researchers.

Pennsylvania Association for the Study of the Unexplained (PASU)
Stan Gordon, Director
6 Oakhill Avenue
Greensburg, PA 15601
Pennsylvania UFO Hotline: (412) 838-7768
*Clearinghouse for reports of UFO sightings and other strange phenomena
in the Pennsylvania area; publishes newsletter.*

Psionics Unlimited
Lewis H. Harrison, Director
P.O. Box 922
New York, NY 10011
*Both scientific and lighthearted investigations into hauntings and the
paranormal.*

Maurice Schwalm
P.O. Box 3522
Kansas City, KS 66103-0522
*Psychic investigator, photographer of supernatural phenomena, writer, lec-
turer, Mensan.*

Richard L. Senate
422 Staunton Street
Camarillo, CA 93010
*Psychic investigator, writer, lecturer; conducts tours of haunted sites in
California.*

Southern Maryland Psychic Investigations
Lori Mellott-Bowles, Director
Lot 58M, Hills Trailer Court
Lexington Park, MD 20653
Aids people in freeing earthbound spirits.

Spiritual Frontiers Fellowship
P.O. Box 7868
Philadelphia, PA 19101
Sponsors, explores, and interprets psychic/mystic experiences; publishes newsletter.

Ed and Lorraine Warren
P.O. Box 41
Monroe, CT 06468
(203) 268-8235
Investigate supernatural events; founders of the New England Society for Psychic Research; Ed Warren lectures and teaches on the paranormal and demonology.

BIBLIOGRAPHY

Akers, Charles. *Abigail Adams*. Boston: Little, Brown, and Co., 1980.

Alleman, Richard. *The Movie Lover's Guide to Hollywood*. New York: Harper Colophon Books, 1985.

Blanchard, Fessenden S. *Ghost Towns of New England*. New York: Dodd, Mead and Co., 1960.

Botting, Douglas. *The Pirates*. Alexandria, Virginia: Time-Life Books, 1978.

Boye, Alan. *A Guide to the Ghosts of Lincoln*, 2nd edition. St. Johnsbury, Vermont: Saltillo Press, 1987.

Brown, Raymond Lamont. *Phantoms of the Sea*. New York: Taplinger Publishing Co., 1972.

Brownlow, Kevin. *The Parade's Gone By*. New York: Alfred A. Knopf, 1968.

Cahill, Robert Ellis. *New England's Ghostly Haunts*. Peabody, Massachusetts: Chandler-Smith Publishing House, Inc., 1983.

Canning, John, ed. *Fifty True Mysteries of the Sea*. New York: Stein and Day, 1980.

Cohen, Daniel. *The Encyclopedia of Ghosts*. New York: Dodd, Mead, and Co., 1984.

Colver, Anne. *Theodosia*. New York: Farrar and Rinehart, 1941.

Daniels, Jonathan. *The Devil's Backbone, The Story of the Natchez Trace*. New York: McGraw-Hill Book Co., Inc., 1962.

Demos, John Putnam. *Entertaining Satan*. New York: Oxford University Press, 1982.

Drake, Samuel Adams. *A Book of New England Legends and Folk Lore*. Boston: Little, Brown, and Co., 1901.

Foote, Shelby. *The Civil War, a Narrative, Fredericksburg to Meridian*. New York: Random House, 1963.

Frazer, Robert W. *Forts of the West*. Norman, Oklahoma: University of Oklahoma Press, 1965.

Frey, Russell W. *Rogues' Hollow History and Legends*. Doylestown, Ohio: Self-published, 1958.

Friedrich, Otto. *City of Nets*. New York: Harper and Row, 1986.

Furnas, J. C. *Voyage to Windward, The Life of Robert Louis Stevenson*. New York: William Sloane Associates, 1951.

Furneaux, Rupert. *Ancient Mysteries*. New York: McGraw-Hill Book Co., 1977.

279

Gassis, Vincent H. *Mysterious Fires and Lights.* New York: David McKay Company, Inc., 1967.

Grayson, G. W., chief; W. David Baird, ed. *A Creek Warrior for the Confederacy.* Norman, Oklahoma: University of Oklahoma Press, 1988.

Gleasner, Diana and Bill. *Florida, Off the Beaten Path.* Charlotte, North Carolina: East Woods Press, 1985.

Gussow, Mel. *Don't Say Yes Until I Finish Talking.* New York: Doubleday and Co., Inc., 1971.

Haley, John Williams. *"The Old Stone Bank" History of Rhode Island,* vol. 3. Providence, Rhode Island: Providence Institution for Savings, 1939.

Hennessy, James Pope. *Robert Louis Stevenson.* New York: Simon and Schuster, 1974.

Holzer, Hans. *Best True Ghost Stories.* Englewood Cliffs, New Jersey: Prentice-Hall, Inc., 1983.

————. *Window to the Past.* New York: Doubleday and Co., Inc., 1969.

————. *Ghosts of the Golden West.* New York: The Bobbs-Merrill Co., 1968.

Johoda, Gloria. *Florida, A Bicentennial History.* New York: W. W. Norton, 1976.

Josephy, Alvin M., Jr., ed. *The American Heritage Book of Indians.* New York: American Heritage Publishing Co., Inc., 1961.

Kopper, Philip. *The Smithsonian Book of North America Indians.* Washington, D.C.: Smithsonian Books, 1986.

Livermore's History of Block Island. Rhode Island: The Block Island Committee of Republication, 1961.

Loftin, Bob. *Spooksville's Ghostlights.* Self-published.

Lomask, Milton. *Aaron Burr.* New York: Farrar, Straus, Giroux, 1979.

McLuhan, T. C. *Touch the Earth.* New York: Outerbridge and Dienstfrey, 1971.

McNeil, W. K. *Ghost Stories from the American South.* Little Rock, Arkansas: August House, 1985.

Martin, MaryJoy. *Twilight Dwellers—The Ghosts, Ghouls and Goblins of Colorado.* Boulder, Colorado: Pruett Publishing.

Mitchell, David. *Pirates.* New York: Dial Press, 1976.

Nadeau, Remi. *Fort Laramie and the Sioux Indians.* Englewood Cliffs, New Jersey: Prentice-Hall, Inc., 1967.

Oppel, Frank. *Tales of the New England Coast.* Secaucus, New Jersey: Castle, 1985.

Parker, Francis. *The Oregon Trail.* New York: The Macmillan Company, 1935.

Peterson, Natasha. *Sacred Sites.* Chicago, Illinois: Contemporary Books, Inc., 1989.

Phillips, David E. *Legendary Connecticut.* Hartford, Connecticut: Spoonwood Press Ltd., 1984.

Pollack, Peter. *The Picture History of Photography.* New York: Harry N. Abrams, 1958.

Scott, Beth and Michael Norman. *Haunted Heartland.* New York: Warner Books, 1987.

Senate, Richard L. *Ghosts of the Haunted Coast.* Ventura, California: Pathfinder Publishing, 1986.

————. *Ghosts of Southern California.* Ventura, California: Pathfinder Publishing, 1985.

Smith, Susy. *Prominent American Ghosts.* Cleveland and New York: The World Publishing Company, 1967.

Stacy, Dennis. *The Marfa Lights.* San Antonio, Texas: self-published, 1989.

Starkey, Marion L. *The Devil in Massachusetts.* Garden City, New York: Anchor Books, Doubleday and Co., Inc., 1969.

Sterry, Iveagh Hunt, and William H. Garrigus. *They Found a Way.* Brattleboro, Vermont: Stephen Daye Press, 1938.

Stevens, Austin N., *Mysterious New England.* Dublin, New Hampshire: Yankee, Inc., 1971.

Sullivan, George. *Discover Archaeology.* New York: Doubleday and Co., Inc., 1980.

Tierney, Gene. *Self-Portrait.* New York: Wyden Books, 1979.

Van Loon, Hendrik. *Life and Times of Petier Stuyvesant.* New York: Henry Holt, 1928.

Waldman, Carl. *Atlas of the North American Indian.* New York: Facts on File Publications, 1985.

Walton, George. *Sentinel of the Plains, Fort Leavenworth and the American West.* Englewood Cliffs, New Jersey: Prentice- Hall, Inc., 1973.

Westervelt, William D. *Hawaiian Legends of Ghosts and Ghost-Gods.* Rutland, Vermont: Charles E. Tuttle Co., 1963.

Whittier, John Greenleaf. *The Poetical Works of John Greenleaf Whittier.* Boston and New York: Houghton, Mifflin and Co., 1887.

Wieneck, Henry. *The Smithsonian Guide to Historic America, Southern New England.* New York: Stewart, Tabori and Chang, 1989.

Williamson, Chilton, Jr. *Saltbound: A Block Island Winter.* New York: Methuen, 1980.

Windham, Kathryn Tucker. *Jeffrey's Latest 13.* Tuscaloosa, Alabama: The University of Alabama Press, 1982.

————. *Thirteen Georgia Ghosts and Jeffrey.* Huntsville. Alabama: The Strode Publishers, 1973.

About the Authors

Literary collaborators for nearly three decades, Joan Bingham and Dolores Riccio have written several non-fiction books together, including *Haunted Houses USA*. Joan lives in eastern Pennsylvania with her husband and Dolores and her husband live in Warwick, Rhode Island.